PMP:
Project Management
Professional
Workbook

D1716704

PMP®:
Project Management Professional Workbook

Claudia Baca

Patti Jansen

San Francisco • London

Associate Publisher: Neil Edde
Acquisitions Editor: Elizabeth Hurley Peterson
Developmental Editor: Heather O'Connor
Production Editor: Dennis Fitzgerald
Technical Editor: Doug Andreen
Copyeditor: Cheryl Hauser
Compositor: Scott Benoit
Graphic Illustrator: Jeff Wilson
Proofreaders: Emily Hsuan, Nancy Riddiough
Indexer: Ted Laux
Book Designer: Bill Gibson
Cover Designer: Archer Design
Cover Illustrator/Photographer: Jeremy Woodhouse, PhotoDisc

Copyright © 2003 SYBEX Inc., 1151 Marina Village Parkway, Alameda, CA 94501. World rights reserved. No part of this publication may be stored in a retrieval system, transmitted, or reproduced in any way, including but not limited to photocopy, photograph, magnetic, or other record, without the prior agreement and written permission of the publisher.

Library of Congress Card Number: 2003104316

ISBN: 0-7821-4240-0

SYBEX and the SYBEX logo are either registered trademarks or trademarks of SYBEX Inc. in the United States and/or other countries.

Sybex is an independent entity from the Project Management Institute (PMI®) and is not affiliated with the Project Management Institute in any manner. Neither the Project Management Institute nor Sybex warrants that use of this publication will ensure passing the relevant exam. The Project Management Professional (PMP®) certification is either a registered trademark or trademark of the Project Management Institute in the United States and/or other countries.

TRADEMARKS: SYBEX has attempted throughout this book to distinguish proprietary trademarks from descriptive terms by following the capitalization style used by the manufacturer.

The author and publisher have made their best efforts to prepare this book, and the content is based upon final release software whenever possible. Portions of the manuscript may be based upon pre-release versions supplied by software manufacturer(s). The author and the publisher make no representation or warranties of any kind with regard to the completeness or accuracy of the contents herein and accept no liability of any kind including but not limited to performance, merchantability, fitness for any particular purpose, or any losses or damages of any kind caused or alleged to be caused directly or indirectly from this book.

Manufactured in the United States of America

10 9 8 7 6 5 4 3 2 1

For our families

Acknowledgments

We couldn't have done this without the support and help of the folks at Sybex who conceived the book, and dedicated a great deal of effort and patience to help two new authors be successful.

First, we would like to thank Elizabeth Hurley, acquisitions editor, who conceived of the workbook as a companion to the *PMP Project Management Professional Study Guide*. As teachers of basic project management courses, we were very excited by the idea, because we realized we could use such a workbook in our own classes. Without Elizabeth and her ideas, enthusiasm, and willingness to work with our ideas, this book simply wouldn't exist. Many thanks to developmental editor, Heather O'Connor. We really appreciate her laborious efforts to rework the workbook styles, her clarifying questions, and her patience with two different authors with two different styles to integrate into one book. Also thanks to Dennis Fitzgerald, production editor, and Cheryl Hauser, copyeditor who made some poor writing into some terrific writing and who found things that neither of us could see in our own work. And because we do not know everything, we must thank Doug Andreen, technical editor, who helped check out the facts and fortify the contents in our exercises. Everyone needs an editor, and all of these people helped fulfill that role better than can be imagined. This book also required some artwork and we appreciate the work of. Jeff Wilson who made the graphics we sent in look so much better in the end. We also thank Scott Benoit, compositor, who laid out the pages and helped the book take its final form.

More than anything we send our love and gratitude to our families who watched us every evening and weekend in front of our computers while they wished we were spending more time with them. And thanks to the folks at QuantumPM who understood when we said we couldn't do the extra work in the evening or over the weekends because we had this book to write. And, more than anything, we want to thank each other. We make a great team, and find mutual support, motivation, and respect in everything we do and this was just one more example of the great team we make. We couldn't have completed this workbook without each other.

Contents at a Glance

Contents

Introduction

We hope you have purchased and started reading the *PMP Project Management Professional Study Guide*. It's a terrific way to study for the PMP exam, and you will want to read what it has to say about taking the exam and take all the practice tests in it. But maybe you are new to project management and some of the concepts you read about are unfamiliar, or some of the knowledge area tools and techniques or outputs are unclear. This workbook supports what you read in the *PMP Project Management Professional Study Guide*, as well as reiterates some of its most important aspects. The *PMP Workbook* can also be used to support basic project management processes and outputs that you need to learn and use in your project management career.

If you are a teacher, you might find this workbook useful to supplement classroom exercises or as homework assignments. You may want your students to complete all exercises from a chapter to help them build a good foundation for the concept you are teaching. You might use the exercises in the order they are presented, or pull some from one chapter, then use one from another chapter based on the order or way you teach your classes. You may also want to use some of the exercises to spark class discussions since some of the exercises might require critical thinking and ideas from real project management experiences.

This workbook does not repeat everything from the *PMP Project Management Professional Study Guide*. We tried to create a book focusing on the most important inputs, tools and techniques, or outputs of the nine knowledge areas from the *Project Management Body of Knowledge Guide (PMBOK Guide)*, or those concepts that might be best learned through critical thinking and practice. Since we are both teachers of beginning project management, we selected many of the same concepts and kinds of exercises we teach in our own classes.

What This Book Covers

This book provides exercises based on concepts from the knowledge areas in the *Project Management Body of Knowledge Guide*. It is organized in order of how the *PMBOK Guide* discusses the knowledge area, except for integration management, which we have at the end since it brings everything else together. This book is organized as follows:

Chapter 1   This chapter covers Scope Management, including justifying proceeding with projects, project selection methods, project initiation and the project charter, creating a scope statement, and creating a scope management plan.

Chapter 2   In this chapter we discuss the most important aspects of Time Management, including creating a WBS, performing activity sequencing, duration activity estimating, developing a schedule, calculating critical path and PERT, and controlling schedule changes.

Chapter 3   The Cost Management chapter covers resource planning, cost estimating, creating a budget and cost baseline, and controlling cost changes.

Chapter 4 This chapter reviews major Quality Management concepts such as planning for quality, quality planning tools, calculating the cost of quality, quality assurance, and quality control.

Chapter 5 This chapter discusses Human Resource Management, including creating a staffing management plan and a RAM, acquiring staff, and team development.

Chapter 6 This chapter covers major Communications Management concepts including understanding your stakeholders, communicating with the team, deciding on information distribution, creating a communications plan, performance reporting, and closing the project.

Chapter 7 This chapter focuses on Risk Management, emphasizing creating a risk management plan, identifying risks, qualitative and quantitative analysis, risk impact and probability matrix, risk response types, and creating a risk response plan.

Chapter 8 The Procurement Management chapter describes deciding on contract types, creating a procurement management plan, creating a SOW, evaluating and selecting a vendor, and creating a contract.

Chapter 9 We finish off the book with Integration Management. Although this is one of the first items covered in the *PMBOK Guide*, it is the application of all of the other knowledge areas to planning, execution, change control, and professional responsibility on a project.

Making the Most of This Book

At the beginning of each chapter of *PMP: Project Management Professional Workbook* you'll find a list of exercises covered within the chapter. Each exercise has the same format: we provide background information about the particular topic. The background might contain terms, examples, and the general steps you might perform to create the deliverable for the exercise. Then, we provide recommended reading from the *PMP Project Management Professional Study Guide* to help support the material. We suggest you read that material as well, to help solidify your understanding. We outline a brief scenario for each exercise. The scenario is set up to describe your role as a project management consultant who will help an organization apply the concepts to their particular situation. You will read the scenario, then answer the questions at the end of each chapter. At the end of the chapter, you will find answers to the exercise questions. Some of the answers will be very specific, while others require interpretation and critical thinking, so the answers in the workbook may not be exactly the same as those you provide.

We sincerely hope the *PMP: Project Management Professional Workbook* helps you in extending your knowledge of project management techniques and concepts. Good luck in your Project Management career!

About the Authors

Claudia Baca has been active in the project management industry since 1984 and has experience in information technology, telecommunications, and e-commerce industries. During her varied career, Claudia has managed many mission critical projects for a major telecommunication company, and several Internet companies. Claudia currently is the Vice President of Consulting Services with QuantumPM. She lectures and teaches for the Project Management Institute chapter in Denver as well as for Colorado State University. Claudia is currently a member of the leadership team that is producing the ANSI standard for Project Management Maturity, OPM3. She has a Masters Certificate in Program Management from Denver University. She earned her PMP in 1995 and has re-certified in 2001. Claudia is a coauthor of a paper "Organizational Project Management Maturity Model (OPM3)" presented at the PMI Global Congress Europe, 2003. She is a technical editor of the *PMP Project Management Professional Study Guide* published by Sybex.

Patti Jansen is a project manager and trainer with QuantumPM and has over 18 years experience in the information technologies industry and 10 years in project and program management. She has managed multimillion dollar, multisystem integration projects for telecommunication and Internet companies. She has a BA from Colorado State University, a Master's in Applied Communication and a certificate in Program Management from the University of Denver. She is a technical editor of the *PMP Project Management Professional Study Guide* and *Project Management JumpStart*, both published by Sybex. She is currently teaching several project management classes at Colorado State University Denver Center.

Chapter

1

Scope Management

THE EXERCISES PRESENTED IN THIS CHAPTER INCLUDE:

- ✓ Exercise 1.1: Justifying a Project—Project Selection Matrix
- ✓ Exercise 1.2: Project Selection Methods—Financial Returns
- ✓ Exercise 1.3: Project Initiation and the Project Charter
- ✓ Exercise 1.4: Creating the Scope Statement
- ✓ Exercise 1.5: Creating a Scope Management Plan and Managing Scope Change

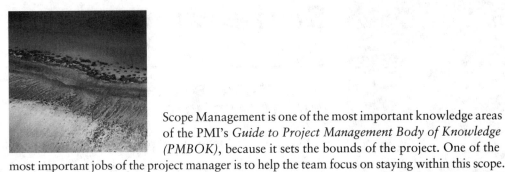

Scope Management is one of the most important knowledge areas of the PMI's *Guide to Project Management Body of Knowledge (PMBOK)*, because it sets the bounds of the project. One of the most important jobs of the project manager is to help the team focus on staying within this scope.

Scope Management involves helping your organization decide on the criteria it wants to use to select projects, then setting up a process to select the projects an organization should pursue. Once the projects are selected, the organization needs to authorize the project and give the project manager the authority to manage the project via the project charter. After being assigned to the project, the project manager needs to ensure a scope statement is created so everyone understands the main objectives and deliverables, as well as constraints and assumptions of the project. Last, the project manager needs to ensure that scope is managed in a standard and consistent fashion. Although a project manager needs to manage many items for scope, the exercises described in this chapter ensure the most fundamental documents or processes of Scope Management are completed. Scope Management is covered in the Initiation, Planning, and Control objectives of the PMP exam.

Exercise 1.1: Justifying a Project—Project Selection Matrix

The objectives for Exercise 1.1 are:

- Describe various project selection criteria.
- Select and justify a project based on a project selection matrix exercise.

Background

Organizations need to be selective in projects they undertake. Otherwise, they would work on all projects proposed in the organization. The projects need to align with the organization's strategy, and provide some kind of return on investment, whether it is financial or some other criteria the organization finds important. A project selection matrix (which could be based on a weighted scoring model), based on well-defined project selection criteria, helps an organization select projects. A project selection committee may use this matrix. First, committee members set up the criteria for selecting projects, and then, for each criterion, they decide what methods to use to measure the project's potential. (For instance, see Exercise 1.2 of this workbook for information on financial return methods.) The matrix allows organizations to make objective decisions (at least, as objective as possible) in deciding which projects to undertake. It also helps the organization prioritize the selected projects—allowing the organization to cut projects if budgets or resources become tight. An organization may have several criteria for selecting projects, and may use several project selection methods. Sometimes, even though a project may look financially risky, it may be worth undertaking, because it will provide a public perception boost the organization needs to regain or improve its market penetration. So, even after using the project selection matrix, a selection committee may choose to proceed with a project based on some other criteria that may not have been part of the initial selection process. In this exercise, you are going to practice using a project selection matrix and learn the criteria for justifying a project. Then, using a scenario involving your company, Terrific Project Management Partners (TPMP), you will put those practices to use.

Recommended Reading: Chapter 3, pp. 86–97, *PMP Project Management Professional Study Guide*, Kim Heldman, PMP (Sybex, 2002).

Using a Project Selection Matrix

When creating a project selection matrix, you must first decide on the project selection criteria and weight the criteria according to the organization's strategic goals and other objectives. Some possible criteria may be:

- Financial return
- Effect on employees/alignment with corporate culture
- Technical advancement or innovation
- Market value/share
- Public perception
- Alignment with/advancement of corporate strategy

For each criterion in your matrix, complete each project's objective or subjective measurements. Table 1.1 provides some possible benefit measurements for sample criteria.

TABLE 1.1 Project Selection Criteria

Criteria	Possible Benefit Measurements
Financial return	• Net present value (NPV) • Cost/benefit analysis • Internal rate of return (IRR)
Cost avoidance	Cost/benefit analysis (calculate savings and all costs)
Technical advancement or innovation	• Will it apply only to the project, the entire organization, or will what is developed during the project be marketable outside the organization? • Will it appear as innovative to others in industry, thus creating prestige for the organization?

TABLE 1.1 Project Selection Criteria *(continued)*

Criteria	Possible Benefit Measurements
Market value/share	Increase value/share according to set formula, research, or surveys
Public perception	• Measure perceived increase/decrease in perception based on focus groups, surveys, or interviews. Estimate the awareness/perception that will be created. • Calculate the number of people affected/made aware
Alignment with organization expertise	• Does the project team have the expertise to do the project? Can the organization acquire the expertise and does it want to? • Will the project efforts help develop some expertise or skill it wants developed?
Needed infrastructure improvement	• Improved productivity—show cost savings if possible • Describe old system/processes that might collapse or slow down and include impact • Compare with other infrastructure projects

Project Justification Criteria

When justifying a project, follow these steps:

1. Select five to seven main criteria to justify your organization's projects. If you select more, this exercise will become difficult to manage. Assign a weighting factor to each criterion according to what is most important to the organization.

2. For each criterion, select the benefit measurement you will use.

3. Create the list of all proposed projects. Note that most should have a written business case to provide more information for the project selection committee.

4. Put the projects in a matrix and rate each project according to the method selected. Then, multiply the weighting factor to each rating received.

5. Eliminate any projects based on any minimum standards or thresholds you have established prior to the ranking exercise (for instance, if the project would lose money and all other rankings are below a 5 average, it automatically is eliminated).

6. Rank the remaining projects.

7. Select the projects you want to proceed with from this ranking.

8. Make sure you document justifications for each project selected based on this process. You can use the justification in your project charter, scope statement, business case, or any other document supporting the project.

Scenario

Your consulting company, Terrific Project Management Partners (TPMP), has been asked to help an established investment company, Best Investments Company (BIC), to create a project justification process for them. The company tends to take on all projects that are proposed, and it has become increasingly difficult to manage the company's project portfolio. You will help them establish a semiannual review process using a project selection matrix based on the company's major project criteria.

BIC has a choice between the following three projects:

- Build investment kiosks and put them in major malls across the United States, known as the kiosk project.

- Create a program to recruit community financial advisors who provide services to investors within a particular territory based on per capita income of various communities, known as the financial advisor project.

- Build franchises that work like fast food restaurants in strip malls , known as the franchise project.

BIC could choose all or one of these projects to increase its presence in the community. After much discussion with the project selection committee, TPMP got agreement that the following are the most important objectives for the company. They also created a weighting factor for each (presented in Table 1.2). These weighting factors will be multiplied by the benefit measurement ratings each of the projects received for the criteria. BIC project managers will meet to determine their rating or score system for each of the criteria.

This process will help rank projects so that those with good rating scores for higher weighted projects will be selected prior to those that might have high ratings for less important criteria.

TABLE 1.2   Best Investments Company Criteria and Weighting

Criteria	Weight Factor
Increase market share as the investment company of choice	5
Good financial return	4
Provide possible innovation in investment tools and techniques	3
Support the corporate culture of employee supporting employee	2
Increase public awareness	1

After applying project measurement ratings for each of the criteria supplied in Table 1.2, the projects were given scores (with 10 being highest possible mark). The kiosk project ratings are represented in Table 1.3.

TABLE 1.3   Kiosk Project Criteria Ratings

Criteria	Rating
Increase market share	5
Good financial return	6
Innovation	9
Support culture	1
Increase public awareness	8

For the financial advisor project, BIC came up with the following ratings represented in Table 1.4.

TABLE 1.4   Financial Advisor Criteria Ratings

Criteria	Rating
Increase market share	7
Good financial return	3
Innovation	5
Support culture	5
Increase public awareness	5

Finally, for the franchise project, BIC created the ratings shown in Table 1.5.

TABLE 1.5   Franchise Criteria Ratings

Criteria	Rating
Increase market share	7
Good financial return	7
Innovation	4
Support culture	3
Increase public awareness	6

Justifying a Project—Project Selection Matrix

Complete the following matrix using the above information. Remember that the actual score for a criterion is the rating times the weighting factor.

1. Fill in the following Best Investment Company project selection matrix based on the information above.

Criteria	Kiosk	Financial Advisor	Franchise
Increase market share			
Good financial return			
Innovation			
Support culture			
Increase public awareness			
Total Score			
Project Rank			

2. If you could choose only one project after this process, which one would it be and why?

_____

_____

_____

3. Does the project ranking determine which project will be selected over the other?

_____

_____

_____

4. Is this a good method for selecting projects? Why or why not?

_____

_____

_____

_____

5. What other criteria might a company use for deciding on projects?

_____

_____

_____

_____

6. What are some potential problems using this method of selecting projects?

_____

_____

_____

_____

Exercise 1.2: Project Selection Methods—Financial Returns

The objectives for Exercise 1.2 are:

- Describe the importance of having a measurement methodology for selecting projects for a particular criteria.
- Describe various financial return methods.
- Use financial return methods to select a project.

Background

Project selection methods help an organization objectively decide what proposed projects to pursue. Project selection methods also help the organization prioritize projects based on the outcome of applying the selected method to the approved projects. The method used is based on the selection criteria an organization uses (as explored in the previous exercise). The more objective methods an organization uses, the better it can justify the selection and sustain the project over time. If your organization does not use selection criteria and project selection methods, projects might be selected according to the person who lobbies the loudest for their project or the organization may overload itself with projects.

In Exercise 1.2, you'll explore methods for project selection, then you'll help Terrific Project Management Partners (TPMP) provide project advice for one of its clients.

Recommended Reading: Chapter 3, pp. 88–97, *PMP Project Management Professional Study Guide*

Before you begin the project selection process, you will have to make a few decisions regarding your approach.

First, decide on the project selection criteria that you want to measure. In Exercise 1.1, we listed several of those criteria. Next, decide on a consistent and standardized approach for measuring benefits for the criteria. For instance, for financial return you could use one or more of the following:

- Payback period
- Net present value (NPV)
- Internal rate of return (IRR)
- Other forms of cost/benefit analysis

Finally, apply the same method for each project using objective measurements.

Subjective measurements, based on expert judgment or some kind of methodology created by the organization or team, work as well as using objective measurements. For instance, how do you measure an increase in public perception? Using previous similar projects as a basis, you could use a focus survey or market research to measure success. These methods offer a way to measure criteria in a consistent and standard approach and have an outcome based on analysis to help you better justify your decision.

Scenario

Your consulting company, Terrific Project Management Partners (TPMP), has been asked to help an established investments company, Best Investments Company (BIC), use project selection methods. Best Investments Company tends to take on any project proposal so it has become increasingly difficult to manage the company's project portfolio. Just as BIC helps its customers achieve the best return for their money, BIC would like to ensure that its three projects have the best financial return; BIC decided to use financial return as their major project selection method.

In order to select the best financial return method, you will take the executives at BIC through several exercises to help them decide which one they should use. They have decided that they want their project managers to be able to calculate these financial return methodologies; they do not want to make the work too complex, but they want the most accurate method possible.

You will take them through the following financial return methods:

Payback period   Payback period is the amount of time it takes a company to recoup its initial investment in the cost of producing a product or service. It is fairly simple to use, but is not as accurate as other methods because it does not consider how the value of money is affected by interest over time. The decision is based on when the payback comes, not on how much the organization will make after that payback point.

Discounted cash flow/net present value (NPV)   Net present value (NPV) brings the value of future monies received into today's dollars minus the initial investment. It is a fairly accurate method because it takes into account the time value of money, but it uses more complicated formulas. You would choose projects with the highest NPV.

Internal rate of return (IRR)   IRR is the discount rate when the present value of the cash inflows equals the original investment. This is a complex but accurate calculation. You should choose projects with the highest IRR value.

When completing Exercise 1.2, you will use the following projects and financial projections to help the company see how these methods work.

Build an investment kiosk.   Initial cost is $5 million to install in targeted locations, and return is expected to be $750,000 the first year, $300,000 per quarter over the next two years, and $750,000 semiannually, thereafter.

Create a program to recruit community financial advisors.   Initial cost is $8 million to recruit and train the advisors, and return is expected to be $1.5 million the first year, $400,000 per quarter over the next three years, and $750,000 semiannually thereafter.

Build franchises that work like fast food restaurants in strip malls.   Initial cost is $11 million to build or convert existing buildings in targeted locations and to hire employees, and return is expected to be $1 million the first six months, $2.5 million the second six months, $500,000 per quarter the second year, $600,000 per quarter the third year, $3 million annually thereafter.

Project Selection Methods—Financial Returns

Determine financial return for the three BIC projects. You might want to create tables for each project.

1.   Based on the three projects, which one has the best payback? Rank them.

_____

_____

_____

_____

2.   Will the project manager be able to calculate this information? Why?

_____

_____

_____

_____

3.   For Best Investments Company, what are some of the advantages/disadvantages of this method?

_____

_____

_____

_____

Based on the kiosk, financial advisor, and franchise projects, use the net present value method to answer Questions 4–6. You may use the same investment and expected financial projection information described in the project setup, but in this case, the time value of money (interest rate) is 5 percent and you will calculate NPV over five years for each project.

You will need to lay out the actual inflows for each year and apply the present value formula to each year, then subtract the initial investment. Also, round to the nearest dollar. To make this easier, check out the following interest rate table.

Year 1: $(1 + .05)^1 = 1.0500$

Year 2: $(1 + .05)^2 = 1.1025$

Year 3: $(1 + .05)^3 = 1.1576$

Year 4: $(1 + .05)^4 = 1.2155$

Year 5: $(1 + .05)^5 = 1.2763$

1. Based on these three projects, which one will provide the best NPV? Rank them.

2. Will the project manager be able to calculate this information?

3. For Best Investment Company, what are some of the advantages/disadvantages of this method?

Finally, for Questions 7–10, you will use IRR without actually calculating IRR. In the case of the three projects, the following shows the IRR value for each project.

- Build an investment kiosk. IRR = 5.5 percent

- Create a program to recruit community financial advisors. IRR = 3 percent

- Build franchises in strip malls that work like a fast food restaurant. IRR = 5 percent

1. Based on the kiosk, financial advisor, and franchise projects, which one will provide the best IRR? Rank them.

   _____

   _____

   _____

   _____

2. Will the project manager be able to calculate this information?

   _____

   _____

   _____

   _____

3. For BIC, what are some of the advantages/disadvantages of this method?

   _____

   _____

   _____

   _____

4. Which financial return method would you recommend for BIC and why?

   _____

   _____

   _____

   _____

Exercise 1.3: Project Initiation and the Project Charter

The objectives for Exercise 1.3 are:

- Describe the need for a project charter.
- Describe the essential elements of a project charter.
- Create parts of a project charter.

Background

A project charter is the official written acknowledgment and recognition that a project exists. It's issued by senior management external to the project and gives the project manager authority to assign organizational resources to the work of the project. When writing a charter, you will capture and document information such as:

- A description of the product and an overview of the project
- Project goals and objectives
- Project deliverables
- The business case or the business need for the project
- Resource and cost estimates
- Feasibility study (optional and not a part of this exercise).

In this exercise, you will learn the steps required for writing a project charter and lead BIC through the process as well.

 Recommended Reading: Chapter 2, pp. 57–61 and Chapter 3, pp. 100–103, *PMP Project Management Professional Study Guide.*

A project charter describes the basic elements of the project and authorizes the project to continue. To write a project charter, follow these steps:

1. Interview the sponsor of the project, any product managers, and any other organizational leaders involved in the project to ensure you understand the product and the purpose of the project. For each succeeding interview, as you listen to the information and take notes, confirm that all of the interviewees concur with the major points you progressively discover.

2. Ask your sponsor and other stakeholders what the main goals and objectives of the project are. Ask questions such as: When you get to the end of this project, what is the product going to look like and what will it do? Have them attempt to define what success looks like for the project.

3. Ask your sponsor and other stakeholders what tangible deliverables will be part of the project. Give them some examples, based on the typical life cycle of your product or service.

4. Collect the business case for your project and attach it to the plan. If it has not been completed, then complete it yourself. Note that you may want to share the major points of the business case with your sponsor and other interviewees, and confirm that all the product justifications have been included, and that your stakeholders agree with the business case.

5. Start an estimate of resource needs and costs. Use previous projects as comparisons; ask your stakeholders for estimates, and based on size and complexity and the kind of industry you are in, start accumulating this information.

6. Write the project charter with all the information you have gathered.

7. Include a description of the authority the project manager will need (can you hire/fire, control budget, reward/punish performance?).

8. Ensure all elements described in the introduction are documented.

9. Ask your sponsor or a senior leader to review and change the charter as needed, and have them sign it and distribute it to leadership and management affected by the project.

10. Have a meeting to ensure concurrence with the charter for all executives and identified team members.

Scenario

Your company, Terrific Project Management Partners (TPMP), has been requested to continue helping the Best Investments Company (BIC) with their project initiation processes. BIC has selected a project and wants to understand how a project charter can help further define and authorize the project. The company has decided to build electronic kiosks in major malls throughout the United States. Jim Thoroughgood has been assigned as project manager, and you will be mentoring him on the project. You will help Jim write a project charter.

BIC expects the kiosk project to deliver most of the standard items for a new investment program, but this one has a twist: BIC is an investment company, not a construction company, and the project involves the construction of a kiosk. The project also involves electronic innovation, specifically, easy computerized menus for mall users. So, some of the things you might need are a software application with an easy user interface, a constructed kiosk, the investment program you will try to sell, advertisements for this new investment program, and other items that will be part of a successful new product. Martha Frederick, your main sponsor, has asked that the first kiosk be in place within nine months and the budget for initial implementation of 25 kiosks should cost no more than $5 million. She says the company doesn't expect anything glitzy—just something efficient and attractive to the average investor.

Project Initiation and the Project Charter

1. Describe the product of the project. Do this in your own words, and don't hesitate to add some of your own thoughts to this description.

    _____

    _____

    _____

2. What are the main goals and objectives of this project? Again, don't hesitate to add some things you know need to be included that may not be included in the exercise setup description.

    _____

    _____

    _____

    _____

3. What are the main, high-level project deliverables?

_____

_____

_____

_____

4. List the responsibility and authority Jim Thoroughgood would require to succeed on this project.

_____

_____

_____

_____

5. Is it a good idea to have the project manager's responsibility and authority written in the project charter? Why?

_____

_____

_____

_____

6. What are the resource and cost estimates?

_____

_____

_____

_____

7. Who signs the charter, and to whom is the charter given?

_____

_____

_____

_____

Exercise 1.4: Creating the Scope Statement

The objectives for Exercise 1.4 are:

- Describe the need for a scope statement.
- Describe the parts essential to a scope statement.
- Create the parts of a scope statement.

Background

The project scope statement is one of the most important items you can create for your project. Without it, you have a project with no bounds. Without it, what the project will accomplish can be anything you or your stakeholders decide along the way. A scope statement acts as your common understanding of the project requirements and deliverables. It is also the baseline of the scope, and if things change, you will follow change procedures to document and plan the changes into your project. If you use a vendor, the scope statement can be used to develop a statement of work (SOW) to describe the work the vendor will perform.

In this exercise, you will learn the elements of a scope statement and the steps involved with creating the scope statement by leading BIC through the scope statement process.

Scope Statement Elements

You will document the following elements for your scope statement:

- Project justification—describe the business need the project is to address.
- Project product—describe the product or service briefly.
- Requirements or specifications—ensure requirements of the product or service are documented. This may be a separate deliverable.
- Project deliverables—list summary-level subproducts for full delivery of the project. This may include a high-level work breakdown structure to show the scope of the project.
- Project objectives—list quantifiable criteria for success and include at least cost, schedule, and quality measures.
- Assumptions—list any assumptions you are making for the project.
- Cost and time estimates.
- Constraints—list any constraints you have for the project.

Recommended Reading. Chapter 4, pp. 120–126, and Chapter 2, pp. 63–66, *PMP Project Management Professional Study Guide.*

The Scope Statement Process

When creating a scope statement, follow these steps:

1. Review the project charter for any items you can reuse for further detail in the scope statement.

2. Work with your project team or other stakeholders to write a brief general statement about the purpose of your project. Try to include a general description of what is in the project, as well as what is not in the project.

3. Include a project justification. This may have been completed in a business case, feasibility study, the project charter, or the project selection work that was completed prior to the project's being approved.

4.   Rewrite or use a product or service description. This is not about the project itself, but the result of the project.

5.   Create a list of major deliverables and create a high-level work breakdown structure to help show the scope of the work. This is a good time to brainstorm with your project team. You might even think of all the deliverables you can on the way to creating your work breakdown structure, and then categorize them into major categories. You want to capture only around seven of the major deliverables (maybe more if the project is complex). Make sure each of these deliverables are measurable and have success criteria tied to them.

6.   List the objective(s) or goals. This is where you describe the goals that help you measure project success. You might think of what must be done for the project to be complete (critical success factors). This needs to be a quantifiable statement, such as "increase shareholder satisfaction by 10 percent." This could be easily measured with pre- and post-implementation surveys. The surveys, of course, would need to be a deliverable of the project.

7.   List assumptions. These are things that you and your project team expect to hold true throughout the project. Sometimes these are statements that seem they should not have to be said: They are obvious. But by documenting them, you can test them as assumptions and ensure stakeholders agree with them. Often these assumptions, if they do not hold true, become risks.

8.   List constraints. These are bounds under which your team will work throughout the project. They restrain or dictate the actions of the project team. For instance, if the team needs to follow some particularly strict safety procedure, it will restrict the team from getting the work done as fast it could otherwise.

9.   You may include requirements in the scope statement or produce them in another document (then refer to them in the scope statement). These requirements are the basis for understanding the amount of work that needs to be done, and for creating a statement of work for a vendor, if you will need to contract some of the work.

10. Include any of the major roles and responsibilities needed for the project.

11. Write the scope statement document, and deliver it to your stakeholders for approval. Have a meeting to review the scope with the team and the stakeholders.

Scenario

You're helping the Best Investments Company (BIC) to continue developing consistent practices in project management in the initiation and planning stages. In particular, a project being managed by Betsy Smith has already been started; since you have been on hand to help advise them of good project management principles, BIC now realizes that it needs a documented scope statement. Betsy is working on a project to increase public awareness and the use of an Internet investment program that has existed for six months, but which is not meeting expected market penetration. Her team has been researching the project for a month, but now the team needs a plan for what to do next. The Internet investment project was expected to increase the overall investment penetration by 10 percent. Right now, no one is sure how much it has increased investment penetration, since overall investment activity by the public has gone down 15 percent in the last year. The team has advertised this service on TV and with Internet pop-up ads. This project has a budget of

$50,000 to develop the plan, and BIC wants the plan within three months. Betsy has already used up about $4,000 in research efforts. Betsy has a team of researchers, part-time software application developers, and the original Internet investment program project manager to call on for help. She is very excited because she has realized the team did not do any advertising for this project in some of the major magazines, such as *Fortune*, and the TV ads were at the wrong times for the target audience. She thinks with this knowledge, she can help the Internet service increase penetration immediately if the team focuses on those areas.

Creating the Scope Statement

1. Write a brief purpose statement for this project. Include a business justification statement. What is the product of this project?

    _____

    _____

    _____

    _____

2. What are some of the major deliverables of the project? Is each deliverable you identify a critical success factor? Why or why not?

    _____

    _____

    _____

    _____

3. Create some goal/objective statements and make sure they are measurable. State what you will put in place to measure them.

    _____

    _____

    _____

    _____

4. Describe some of the assumptions you have for this project.

    _____

    _____

    _____

    _____

5. Describe some constraints.

    _____

    _____

    _____

    _____

6. Will you need a statement of work? Why or why not?

_____

_____

_____

_____

Exercise 1.5: Creating a Scope Management Plan and Managing Scope Change

The objectives for Exercise 1.5 are:

- Describe the need for a scope management plan.
- Describe the parts of a scope management plan.
- Be able to create a scope management plan.
- Learn how to manage scope change.

Background

Is the scope of your project well defined? If the scope changes for your project, what will you do? Do your stakeholders know what to do if they need to suggest a change to the scope of your project? When should you change the scope of your project versus not changing it? All of these questions (and many more) will be answered if you create a scope management plan. As with all PMI's knowledge areas, PMI suggests using documentation to manage that knowledge area. If criteria don't get written down early in the planning process, you will tend to make them up along the way. Maintaining and documenting changes to the scope prevents you from becoming disorganized and helps you manage the project consistently. It also means you and your team can more easily manage scope change and will not allow change that shouldn't occur.

For the scope management plan, you need to identify the stability of the scope at the time you document the plan, how often the scope could change, and the impact to your project if the scope does change. You also need to document how you will manage change. For instance, will you have a form that must be completed, or can people just send e-mail? Whose approval will you need and when? Are there some scope changes the project can absorb without too much impact?

In Exercise 1.5, you will learn the elements that make up a scope statement, and the methods for creating a scope management plan. Finally, you will continue to help the Best Investment Company (BIC) in its project management endeavors.

Scope Management Plan Elements

You will document the following elements for your scope management plan:

- What is the stability of the project scope? Is it early in the plan and, thus, likely to change as you build more information about your project? Or is it simple and well defined, or later in the project planning to indicate a more stable scope?

- How often do you estimate the scope might change, and why?

- If the scope changes, what will the impact be to your project? Do some scope changes have more impact than others? Why?

For managing scope change you will want to ensure you answer the following questions:

- What kind of information about the change needs to be captured?

- Are there specific processes you will use? How will you log, track, and ensure change is incorporated into the project? How will you manage scope changes not accepted for this phase of the project?

- Who needs to approve change?

- How often will scope changes be reviewed?

 Recommended Reading, Chapter 4, pp. 127–129, *PMP Project Management Professional Study Guide.*

Creating a Scope Management Plan

When creating a scope management plan, follow these steps:

Review your scope statement and make some informed judgments about its stability.   Has everyone approved your statement? Will you have new stakeholders join the project over time? Does it still need some clarity? Have you been able to thoroughly document its assumptions and constraints? Have you been able to easily identify success criteria and create objective measurements for its goal statements? Is the project simple and of short duration? If the answer is "no" to any of these, you may need to say the scope is not stable and you will see more changes. Give the scope stability a confidence factor rating, and list the steps you will take to progressively stabilize the scope.

Are the deliverables well defined? Is the project small or short in duration? Is it later in the project phase? Is it just like a similar project done before or a cookie cutter type of project? If the answer is "yes" to any of these, then you may be able to rate the scope stability as high.

Provide in the plan the probability of scope changes and their frequency.   This might be based on the phase you are in or the stability confidence factor you created. You could use this information to estimate how much time you will need for project administration of scope changes. You might create a table with various dates on which you will perform a scope review so you can have the team review the scope and its stability and then reflect changing stability after these reviews.

Describe how scope changes will impact the project.   If you are under a very tight schedule, you might describe how any scope addition will change the end date. Or if quality is one of the important driving factors, that additions to the scope will have to also include additional quality assurance.

Document the scope change process.   You will want to integrate the scope change process into your overall change control procedures that will be described in a later exercise. You will need to document the following data and processes whether it is an increase or decrease in the scope of the project:

a.   General information about change, such as date, brief description, and who is requesting the change.

b.   Business, technical, or other need for the change.

c.   Describe the resulting analysis of the change (a subject matter expert needs to document impact/analysis). The following items might be a part of that analysis.

  - Impact on scope, resources, cost, quality, schedule, a deliverable, goal, or any other item in the project that will change.

  - Are any new risks introduced, or old risks impacted? What are some of the issues or impacts to existing requirements of the service or product that could occur due to the scope change?

  - Will the change affect other dependencies, such as another project or business processes?

d.   What are the levels of review and approval for the change and how is the change (or reason the change was not accepted) communicated to everyone (whether affected or not)? You might set up a matrix for levels of approval in the scope change plan or in the overall change control plan. The thresholds for approval will vary greatly depending on the complexity of the project. For instance, a five-month project may be able to tolerate a week's slippage and thus may not require a high-level approval. But a one week slippage for a two-month project is relatively significant.

e.   How will the change be integrated into the scope and now managed and tracked as part of the project plan?

Communicate the scope management plan and the scope change process to your project team.   Have a meeting to describe the scope management plan, and hold a training session to make sure everyone knows how to follow your processes to change scope.

Scenario

You're helping the BIC to continue in developing consistent practices in project management planning stages. In particular, a project being managed by Betsy Smith has already been started, but it doesn't have a scope management plan. The project is to create a plan that will increase public awareness and use of an Internet investment program that has existed for six months, but which is not meeting expected market penetration. She has created a scope statement with your help. The project budget is $50,000, is expected to take three months, and includes deliverables of in-house research and a focus survey. The end result is a plan that the sponsor, director of marketing Harriet Freeman, feels must be backed up by excellent marketing research, and which is easily implementable. During the introduction of the scope statement, two key stakeholders were missing, and Betsy has tried to get their approval, but has not been able to do so yet. The project has already started, and most of the research has been completed. Betsy is finding evidence that some major marketing steps were not originally done in the project; plus the market has changed due to the downturn in the economy, so some extra marketing steps need to be taken, including more Internet and TV advertising.

Creating a Scope Management Plan and Managing Scope Change

1. Rate the stability of the scope. Base this on your own confidence factor and describe what you think makes the scope stable and/or unstable.

    _____

    _____

    _____

    _____

2. What are some reasons the scope might change? How often do you think the scope might change? Why?

    _____

    _____

    _____

    _____

3. Fred Arlington, the project manager from the original project, thinks that the project needs to include hiring an independent auditor to review the market research findings because he does not think the research team is coming to the right conclusions. Describe potential impacts to schedule, quality, the people, or any other important elements of the project this change might cause.

    _____

    _____

    _____

    _____

4. What must Fred do to request this change? What data do you need to capture for this scope change request?

    _____

    _____

    _____

    _____

5. Who do you think needs to approve the change, and when should the change reviews occur?

_____

_____

_____

_____

6. Why is a scope management plan important?

_____

_____

_____

_____

Answers to Exercise Questions

Answers to Exercise 1.1

Your answers should be similar to the following:

1. The following shows you how the Best Investments Company project selection matrix would be completed. Note that the answers you have do not need to match the answers provided. You may think of other information or justifications besides those given.

Criteria	Kiosk	Financial Advisor	Franchise
Increase market share	5 x 5 = 25	7 x 5 = 35	7 x 5 = 35
Good financial return	6 x 4 = 24	3 x 4 = 12	7 x 4 = 28
Innovation	9 x 3 = 27	5 x 3 = 15	4 x 3 = 12
Support culture	1 x 2 = 2	5 x 2 = 10	3 x 2 = 6
Increase public awareness	8 x 1 = 8	5 x 1 = 5	6 x 1 = 6
Total Score	86	77	87
Project Rank	2	3	1

2. The franchise project provides the greater increase in the market share and financial return, although the kiosk project is so close in overall ranking and may be considered. By looking at the details of what was rated so high, you can see that innovation is what made the kiosk project achieve a higher rating, which is a lower weighted criteria.

3. The project ranking certainly provides a good way of ranking projects and is clearly demonstrated in this exercise. However, in this case, if the company found that the innovation of the kiosk project was important to the company's strategic advancement, it might choose the kiosk project over the franchise project. Or perhaps it would decide to undertake both projects, because the innovation of the kiosk project is so compelling. At any rate, this process provides a consistent and objective method of selection, but it may not be the only factor in choosing one project over the other.

4. Yes, the project ranking is an excellent method. There may be other kinds of selection methods, but this provides a consistent approach to ranking projects. There may be some projects that could have the same ratings, and there would need to be a method for breaking ties, as well.

5. Some other criteria a company might use are: Cost avoidance (Cost/benefit analysis—calculate savings and all costs)

   Alignment with company expertise. (Does the project team have the expertise to do the project? Can the company acquire the expertise and does it want to? Will the project efforts help develop some expertise it wants developed?)

   Needed infrastructure improvement. (Improved productivity—show cost savings if possible. Describe old system/processes that might collapse or slow down and include impact. Compare with other infrastructure projects.)

6. Some possible problems include:

   It is possible that each project would not be rated consistently. The project selection method and the way it is applied needs to be consistent. Also, there may be times when a project may rate and rank low, but there is some intrinsic value that might be ignored. The project selection committee must use good judgment and instinct to think about projects. It is also possible that the selection process can be overridden by leaders or politics in the company. This may be okay, or it may undermine the selection process.

Answers to Exercise 1.2

The best way to answer this exercise is by setting up a year-by-year expected cash flow matrix. It would look something like the following set of tables. You may think of other information or justification besides those given.

The first table shows Kiosk cash inflows with an initial investment of $5,000,000.

Year	Cash Inflow in Dollars
1	750,000
2	1,200,000
3	1,200,000
4	2,000,000
5	1,500,000
6	1,500,000

The next table shows financial advisor cash inflows with an initial investment of $8,000,000.

Year	Cash Inflow in Dollars
1	1,500,000
2	1,600,000
3	1,600,000
4	1,600,000
5	1,500,000
6	1,500,000

This last table shows franchise cash inflows with an initial investment of $11,000,000.

Year	Cash Inflow in Dollars
1	3,500,000
2	2,000,000
3	2,400,000
4	3,000,000
5	3,000,000
6	3,000,000

1. The Kiosk project has the best payback, which would be early in the fourth year. The original investment was $5 million, and by adding each year's totals incrementally, the payback of $5,150,000 would occur in the fourth year. This would rank number 1.

   The franchise project has the second best payback, which would be early in the fifth year. The original investment was $11 million, and by adding each year's totals incrementally, the payback of $13,900,000 would occur in the fifth year (it would be paid back early in that year). This would rank number 2.

   The financial advisor project has the third best payback, which would be in the sixth year. The original investment was $8 million, and by adding each year's totals incrementally, the payback of $9,300,000 would occur in the sixth year. This would rank number 3.

2. Yes, the project manager could do this calculation. It is one of the simplest financial return calculations. After the cash inflows are projected, the project manager can make this calculation with simple addition/subtraction.

3. Some advantages of the payback period method are that it is simple to calculate and easy to understand. A major disadvantage is that it does not take into account the time value of money (interest) and thus, it is not as accurate as the other methods.

4. The best NPV is the franchise project, and the second is the kiosk project. Since the financial advisor project has a negative NPV, it should not be considered in a ranking. The following tables describe how the NPV was calculated for each.

The first table shows NPV for kiosk inflow based on the initial investment of $5,000,000.

Year	Cash Inflow in Dollars	Calculation	Totals
1	750,000	750,000 ÷ 1.0500 =	714,286
2	1,200,000	1,200,000 ÷ 1.1025 =	1,088,435
3	1,200,000	1,200,000 ÷ 1.1576 =	1,036,628
4	2,000,000	2,000,000 ÷ 1.2155 =	1,645,413
5	1,500,000	1,500,000 ÷ 1.2763 =	1,175,272
Total			5,660,034
Less Investment			(5,000,000)
NPV			660,034

The next table shows NPV for the recruitment project based on the initial investment of $8,000,000.

Year	Cash Inflow in Dollars	Calculation	Totals
1	1,500,000	1,500,000 ÷ 1.0500 =	1,428,571
2	1,600,000	1,600,000 ÷ 1.1025 =	1,451,247
3	1,600,000	1,600,000 ÷ 1.1576 =	1,382,170
4	1,600,000	1,600,000 ÷ 1.2155 =	1,316,331
5	1,500,000	1,500,000 ÷ 1.2763 =	1,175,272
Total			6,753,591
Less Investment			(8,000,000)
NPV			(1,246,409)

The last table shows the NPV for the franchise project based on the initial $11,000,000 investment.

Year	Cash Inflow in Dollars	Calculation	Totals
1	3,500,000	3,500,000 ÷ 1.0500 =	3,333,333
2	2,000,000	2,000,000 ÷ 1.1025 =	1,814,059

Year	Cash Inflow in Dollars	Calculation	Totals
3	2,400,000	2,400,000 ÷ 1.1576 =	2,073,255
4	3,000,000	3,000,000 ÷ 1.2155 =	2,468,120
5	3,000,000	3,000,000 ÷ 1.2763 =	2,350,545
Total			12,039,312
Less Investment			(11,000,000)
NPV			1,039,312

5. No, NPV is not as simple to calculate as payback period so it may be difficult for some project managers to calculate. It will require a certain amount of financial acumen.

6. An advantage of the NPV method is that it is more accurate because it includes the time value of money. A disadvantage is that it is more complex to calculate.

7. Since the kiosk project has the highest internal rate of return at 5.5 percent, it ranks number 1. The franchise project ranks second with 5 percent IRR. The financial advisor project ranks last at 3 percent IRR.

8. No, it's complex to calculate IRR in this situation. IRR requires a financial calculator and thus it may be difficult for the project manager to calculate.

9. An advantage of IRR is that it is more accurate. A disadvantage is that it is more complex to calculate.

10. We recommend the NPV method. Since the managers at Best Investments Company stated that they are interested in an accurate method, providing the best investments as they hope to do for their clients, you might recommend the NPV method. Using the payback method, the kiosk project seemed to be the best selection, but when you look at NPV, it is evident that the franchise project is the best investment when comparing over the same amount of time.

Answers to Exercise 1.3

Your answers should be similar to the following:

1. A sample product description:

   Create kiosks that provide investment solutions to new and returning customers shopping at America's major malls. This kiosk must be attractive and easy to use in order to bring in new customers to our investment portfolio. The kiosk must have an easy-to-use interface for customers to start their investment portfolios. The kiosk will include a new and innovative application that allows customers to analyze and create a portfolio using our current investment products. The main customers for this product are those people who do not have computers in their homes, and those browsing the malls. The kiosk must be compelling enough to grab the customer's attention. The main reason for creating this kiosk is to increase our market by 10 percent.

Note that a product statement evolves as the project progresses, and the description may become far more detailed. Also, this description would need to be in greater detail if a vendor would be used to do the work (or portions of the work).

2. Some possible objectives might be:

   (A) We will increase our total investment penetration based on this innovative product by 10 percent within two years. (B) With the innovation created by our new application and interface, we will increase our image within the industry within six months by having at least three independent articles printed in major industry magazines lauding our kiosks. (C) The application must be secure for the customer, and must use basic information, so that the customer does not have to have a lot of information to start their portfolio.

3. Some of the deliverables might be:

   Design, construction, and testing of the kiosk. Concept, design, and implementation (including testing) of the interface and new investment application.

   Marketing of the kiosk concept. Also, surveys and market research to ensure that market increase is achieved, and that the designs will be innovative.

4. Jim's responsibilities will be to ensure that the project is properly planned, executed, and managed. Specifically his responsibilities should include:

   - Set standards and policies for the project's work and establish and communicate the project procedures to the project team and stakeholders and any contractors used on the project.

   - Identify activities and tasks, resource requirements, project costs, project requirements, and performance measures.

   - Ensure all project information is documented.

   - Communicate status to management, stakeholders, and the team as needed.

   - As the project proceeds, ensure that the ongoing plan and schedule accurately reflect cost, time, and performance as the plan is executed and make any corrective steps as necessary.

   For authority, Jim could require the following:

   - Control over the budget.

   - The ability to choose, add, and remove members from the team.

   - Authority to negotiate and manage the contract terms and the contractor. Contract management might include requiring status and specific performance measurements from the contractor. Also, the project manager should have input into performance reviews for the work performed on the project.

   - Help from management to escalate and solve major project issues.

   - Work on an equal basis with functional managers within the company to get issues solved.

   - Create, change (with appropriate approval), and communicate the project plan and focus as needed.

5. Yes, it is an excellent idea to write the project manager's responsibility and authority into the charter (as well as other roles and responsibilities, if possible). It is better to have it in writing rather than just assumed. If issues come up in the project in which he or she needs to assert authority, the project manager will then be able to point to the charter to help support his or her actions.

6. You have been given a budget estimate of $5 million, and you can start with that as your cost estimate, although you will need to state that one of your planning deliverables will be to create a more accurate cost estimate. For resources, you might initially list in the charter that you will need a market researcher, functional team members (from the investment portfolio department and IT groups), kiosk builders (you might consider a contractor with this experience), and marketing/sales people to sell the kiosks at the malls.

7. Martha Frederick or a senior manager actually issues the project charter. Jim Thoroughgood, the project sponsor, key stakeholders, and other key major senior managers will sign the project charter.

Answers to Exercise 1.4

Note that the answers you have do not need to match the answers provided. You may think of other information or justifications besides those given.

1. A sample purpose statement:

    The purpose of this project is to create a plan to help increase investment penetration by 10 percent and include a way to measure it. The project will research the market demand for the Internet investment project. The product of the project is actually just a plan based on solid market research and a measurement method to ensure the market increase can be quantified.

    Note: It may appear that the team's purpose is to increase market share, but it is solely *to create a plan* to increase market share.

2. The following are some possible deliverables. You may think of others.

    ▪ A market research report. This would be a critical success factor, because without it, you would not know the competition or the market share you could obtain. If research was done for the original project, you would want to update or include it in this document.

    ▪ A survey to find out why people aren't using the current program. This survey is not required—your plan could use the research as a baseline, and this might add a great deal to the quality of your plan.

    ▪ A recommendation. This could be part of the plan, but the recommendation could supply what steps you would include in the plan, such as particular advertising, or improvement of the Internet program, and support for why they should be done. This may not be a critical success factor but again would help with the quality of the plan.

    ▪ A plan. This is a critical success factor—the product of the project.

    ▪ A way to measure the current market share of investment programs, and a way to measure the market share after the plan is implemented. This is a critical success factor.

3. Some possible objectives might be:

- Create an implementable plan to increase Internet program market share by 10 percent within three months. You may measure whether the plan is implementable by ensuring time and resources are applied, and that all tasks are approved by possible owners of the tasks. All the tasks should be based on specific research or survey results.

- Create a tool that can be systematically applied to measure market improvement for the program at predefined times during the plan's implementation to show increase or decrease from baseline.

4. Some assumptions might be:

- The output of this project is only a plan. No steps will be taken to actually improve market share at this time.

- The market research will be as accurate and timely as possible.

- A survey will accurately reflect the attitudes of typical users of the Internet program.

- You have the expertise on the team to know what kind of tasks to implement to increase market share for the program.

5. Some constraints might be:

- The team is constrained by the remaining budget to do the research, survey, and plan creation.

- The research team must use only the tools and knowledge it has. (Note: This is a good test to see if the stakeholders would consider getting some expert research help for the team.)

6. No, you will probably not need a statement of work (SOW) because you will not be using any outside contractors. Sometimes people call this scope statement an SOW, but it is usually used for contractors. If you use some kind of outside help to perform the survey to gather data about issues with the current Internet program, you would need to create an SOW for their part of the work.

Answers to Exercise 1.5

Note that the answers you have do not need to match the answers provided. You may think of other information or justifications besides those given.

1. The stability of the scope might be around 60 percent confidence factor. It is very well defined and of short duration. The team is already a month into the project, so it should have a fairly high confidence factor. But because two key stakeholders have not approved the scope statement you cannot give the stability a high rating. This is especially true based on the success statement that the sponsor has provided. The key stakeholders as well as the project team will probably need a more measurable success definition to understand what excellent market research and implementable plan mean.

2. Some reasons the scope might change:

   During market research, the team may find an alternative research path it did not originally think of, requiring more time to include more research. Another scope change might be that the team may find that it needs someone to audit the completed plan, to ensure that all tasks listed can be implemented. The project team may be asked to actually start implementing some of the tasks it has included in the plan before the plan is actually signed off or this project is over. The sponsor might start getting anxious and ask the team to get the work done more quickly because the market is turning so quickly.

With a stability factor of 60 percent, the scope could change quite often. Since two stakeholders have not approved it, the scope could change a great deal in the next two weeks (and if so, adjustments would need to be made to the plan). Once the stakeholders approve the plan, stability may go up to 90 percent, and the scope might change only about every two weeks or once a month.

3. Fred's decision to hire an independent contractor would have an impact on the in-house researchers. They may feel their integrity and research methods are under question. This could impact the results of the project, with the team slowing to figure out why this independent research is necessary and to analyze what value another research effort will bring the project. Of course it would increase the schedule and budget. It will take time to find a firm, define the statement of work, hire the firm, and manage them. This could increase the project's schedule to at least a month or more. It will increase the project budget since it will cost money to hire the firm and time to manage the vendor. It would change the quality of the work—it could actually increase it or decrease it, depending on the standards and reputation of the firm hired.

4. To request the change and hire an independent contractor, Fred needs to go through the formal change request process that Betsy will create in the scope management plan. In that plan, she will describe how people are supposed to submit change requests. The data requested and what needs to be included in the analysis should be:

   - What is the requested change.

   - Why is the change needed. Fred will need to document a compelling business justification to find support for this change.

   - What is the impact on schedule, budget, quality, deliverables, or goal. Include any analysis about the change. Include any information about who has reviewed this impact to ensure a good analysis was completed.

5. Before she can approve the change, Betsy will need to come up with some kind of scope approval authority matrix for estimated impacts. The following table illustrates such a matrix.

Approval/Impact	Cost	Schedule	Quality
Project manager	<$200	< one week	Include or exclude some quality measures
Management stakeholder	$200 to < $500	< one week	No approval needed
Sponsor	= or > $500	> one week	No approval needed
Customer	No approval needed	> one week	Include or exclude some quality measures

This matrix shows the various criteria that a person needs to approve based on a schedule of three months and a budget of $50,000. In this case, the project manager needs to approve everything, but could approve a change under $200 without its being approved by anyone else (and if there weren't many of them!). However, if the schedule changes or a cost change is greater than $200, the project manager would need to get a management stakeholder's approval as well.

Betsy might set up biweekly change reviews, based on how often she thinks change might occur and how often she needs a change review board to look at the submitted changes.

6. The scope management plan is important because the project manager and the team know how to react to requests for change when they occur. The team members will be able to manage change (which is inevitable), rather than let the change manage them. It will describe the criteria needed to analyze the change, and the thresholds for approval of the change. In this manner change will be organized, managed consistently, and communicated regularly and equally to all stakeholders.

Chapter

2

Time Management

THE EXERCISES PRESENTED IN THIS CHAPTER INCLUDE:

- ✓ Exercise 2.1: Creating the Work Breakdown Structure (WBS)
- ✓ Exercise 2.2: Activity Sequencing
- ✓ Exercise 2.3: Estimating Duration Activity
- ✓ Exercise 2.4: Calculating Critical Path
- ✓ Exercise 2.5: Calculating PERT
- ✓ Exercise 2.6: Duration Compression
- ✓ Exercise 2.7: Creating Gantt Charts
- ✓ Exercise 2.8: Controlling Schedule Changes

This section covers Project Time Management, one of the knowledge areas found in PMI's *Guide to the Project Management Body of Knowledge (PMBOK)*. The backbone of project management is the ability to plan, schedule, and control. This chapter sets the foundation for creating a workable schedule. It starts with creating a work breakdown structure and takes you through each level of decomposition and analysis until you are able to create a baseline schedule.

In this chapter, you'll be faced with new challenges in regard to your fictional company, Terrific Project Management Partners (TPMP). You'll learn and practice Project Time Management techniques, such as building a work breakdown structure and sequencing activities. Since the processes of time management build on each other, you'll notice we use the same scenario throughout this chapter and ask you to build on each step of the planning process.

Exercise 2.1: Creating the Work Breakdown Structure (WBS)

The objectives for Exercise 2.1 are:

- Describe the need for a work breakdown structure.
- Describe the essential elements of a work breakdown structure.
- Create a work breakdown structure.

Background

A work breakdown structure (WBS) is a tool and technique used to decompose project scope components into smaller and more manageable components or work packages. The project manager creates it with project team members, and it has many purposes. First, the WBS helps to identify the major deliverables of the project. It creates a total view of the project in small, manageable components and, finally, the WBS helps create a common understanding of the project deliverables.

A work breakdown structure is composed of two elements. The first is levels of work, of which there are three. The highest level is usually the project name or the major task. Intermediate levels of work are subcomponents or higher level tasks, sometimes called summary tasks. Summary tasks are used to sum up the type of tasks below them. Summary tasks help you categorize your thoughts. Two examples of possible summary level tasks are the departments of an organization or geographic boundaries. Finally, work packages are the lowest level of work, sometimes just called the work task.

The other element of the WBS is a unique number identifier. Figure 2.1 shows the three levels of work and the unique number identifiers.

FIGURE 2.1   WBS with three levels

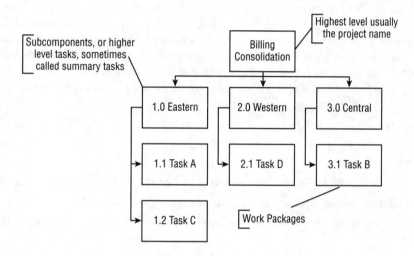

There are eight steps to create a work breakdown structure:

1. Determine the format used in creating the WBS. You can use either a tree structure or an outline.

2. Determine how many levels of decomposition are appropriate for your project.

3. Determine how the levels of the work breakdown structure will be organized.

4. Label level one the project name.

5. At level two, decompose the project into a set of deliverables.

6. For each subsequent level, decompose the level above into smaller components.

7. Create the lowest level of decomposition. This level, called the work package, should be small enough to easily assign to one person to complete. You also will be able to easily create time and cost estimates for this level.

8. Create a unique numerical identifier for each component on the work breakdown structure. The numbering scheme starts at the left side of the WBS and works the same as a numeric outline (e.g., 1.0, 1.1, 1.1.2, etc.).

Recommended Reading: Chapter 4, pp. 130–137, *PMP Project Management Professional Study Guide.*

In Exercise 2.1, you'll guide a TPMP project manager through creating a work breakdown structure in order to help a client reach its goals with the credit card validation project.

Scenario

Your company, Terrific Project Management Partners (TPMP), has just placed you at Systems-Delivery, Inc., as a temporary project manager. You've been assigned the credit card validation project. This project is designed to be the next big thing in credit card fraud prevention. The management of SystemsDelivery believes that this product will be in high demand at every major retailer in the country. Of course the management needs this product to go to market as quickly as possible. On your first day, the project sponsor hands you several documents about the project. One of these documents is a scope statement the last project manager created before he quit. The scope statement includes the following items:

- The validation system will be housed in a device that attaches to all electronic cash registers.
- The validation system must be updated daily using a telephone line and a special toll-free number.
- The validation system contains both software and hardware components.
- The validation system must validate a credit card in 30 seconds or less.
- The validation system must be ready for the U.S. market first, Canadian second, and European third.
- Different devices and software will be needed for each market.

Creating the Work Breakdown Structure

Follow the scope information provided for the credit card validation project and create the work breakdown structure.

1. What format will you use to create your work breakdown structure?

    _____

    _____

2. What is the name of the highest level component of the work breakdown structure?

    _____

    _____

3. What are the main project deliverables on the second level of the work breakdown structure? This is high level.

    _____

    _____

    _____

4. Now that you have the main project deliverables defined, analyze each one and determine the substeps that make up each. These new substeps are level three. Draw them.

5. Examine each level as you create it and determine the substeps until you have tasks that are easily assigned to one person. How many levels did you create for this work breakdown structure? Display your work.

_____

_____

6. Uniquely number each component of the work breakdown structure. Draw your answer.

Exercise 2.2: Activity Sequencing

The objectives for Exercise 2.2 are:

- Describe the different types of dependencies.
- Describe the differences between the precedence diagramming method (PDM) and the arrow diagramming method (ADM).
- Define the four types of dependency relationships.
- Create a network diagram.

Background

Activity Sequencing is a time management planning process used to determine how the work of the project will progress. In other words, it is the sequence of the tasks of the project. In Activity Sequencing you take the activity list created by the work breakdown structure, then use tools and techniques to decide on the progression of the work, which results in the creation of a network diagram.

Components of Activity Sequencing

In order to begin the sequencing process, you must first understand the elements that make it possible, including activity lists, dependencies, and diagramming methods.

Activity List

In the last chapter, we talked about the lowest level of work on the WBS. That lowest level is called a work package. It is also called the activity list.

Dependencies

The first component of Activity Sequencing is determining the dependencies of the work to be done. A dependency describes the relationship between two tasks. There are three types of dependencies. They are:

Mandatory dependencies   Are inherent in the work to be done. You cannot road test a new tire until the tire is manufactured.

Discretionary dependencies   Created by the project team. On the new tire you are creating, you want a ½-inch tread. Because of the size of the tread, you'll need to use a new tire mold that won't be ready for six weeks. You've just created a discretionary dependency.

External dependencies   Come from outside of your project. On your new tire, you are using a special rubber formula that is being shipped from Japan. The next ship to leave for the United States doesn't leave for two more days. You now have an external dependency on that shipment.

Diagramming Methods

Once you understand dependencies, you will need to know which tool and technique to use to depict the sequence of the work. There are two diagramming methods that are most commonly used for sequencing. The first is the precedence diagramming method (PDM), also known as activity on node (AON). In this type of diagram, shown in Figure 2.2, the nodes (boxes) depict the task and the arrows depict the dependency.

FIGURE 2.2   Precedence diagramming method

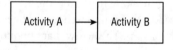

Precedence diagramming uses four types of logical relationships to determine the dependencies between the activities. They are:

1.   In the finish to start relationship, illustrated in Figure 2.2 Activity B cannot start until Activity A is completed.

2. In the start to finish relationship, illustrated below, Activity B cannot finish until Activity A has started.

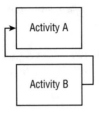

3. In the finish to finish relationship, pictured below, Activity B cannot be completed until Activity A is completed.

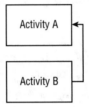

4. Finally, in the start to start relationship, Activity B cannot start until Activity A starts. The following is an example of the start to start relationship.

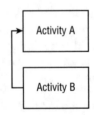

The other commonly used diagramming method is the arrow diagramming method (ADM), also known as activity on arrow (AOA). In this method, the lines are the activities and the circles are the nodes that depict the relationship. The arrow diagramming method, shown in Figure 2.3, uses a finish to start relationship.

FIGURE 2.3   Arrow diagramming method

The Network Diagram

Once you know the components of Activity Sequencing, you can create a network diagram, like the one shown in Figure 2.4, which depicts the progression of work on a project. You will need to create a start and finish node so that all nodes on the network diagram are connected.

FIGURE 2.4   Network diagram

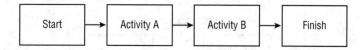

Here are the steps to make a network diagram using Activity Sequencing.

1. Determine whether the WBS needs to be decomposed into smaller activities, called an activity list. These should be small activities that can be assigned to one person.

2. Understand each activity well enough to determine the dependencies between them. Are they mandatory, discretionary, or external?

3. Determine the method of diagramming you will use: precedence or arrow diagramming.

4. Understand the dependencies well enough to know the type of logical relationship between the activities.

5. Create a start and finish node.

6. Sequence the lowest level activities or tasks between the start and finish nodes. Do not sequence the higher levels of the work breakdown structure, that is, the summary level activities.

Recommended Reading: Chapter 5, pp. 165–169, *PMP Project Management Professional Study Guide.*

In Exercise 2.2, you're going to continue your work with SystemsDelivery on the credit card validation project, by determining dependencies and logical relationships and by choosing diagramming methods to create a network diagram.

Scenario

Your company, Terrific Project Management Partners (TPMP), has just placed you at Systems-Delivery, Inc. as a temporary project manager. You've been assigned the Credit Card Validation project. This project is designed to be the next best thing in credit card fraud prevention. The management of SystemsDelivery believes that this product will be in high demand at every major retailer in the country. Of course the management needs this product to go to market as quickly as possible. You have been on the project for two weeks now. You have created the work breakdown structure illustrated in Figure 2.5 for producing the Canadian product. This WBS was created at the lowest possible level, the activity list.

FIGURE 2.5   Canadian device WBS

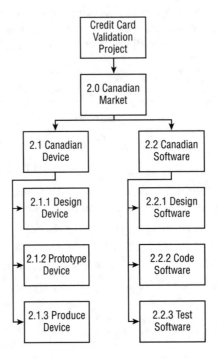

Activity Sequencing

Use the work breakdown structure provided in Figure 2.5 for the credit card validation project and start Activity Sequencing.

1. How many activities have been created at the lowest level of the work breakdown structure (the activity list level)?

    _____

    _____

2. Analyze the dependencies between the activities. Are these dependencies mandatory, discretionary, or external?

    _____

    _____

3. Analyze the dependencies. What is the one logical relationship between each activity for the Canadian software?

    _____

    _____

4. Determine the best method to diagram these activities. Will you use the precedence diagramming method or the arrow diagramming method?

_____

_____

5. Sequence the lowest level activities between a start and finish node. Draw your answer.

Exercise 2.3: Estimating Duration Activity

The objectives for Exercise 2.3 are:

- Describe the meaning of duration.
- Describe the four types of tools and techniques used to create a duration estimate.
- Create duration estimates.

Background

Activity Duration Estimating is a time management planning process that helps determine the amount of time an activity will take. Time in this context means how many work periods (days, weeks, hours, etc.) for the activity to be performed and takes into account elapsed time. For example, you start work at 8:00 AM and begin a task immediately. If you do your normal daily routine, you take a break at 10:00 AM and 2:00 PM and have lunch at noon for an hour. You started the work at 8:00 AM and complete the first draft at 11:00 AM. You have your boss review your work from 11:00 AM till 3:30 PM. At 3:30 PM you put some finishing touches on the report and hand it in at 5:00 PM and go home. You would call this a one-day duration even though you only worked on it from 8:00 AM until 10:00 AM, 10:15 until 11:00 AM, and 3:30 PM until 5:00 PM.

To create an activity duration estimate, you take the inputs of the work breakdown structure activity list created in Exercise 2.1 and resource requirements, and you then determine the estimated time expected for each activity.

Elements of Duration Estimates

You can use several tools and techniques to determine the duration estimates. The first is called expert judgment. In this technique, you ask the people who will perform the task to provide the estimates.

The second technique is called analogous estimating, sometimes called top-down estimating. In this technique, you find other similar tasks that were performed before and use this historical information to create the estimates.

The next technique is quantitatively based durations. It uses a unit of work multiplied by the productivity of the worker. Say, for example, you are estimating a street-paving project. You know that one paving truck can pave 100 feet in 2 hours. You also know the length of the street is 300 feet. Therefore the duration for paving this street is 6 hours.

The last technique used in activity duration estimating is reserve time, also called contingency. Reserve time is a unit of measure that is added to the original estimate to allow for any schedule risk. The unit of measure can either be more hours or a percentage. On our paving example, you know the truck you're using has been having some problems. Because of this you will add 2 more hours to the 6-hour estimate as reserve time.

Creating a Duration Estimate

There are seven steps to creating duration activity estimates.

1. Determine if the WBS needs to be decomposed into smaller activities, called an activity list. These activities should be small enough to be assigned to one person.

2. Understand the resource requirements for each activity.

3. Determine whether it would be best to use expert judgment, analogous estimating, or quantitatively based durations for each activity.

4. Determine the proper duration estimate for each activity.

5. Analyze each activity for schedule risk.

6. Determine what type of reserve time you might apply: a work unit or percentage.

7. Add reserve time to each activity where appropriate.

In this exercise, we're going to continue building our time management information at SystemsDelivery by creating duration estimates for the credit card validation project.

Recommended Reading: Chapter 5, pp. 169–171, *PMP Project Management Professional Study Guide.*

Scenario

Your company, TPMP, has just placed you at SystemsDelivery, Inc. as a temporary project manager. You've been assigned the Credit Card Validation project. This project is designed to be the next best thing in credit card fraud prevention. The management of SystemsDelivery believes that this product will be in high demand at every major retailer in the country. Of course the management needs this product to go to market as quickly as possible. You have been on the project for two weeks now. You have created the work breakdown structure illustrated in Figure 2.6 for producing the Canadian product. This WBS was created at the lowest possible level, the activity list.

FIGURE 2.6   Canadian device WBS

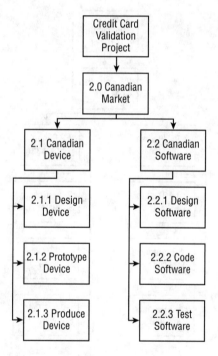

Estimating Duration Activity

Use the work breakdown structure provided in Figure 2.6 for the credit card validation project and start creating duration estimates.

1. How many activities have been created at the lowest level of the work breakdown structure (the activity list level)?

_____

_____

2.   What types of people will be needed to perform these activities?

_____

_____

3.   What tool and technique will you use to derive the estimate?

_____

_____

4.   Determine the duration estimate for each activity. Please place your answer on the WBS below.

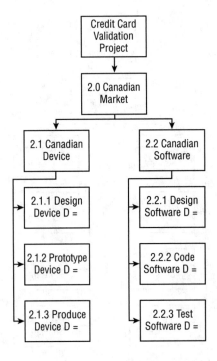

5.   Determine what type of reserve time you might apply to the tasks at risk.

_____

_____

_____

_____

6. Add the reserve time to the appropriate estimates. Place new duration estimates on the WBS below.

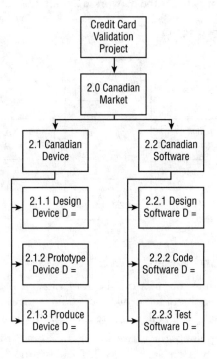

Exercise 2.4: Calculating Critical Path

The objectives for Exercise 2.4 are:

- Describe the meaning of float.
- Understand the three steps of calculating critical path.

Background

When you create a network diagram, you also create a critical path for your project. The critical path is defined as the longest path through the project and has no float, or slack time—meaning the amount of time you can delay the early start of the project without affecting the planned finish date of the project. Looking at your network diagram, the critical path or tasks with float may not be obvious. You'll want to manage the critical path, because if a task on the critical path slips, the end date of the project slips. To determine the critical path for your project, you use a mathematical analysis tool and technique of the schedule development process called Critical Path Method (CPM).

CPM calculates a single critical path for the project. It requires that you perform a forward pass, backward pass, and calculate float for the entire network diagram.

Let's calculate the critical path for the network diagram illustrated in Figure 2.7.

FIGURE 2.7   Network diagram

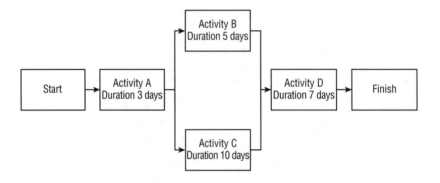

Calculating a Forward Pass

To calculate the critical path for our network diagram, first, we'll have to compute a forward pass. Starting at the earliest point of the network diagram, a forward pass calculates the early start and early finish for each task. Following are the steps to calculating a forward pass:

1.   Starting at the earliest point of the network diagram from Figure 2.7, look at Activity A. The earliest time Activity A can start is day 0. Therefore the early start is zero. Add the duration to the early start. The early finish is 3. 0 + 3 = 3.

2.   Continue through the network diagram and calculate the early start and early finish for each task.

3.   When you get to Activity D, use the largest early finish from Activity B or Activity C for the early start of Activity D. Table 2.1 illustrates the early start and early finish days for our network diagram.

TABLE 2.1   Early start and early finish for each activity

Activity	Early Start	Early Finish
A	0	3
B	3	8
C	3	13
D	13	20

Calculating a Backward Pass

Calculate the backward pass by starting at the latest point of the network diagram; a backward pass determines the late start and late finish for each task. Following are the steps for computing a backward pass.

1. Starting at the latest point of the network diagram, look at the final activity, in this case, Activity D. The latest time it can finish is day 20. Day 20 is the early finish from the forward pass. Therefore, the late finish is 20. Subtract the duration from the late finish. The late start is 13. 20 – 7 = 13.

2. Continue through the network diagram and calculate the late start and late finish for each task.

3. When you get to Activity A, use the smallest late start from Activity B or Activity C for the late finish of Activity A. Table 2.2 illustrates the late start and late finish for our network diagram.

TABLE 2.2 Late start and late finish for each activity

Activity	Late Start	Late Finish
D	13	20
C	3	13
B	8	13
A	0	3

Calculating Float

Finally, you can calculate float by subtracting the early start from the late start or subtracting the early finish from the late finish.

1. Starting at the earliest point of the network diagram, look at Activity A. The late start is zero and the early start is zero. Subtract the early start form the late start. Therefore the float is zero. 0 – 0 = 0.

2. Continue through the network diagram and calculate the float for each task. Table 2.3 depicts the float available for each activity of our network diagram.

TABLE 2.3 Float available for each activity

Activity	Float
A	0
B	5

TABLE 2.3 Float available for each activity *(continued)*

Activity	Float
C	0
D	0

Using the Critical Path Method

If you look at the network diagram shown in Figure 2.7 and take into account the forward, backward, and float calculations, you determine the critical path for the project. Here's how you calculate the critical path:

1. Take the network diagram for your project. Perform a forward pass. Starting at the earliest point, day 0, determine the early start and early finish for each task.

2. Perform a backward pass. Starting at the latest point of the network diagram, determine the late start and late finish for each task.

3. Subtract the early start from the late start to determine the float.

4. Determine which tasks have zero float.

The critical path of our network diagram in Figure 2.7 is Activity A, C, and D, because the critical path has zero float. Figure 2.8 illustrates the critical path for the network diagram from Figure 2.7.

FIGURE 2.8 Critical path

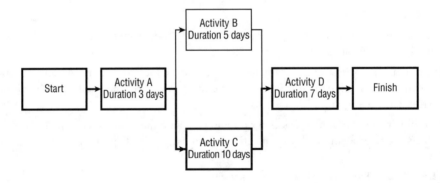

Recommended Reading: Chapter 7, pp. 249–252, *PMP Project Management Professional Study Guide*.

Now it's time to put the critical path method into action. In calculating critical path, TPMP is going to help SystemsDelivery determine the critical path for credit card validation Project.

Scenario

Your company, TPMP, has just placed you at SystemsDelivery, Inc. as a temporary project manager. You've been assigned the Credit Card Validation project. This project is designed to be the next best thing in credit card fraud prevention. The management of SystemsDelivery believes that this product will be in high demand at every major retailer in the country. Of course the management needs this product to go to market as quickly as possible. You have been on the project for two weeks now. You have created the network diagram shown in Figure 2.9. You've decided to determine the critical path. You know that this information will help you manage the project more effectively.

FIGURE 2.9   Canadian device network diagram

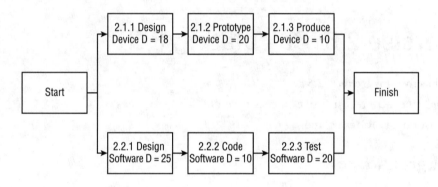

Calculating Critical Path

Use the work breakdown structure provided in Figure 2.9 for the credit card validation project and calculate the critical path.

1. Do a forward pass on the network diagram. What is the early start for tasks 2.1.1 and 2.2.1?

    _____

2. What is the early start for task 2.2.2?

    _____

3. Do a backward pass on the network diagram. What is the largest early finish between tasks 2.1.3 and 2.2.3? It is also the late finish.

    _____

    _____

4. What is the late finish for task 2.1.2?

_____

_____

5. What is the definition of float?

_____

_____

6. Calculate the float for the network diagram. What is the float on task 2.1.1?

_____

_____

7. Which tasks comprise the critical path?

_____

_____

Exercise 2.5: Calculating PERT

The objectives for Exercise 2.5 are:

- Describe the three types of estimates for a PERT calculation.
- Perform a PERT calculation.

Background

Another mathematical analysis tool and technique of the schedule development process is the Program Evaluation and Review Technique (PERT). Like CPM it focuses on determining the project's duration, but it uses expected values or weighted averages to perform the calculations instead of a most likely duration estimate like CPM. PERT relies heavily on the mathematics of probability and statistical bell curves. PERT can be used to provide more confidence to duration estimates that may be shaky. It can be applied to every task, to certain risky tasks, or to the critical path.

To do a PERT calculation, you must start with three separate estimates:

Optimistic   If everything goes well, how long the task will take.

Pessimistic   If everything goes poorly, how long the task will take.

Most likely   The original estimate provided. Sometimes called a best guess.

Once you know the three estimates, you then do a calculation to determine the mean. In statistics, the mean represents the average of all estimates for a particular task. Next, you determine the standard deviation. This calculation will be used to determine the amount of additional time that can be added to the estimates to provide more confidence. Last, you add the mean to as many standard deviations as you need to provide the confidence you are looking for.

Let's take our previous network diagram shown in Figure 2.10 and do a PERT calculation for each task using the following steps.

FIGURE 2.10   Network diagram

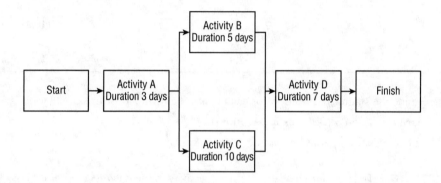

1.   Determine the optimistic and pessimistic estimates. The most likely estimates were created in Exercise 2.3: Estimating Duration Activity. Ask the experts who provided the first estimate to determine the optimistic and pessimistic estimates. Table 2.4 shows the estimates that our experts created.

TABLE 2.4   Optimistic, pessimistic, and most likely estimates for the network diagram

Activity	Most Likely	Optimistic	Pessimistic
A	3	2	5
B	5	4	8
C	10	7	15
D	7	5	10

2.   Determine the mean for each task. The formula for this calculation is:

Mean = (Optimistic + (4 * Most Likely) + Pessimistic) / 6

Table 2.5 illustrates the mean calculations for the network diagram.

TABLE 2.5   The mean for each activity in the network diagram

Activity	Most Likely	Optimistic	Pessimistic	Mean
A	3	2	5	3.2
B	5	4	8	5.3
C	10	7	15	10.3
D	7	5	10	7.2

3. Determine the standard deviation for each task. The formula for this calculation is:

    Standard Deviation = (Pessimistic – Optimistic) / 6

    Table 2.6 shows the standard deviation for each task.

TABLE 2.6   The standard deviation for each activity in the network diagram

Activity	Most Likely	Optimistic	Pessimistic	Mean	SD
A	3	2	5	3.2	.5
B	5	4	8	5.3	.7
C	10	7	15	10.3	1.3
D	7	5	10	7.2	.8

4. Determine the confidence level you want to achieve. Add the mean to a standard factor multiplied by the standard deviation. Table 2.7 shows the standard factor and formula for each confidence level.

TABLE 2.7   Standard factors and formulas for each confidence level

Confidence level	Standard Factor	Formula
50%	0	Mean
60%	0.25	Mean + (.25*SD)
70%	0.53	Mean + (.53*SD)

TABLE 2.7   Standard factors and formulas for each confidence level *(continued)*

Confidence level	Standard Factor	Formula
80%	0.84	Mean + (.84*SD)
90%	1.28	Mean + (1.28*SD)
95%	1.65	Mean + (1.65*SD)
99%	2.33	Mean + (2.33*SD)

Using the 99 percent confidence shown in Table 2.7, you would be able to complete your PERT calculation in Table 2.8.

TABLE 2.8   New estimate using 99 percent confidence

Activity	Most likely	Optimistic	Pessimistic	Mean	SD	New
A	3	2	5	3.2	.5	4.5
B	5	4	8	5.3	.7	7
C	10	7	15	10.3	1.3	13.5
D	7	5	10	7.2	.8	9

Recommended Reading: Chapter 7, pp. 253–256, *PMP Project Management Professional Study Guide.*

Now, you'll get a chance to calculate PERT for the credit card validation project.

Scenario

TPMP has just placed you at SystemsDelivery, Inc. as a temporary project manager. You've been assigned the Credit Card Validation project. This project is designed to be the next best thing in credit card fraud prevention. The management of SystemsDelivery believes that this product will be in high demand at every major retailer in the country. Of course the management needs this product to go to market as quickly as possible. You have been on the project for a while now. You've been developing your schedule and you're very worried about a couple of the estimates that have been provided. You've decided to use the PERT technique to create some new estimates that will provide more confidence in the completion date of the project. Figure 2.11 illustrates the critical path you've created for the Canadian device. You'll use this critical path as the basis for calculating PERT.

FIGURE 2.11   Canadian device network diagram

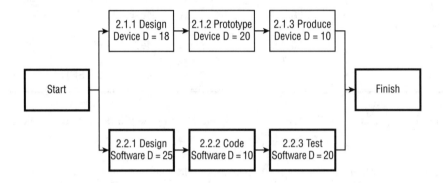

Calculating PERT

Use the critical path diagram provided in Figure 2.11 for the credit card validation project and start a PERT calculation.

1. What are the three types of estimates used for a PERT calculation?

   _____

   _____

   _____

2. What is the most likely estimate for task 2.2.2?

   _____

   _____

3. You and your team have determined that the pessimistic estimate is 13 and the optimistic estimate is 9. What is the mean?

   _____

   _____

4. What is the standard deviation for task 2.2.2?

   _____

   _____

5. What is the standard factor for 80 percent confidence?

_____

_____

_____

6. What is the new estimate for this task using 80 percent confidence?

_____

_____

_____

Exercise 2.6: Duration Compression

The objectives for Exercise 2.6 are:

- Describe the two types of duration compression.
- Describe the steps performed to crash a project.
- Describe the steps performed to fast track a project.

Background

You have put your schedule together, and you now know the end date. Your sponsor requested that the project be completed in the fourth quarter of this year. Your end date is first quarter of next year. This is when you employ another set of schedule development tools and techniques—duration compression. There are two popular techniques to achieve duration compression. The first is crashing. The second is fast tracking. We'll spend some time on each of these topics.

Crashing

Crashing is an analysis method that looks at trade-offs between the schedule and the cost of the project. In crashing, you analyze the critical path and determine what you can do to shorten it. It's best to get your team together to do this activity. You'll need your experts to help analyze the schedule.

Crashing may or may not result in a shorter schedule. It also may affect the project's budget beyond the acceptable range.

Let's take our previous network diagram illustrated again in Figure 2.12 and do a crashing exercise.

FIGURE 2.12   Network diagram

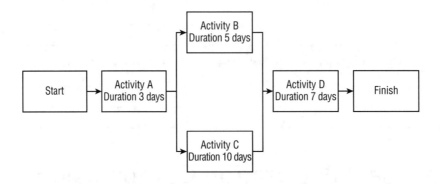

1. If you haven't already determined the critical path, you'll need to do that. You won't shorten the project duration if you don't work on the critical path. The critical path we created in Exercise 2.4 is illustrated in Figure 2.13.

FIGURE 2.13   Network diagram with critical path

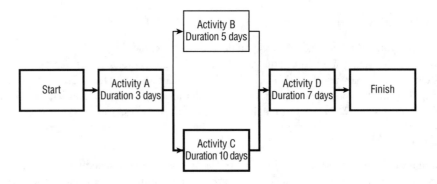

2. Now analyze each task for compression possibilities. You are looking for opportunities to:

   - Add more resources to shorten the task duration.
   - Reduce the scope of the project and subsequently these critical path tasks.
   - Find a different way of sequencing the tasks that will reduce the duration.

3. Determine whether the schedule and cost trade-off are acceptable. For example, you've decided to add another resource to Activity C. Adding the other resource changes the work of the task as illustrated in Table 2.9.

TABLE 2.9   Adding another resource

Activity	Duration	Cost
Do 10 days of work with one person	10 days	$1,000
Do five days of work per person and one day to consolidate the results.	6 days	$1,200

That's it! Adding another $200 to the budget is not a problem and you've decreased the duration of the project by four days.

Fast Tracking

Fast tracking is another analysis method that may enable you to reduce the duration of your projects. In fast tracking, you look for opportunities to have tasks worked in parallel instead of sequentially. Again, you only look for opportunities on the critical path. It would be best to do this analysis with the people who will perform these tasks. They are the experts and can determine if this technique will work.

Fast tracking may indeed result in a shorter schedule than your original critical path, but it may raise the risks beyond the acceptable range.

Let's take our faithful network diagram and run through the steps of fast tracking. Take a look at Figure 2.12 again.

1. Determine the critical path of the project. We did this already in Exercise 2.4, but take another look at Figure 2.13. You won't shorten the project duration if you don't work on the critical path.

2. Analyze each task on the critical path for the ability to work it at the same time as another task.

3. Determine if the risks associated with your schedule changes are acceptable.

Recommended Reading: Chapter 7, pp. 256–257, *PMP Project Management Professional Study Guide.*

Crashing and fast tracking are effective tools to compress the duration of a project. Now, you'll get a chance now to use those tools on the credit card validation project.

Scenario

TPMP has just placed you at SystemsDelivery, Inc. as a temporary project manager. You've been assigned the Credit Card Validation project. This project is designed to be the next best thing in credit card fraud prevention. The management of SystemsDelivery believes that this product will be in high demand at every major retailer in the country. Of course the management needs this product to go to market as quickly as possible. You have been on the project for a while now. You've completed your schedule and critical path shown in Figure 2.14 and realize that the Canadian device won't hit in the market window SystemsDelivery has targeted. You've decided to compress the duration of the project.

FIGURE 2.14   Canadian device critical path

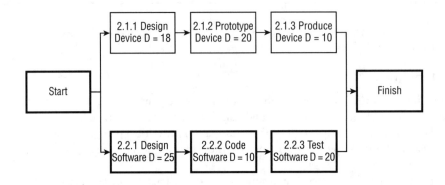

Duration Compression

Use the critical path diagram provided in Figure 2.14 for the credit card validation project and compress the project duration.

1. What are the two types of duration compression?

_____

_____

2. Describe crashing.

_____

_____

3. Describe fast tracking.

_____

_____

4. Compare the network diagram below to Figure 2.14. This is an example of which technique?

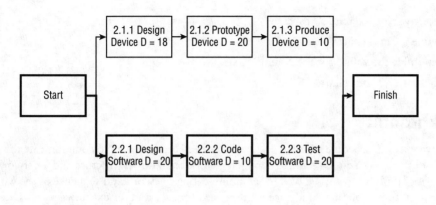

_____

_____

5. Compare the network diagram below to Figure 2.14. This is an example of which technique?

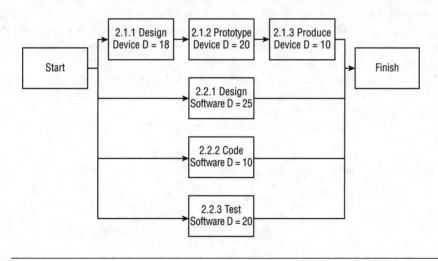

_____

_____

6. What is the new critical path for the graphic above?

_____

_____

Exercise 2.7: Creating Gantt Charts

The objectives for Exercise 2.7 are:

- Define a Gantt chart.
- Determine the values for the X and Y axes.
- Construct a Gantt chart.

Background

You have put your schedule together and you now need a simple way to communicate the activities of your project. You have already created a work breakdown structure and a network diagram. Those tools have worked well for communicating the work and sequence of the work to your project team. Your next audience is the project sponsor and the executive team. These are people who do not need to know every single task but need to know the general flow of the work. They may be more interested in the bottom line than the details. This is probably the right time to create a Gantt chant, also known as a bar chart. The *Guide to the PMBOK* describes a Gantt chart as a "graphic display of schedule related information." It normally depicts the project elements down the left side of the chart (Y axis) and a time scale across the top or bottom of the chart (X axis). Tasks with a duration are shown as date-placed horizontal bars. Most project managers use a project management software system for creating a Gantt chart. You may need to understand how a Gantt chart is constructed for the exam.

To create a Gantt chart you must, first, determine the time scale you will use to display the information. Second, you will determine the level of the tasks that will be displayed. Last, draw the chart and place the tasks on the chart.

Let's take our network diagram illustrated in Figure 2.15 and turn it into a Gantt chart using the following four steps.

FIGURE 2.15 Network diagram

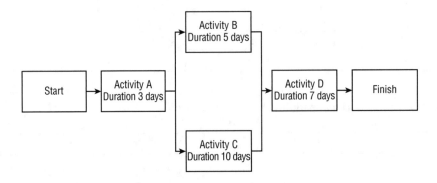

1. Determine the time scale you will use for your Gantt chart. Analyzing the network diagram, you determine that the time scale used is days. You also look at the critical path. You determine that the critical path is 20 days in length. That should create a chart that fits nicely on one page. Having these two pieces of information, you decide to use a time scale of days for the Gantt chart.

2. Now analyze the tasks for the appropriate level to depict on your chart. If your audience is looking for the bottom line, you would not show every task in a 200-task project. You would find a way to summarize the information. You may find it helpful to go back to your work breakdown structure and look at the upper levels. These are the levels you used to decompose the rest of the project's tasks. Use these summary tasks or others that you believe will be the best way to depict the information.

3. Draw the chart. The activities should go on the left side of the bar chart and the time scale across the top or bottom. The figure below illustrates this Gantt chart.

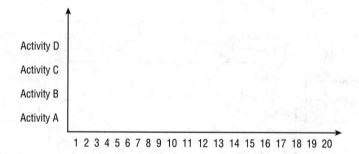

4. Place the tasks on the chart. On the network diagram we are using, Activity A has a three-day duration. You draw that task as a horizontal bar on the chart crossing over days 1, 2, and 3. When through, your diagram would look like the one below.

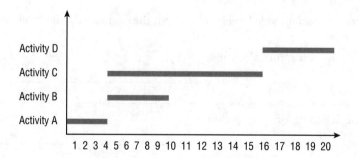

Recommended Reading: Chapter 7, p. 262, *PMP Project Management Professional Study Guide.*

Scenario

Your company, Terrific Project Management Partners, has just placed you at SystemsDelivery, Inc. as a temporary project manager. You've been assigned the Credit Card Validation project. This project is designed to be the next best thing in credit card fraud prevention. The management of SystemsDelivery believes that this product will be in high demand at every major retailer in the country. Of course the management needs this product to go to market as quickly as possible. You have been on the project for a while now. You've completed your schedule, which is shown in Figure 2.16, and have compressed the duration so that the project will complete in the desired time frame. You have a status presentation in a few days to the project sponsor and the executives in the marketing department. You want to make sure that they understand the sequence of activities and the time line to complete the project. You've decided the best way to communicate the time line is via a Gantt chart.

FIGURE 2.16   Canadian device critical path

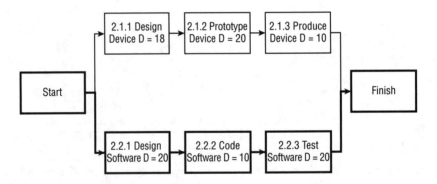

Creating Gantt Charts

Use the network diagram provided in Figure 2.16 for the credit card validation project and create a Gantt chart.

1.   Gantt charts are sometimes also called

_____

_____

2.   What is the definition of a Gantt chart?

_____

_____

_____

_____

3. Determine the best time scale for your project. What is it?

_____

_____

4. How many activities will you show for this audience?

_____

_____

5. Draw your Gantt chart.

Exercise 2.8: Controlling Schedule Changes

The objectives for Exercise 2.8 are:

- Describe the steps required to control schedule changes.
- Describe the key elements of a schedule management plan.
- Describe the concept of a baseline.

Background

You have completed putting your schedule together and have gotten approval from the executive sponsor. Now it's time to work the plan you've created. You know that if you execute the schedule exactly as you have planned, you will complete this project on time, on budget, and with the quality the sponsor has requested. Now, how do you keep that schedule from changing? First, you must plan for change; second, you must determine whether the schedule has changed;

and third, you must manage the actual changes that happen on your project. These steps describe the *Guide to the PMBOK* process, Schedule Control. Schedule Control is a controlling process. Controlling processes describe how you monitor and measure project results, and what actions you take so the project completes as planned. Schedule Control is highly related to another controlling process called Integrated Change Control. You need to know how these two processes interrelate for the PMP exam. Integrated Change Control is covered in Exercise 9.3.

Let's go back to the components of Schedule Control and spend some time on each of them.

Plan for Change

As you were developing your schedule, you were aware of many factors that influenced your schedule. Some of those items were assumptions and constraints. You also know that some of those assumptions may not be true and will possibly disrupt your plan. As you finalize the schedule, you need to create a schedule management plan. This plan will document the assumptions and constraints as well as other important aspects of the larger plan. It documents how you will control the changes that impact the schedule. The schedule management plan can be as detailed or as simple as you need. The key here is to plan for change and determine how you will react when those changes occur. Your plan should cover items like:

- Who can request a change?
- How will you determine the impact of the change to the schedule?
- Is there a specific form for requesting a change?
- Who can approve the change?
- What is the reason for the change?
- If the change is denied, how is the requestor notified?
- What are the advantages or disadvantages for allowing the change?
- If the change is approved, how is the schedule updated?
- Will the change be logged and tracked?
- If the change is approved, how are the team and the requestor notified?
- Who will review the change?

Once the schedule management plan is set, you are ready to begin executing your schedule.

Has the Schedule Changed?

The second step in Schedule Control is determining whether the schedule has changed. In order for you to know if the schedule has changed, you must know:

- What you planned on doing (in other words, the original schedule for the project).

- Where you currently are in the process.
- The variance between the two.

What You Planned on Doing

Just before you begin the execution of the schedule, you must set the baseline. The baseline is a copy of your plan that shows the original schedule for the project. You set aside this copy as a reference point to be used for analysis across the remainder of the project. Most project managers use a project management software system to plan and track their projects. Almost all systems have a simple command that saves a baseline for comparison purposes. If you are creating and tracking your project manually, you need to keep a copy of your project prior to execution.

Where You Currently Are

Before you begin to execute your project plan, you need to determine how you will track what has been accomplished. This tracking is usually done via some type of status update where the people working on the project report the time worked on specific tasks. This time reporting can be done in several ways.

1. Report % complete on a task.
2. Report the time spent on task.
3. Report the time spent and the time remaining on a task.

You should determine the frequency of the status reports. Here is a rule of thumb for establishing the frequency. Ask yourself, "How long can a task be out of control and the project manager not know it?" Based on the answer to this question, you might set the frequency at once a week, once every two weeks, or once a month. Applying the actual time to the schedule is how you determine where you are.

The Variance between the Two

You have created a baseline of what you planned to do. You have also applied the actual time spent to your project schedule. Now it's time to compare the two plans to each other. This is called variance analysis. Variance analysis is a tool and technique of the schedule development process. In variance analysis, you look at several factors and determine whether your project will complete on time. There are several areas that you should examine:

Late starts and late finishes   Have any of the tasks on the critical path started late or finished late?

Remaining work   Do any of the tasks on the critical path have remaining work that will force them to finish late?

Completion date   Is the completion date for the project the same one you had planned?

Managing Changes

The third and last component of Schedule Control is managing the actual changes on your project. In this final step, you will take action to keep your project on track. Managing changes proactively will help you respond to:

- Requested changes to your project.
- Variances to schedule completion.

If you plan for change and assess how the schedule has changed appropriately, then managing changes will be easy. You are simply working the processes that you defined. For requested changes, you will use the change control process that you defined earlier in this exercise. For variances, you are using the process established when assessing how the schedule has changed. Your analysis, decisions, and corrective actions regarding changes and variances will help you manage the project to a successful completion.

Recommended Reading: Chapter 10, pp. 375–376, *PMP Project Management Professional Study Guide.*

You'll get a chance now to practice controlling changes to your credit card validation project in Exercise 2.8.

Scenario

TPMP has just placed you at SystemsDelivery, Inc. as a temporary project manager. You've been assigned the Credit Card Validation project. This project is designed to be the next best thing in credit card fraud prevention. The management of SystemsDelivery believes that this product will be in high demand at every major retailer in the country. Of course the management needs this product to go to market as quickly as possible. You have been on the project for a while now. You've completed your schedule and have compressed the duration so that the project will complete in the desired time frame. You've just gotten approval from your executive sponsor on your plan. He is pleased with your delivery date and has told you that you will receive a bonus if you deliver on schedule. You know you're going to need to control the schedule to get that bonus.

Controlling Schedule Changes

1. Name four of the key elements of a schedule management plan.

    _____

    _____

    _____

    _____

2. What are the three things you must know to determine if the schedule has changed?

_____

_____

_____

_____

3. A copy of your plan that shows exactly what you planned on doing is also called a

_____

_____

4. What are the three steps of Schedule Control?

_____

_____

_____

_____

Answers to Exercise Questions

Answers to Exercise 2.1

1. The tree structure is the best way to set up the work breakdown structure for the credit card validation project.

2. The highest level component of the WBS is credit card validation project.

3. The main project deliverables that will be on the second level of the work breakdown structure are U.S. market, Canadian market, and European market.

4. Your answer should look like the graphic below.

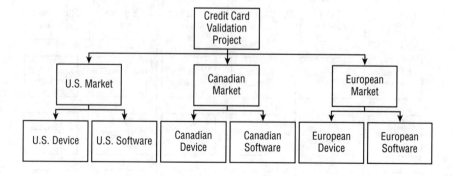

5. You should create four levels for this work breakdown structure. The level three substeps should look like the graphic below.

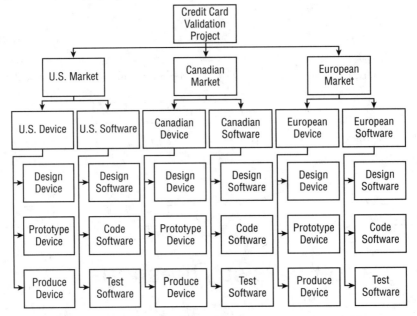

6. If you uniquely number each component of the work breakdown structure, your answer would look like the graphic below.

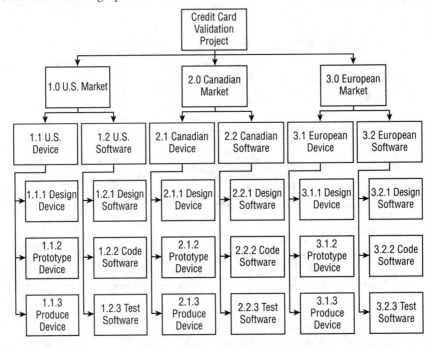

Answers to Exercise 2.2

1. Six activities have been created at the lowest level of the work breakdown structure (the activity list level).

2. Of the six activities, the dependencies are mandatory.

3. Finish to start is the one logical relationship between each activity for the Canadian software.

4. Precedence diagramming method is the best method to diagram these activities.

5. If you sequence the lowest level activities between a start and finish node, your answer should look like the graphic below.

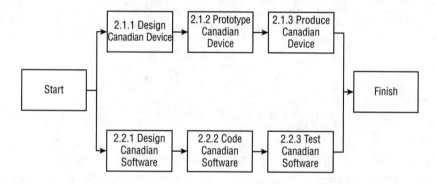

Answers to Exercise 2.3

1. Six activities have been created at the lowest level of the work breakdown structure (the activity list level).

2. Programmers and product engineers are the types of people needed to perform these activities.

3. Your best tool and technique to derive the estimate is expert judgment.

4. When you determine the duration estimate for each activity, your answer will look like the graphic below.

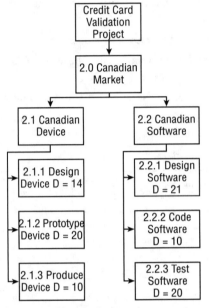

5. The type of reserve time you might apply to the tasks at risk is a work unit.

6. If you add the reserve time to the appropriate estimates, your answer will look like the graphic below.

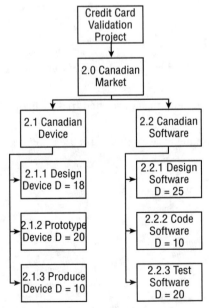

Answers to Exercise 2.4

1. When you do a forward pass on the network diagram, the early start for tasks 2.1.1 and 2.2.1 is zero.

2. The early start for task 2.2.2 is 25.

3. When you do a backward pass on the network diagram, the largest early finish between tasks 2.1.3 and 2.2.3 is 55. It is also the late finish.

4. The late finish for task 2.1.2 is 45.

5. Float is the amount of time that an activity may be delayed from the early start without delaying the project finish date.

6. If you calculate the float for the network diagram, the float on task 2.1.1 is 7.

7. Tasks 2.1.1, 2.1.2 and 2.1.3 comprise the critical path.

Answers to Exercise 2.5

1. The three types of estimates used for a PERT calculation are most likely, optimistic, and pessimistic.

2. The most likely estimate for task 2.2.2 is 10.

3. When you and your team determine that the pessimistic estimate is 13 and the optimistic estimate is 9, then the mean is 10.3.

4. The standard deviation for task 2.2.2 is .7.

5. The standard factor for 80 percent confidence is .84.

6. Using 80 percent confidence, the new estimate for this task is 11.

Answers to Exercise 2.6

1. The two types of duration compression are crashing and fast tracking.

2. Crashing is an analysis method that looks at trade-offs between the schedule and the cost of the project. In crashing, you analyze the critical path and determine what you can do to shorten it.

3. In fast tracking, you look for opportunities to have tasks worked in parallel instead of sequentially.

4. Comparing the network diagram to Figure 2.14, you'll notice this is an example of crashing.

5. Comparing the network diagram to Figure 2.14, you'll notice this is an example of fast tracking.

6. The new critical path for the new graphic is 2.1.1, 2.1.2, and 2.1.3.

Answers to Exercise 2.7

1. Gantt charts are sometimes also called bar charts.
2. A Gantt chart is a graphic display of schedule related information.
3. The best time scale for your project is days.
4. You will show six activities for this audience.
5. Your Gantt chart should look like the chart below.

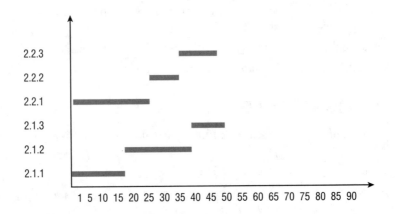

Answers to Exercise 2.8

1. Four key elements of a schedule management plan may include the following:

Who can request a change?

Is there a specific form for requesting a change?

What is the reason for the change?

What are the advantages or disadvantages for allowing the change?

Will the change be logged and tracked?

Who will review the change?

How will you determine the impact of the change to the schedule?

Who can approve the change?

If the change is denied, how is the requestor notified?

If the change is approved, how is the schedule updated?

If the change is approved, how are the team and the requestor notified?

2. The three things you must know to determine if the schedule has changed are what you planned on doing, where you currently are in the process, and the variance between the two.

3. A copy of your plan that shows exactly what you planned on doing is also called a baseline.

4. The three steps of Schedule Control are planning for change, determining if the schedule has changed, and managing the actual changes that happen on your project.

Chapter

3

Cost Management

THE EXERCISES PRESENTED IN THIS CHAPTER INCLUDE:

- ✓ Exercise 3.1: Resource Planning
- ✓ Exercise 3.2: Types of Cost Estimates
- ✓ Exercise 3.3: Cost Estimating
- ✓ Exercise 3.4: Creating a Budget and Cost Baseline
- ✓ Exercise 3.5: Controlling Cost Changes

This section covers Project Cost Management, one of the knowledge areas found in PMI's *Guide to the Project Management Body of Knowledge*. Project Cost Management sets the foundation for creating and controlling the costs of a project. In this chapter, we will begin by discussing Resource Planning. From there, we will introduce the steps of the cost planning process and cover the components of creating a budget and cost baseline. Finally, we conclude this chapter by discussing controlling cost changes.

Throughout this chapter, you will see that Terrific Project Management Partners has a new challenge, this time at the Pinnacle Candy Company. As in Chapter 2, "Time Management," we have used one scenario throughout the chapter. This set-up allows you to build the costs for the project step by step.

Exercise 3.1: Resource Planning

The objective for Exercise 3.1 is:

- Describe the three types of resources.

Background

Resource Planning is a planning process done at the beginning of the Cost Management process to establish the costs of a project. Resource Planning requires that you determine what resources are needed on your project and determine how many of each type of resource are needed.

The Resource Planning process incorporates the work breakdown structure, the scope statement, and resource pool descriptions. Using expert judgment, the project manager can determine the resource requirements for the project.

When we talk about resources in Resource Planning we are not talking about actual individual people. In fact, we won't talk about specific resources until we get to the staff acquisition or procurement processes. Instead, with Resource Planning we are talking about types of resources. There are three commonly known types of resources: people, equipment, and materials. People can be individuals that work in your department or your company, or vendors you hire to complete the work—basically any skilled resource. Equipment refers to items such as a forklift, a dump truck, a computer, or other nonconsumable resources. Materials are things like water, power, and other consumables.

Let's examine each of the primary inputs to the Resource Planning process. The first input is the WBS, which you learned about in Chapter 1, "Scope Management," and built on in

Chapter 2, "Time Management." This is the same WBS that was created in the activity definition process of time management. You should have already completed duration estimates for each task. Figure 3.1 shows a typical WBS with duration estimates.

FIGURE 3.1   WBS with duration estimates

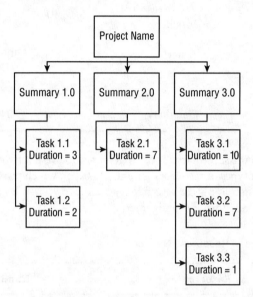

The second input into the Resource Planning process is the scope statement that was created in the Scope Planning process. You will use this scope statement as a means of verifying that your Resource Planning has been done within the scope of what you have been asked to do.

The last input into the Resource Planning process is the resource pool description. This description may or may not exist at your company. You'll want to create or modify it depending on what you find. It should contain a list of the resource types in the company as well as the actual number of resources for each category. Table 3.1 shows a sample resource pool description.

TABLE 3.1   Resource Pool Description

Resource Type	Name	Number
Skilled resources	Accountant	2
	Office manager	1
	Forklift operator	4
	Warehouse supervisor	1
	Heavy equipment operator	5

TABLE 3.1 Resource Pool Description *(continued)*

Resource Type	Name	Number
Equipment	Backhoe	2
	Forklift	3
Materials	Water	100 gallons
	Gas	1,000 gallons
	Electricity	10 kilowatt hours

Once you have your three primary inputs together, you are ready to use your expert judgment to determine what types of resources should be used on which tasks of your project. When you are through, you might apply the resource type name to your WBS or you might just create a table like Table 3.2 that shows the assignment.

TABLE 3.2 Types of Resources Needed

Task	Resource	Number of Resources
1.1	Forklift	1
	Forklift operator	1
1.2	Backhoe	2
	Heavy equipment operator	2
	Water	50 gallons
2.1	Accountant	1
3.1	Office manager	1
3.2	Warehouse supervisor	1
3.3	Forklift	1
	Forklift operator	1

The last step in creating your resource assignments involves your scope statement. Take both the resource requirements table and the scope statement and analyze whether you are still in scope or out of scope.

Recommended Reading: Chapter 5, pp. 156–157, *PMP Project Management Professional Study Guide.*

Scenario

TPMP has just placed you at the Pinnacle Candy Company as a temporary project manager. You have been assigned the EspressoFix Bar project. This project is going to create a new candy that will satisfy every coffee addict's need for coffee all wrapped up in a candy bar. The management at Pinnacle only wants to see if this new candy bar is marketable. Production of the finished product will be another project initiated later. You have been on the job long enough to have created a scope statement and the work breakdown structure that is shown in Figure 3.2. You and your team have also completed the duration estimates for each task.

FIGURE 3.2   EspressoFix WBS with duration estimates

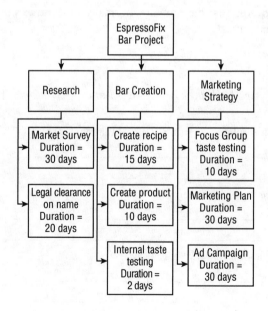

You asked the project team if there is a documented resource pool for the company. You find out that nothing exists so you get some reports from human resources and you and your team brainstorm to create the resource pool illustrated in Table 3.3.

TABLE 3.3 Resource Pool with Human Resources Information

Resource Type	Name	Number
Skilled resources	Marketing	5
	Advertising	4
	Legal	2
	Chefs	2
	Employees	35
	Vendor—Focused Marketing, Inc.	Unlimited
Equipment	Test kitchen	1

You have also discovered that the company normally subcontracts the focus group work with Focused Marketing, Inc.

Resource Planning

Using the information provided for the EspressoFix Bar project, answer the following questions about Resource Planning.

1. Resource Planning is what step in the Cost Management process?

    _____

    _____

2. What are the three types of resources?

    _____

    _____

3. What is an example of a material resource?

    _____

    _____

4. What are the three primary inputs used in Resource Planning?

_____

_____

5. What is the output of Resource Planning?

_____

_____

6. Create a resource requirement table for the EspressoFix Bar with the resource pool shown in Table 3.3.

Task	Resource	Number of Resources

Exercise 3.2: Types of Cost Estimates

The objectives for Exercise 3.2 are:

- Describe the three types of cost estimates.
- Describe when each estimate type is used.

Background

You have completed the Resource Planning for your project and now you are ready to do Cost Estimating. Before you do, let's define the different types of cost estimates and in what phase of the project they are typically done. There are three types of cost estimates: order of magnitude, budget, and definitive. These types originated in the engineering and construction industries but PMI recommends applying them to any industry.

Order of magnitude estimates   Are usually done at the very beginning of a project, sometimes as early as the Initiation phase. These estimates are usually derived from information for similar or previous projects. For example, you had a project two years ago that took one year and $1 million to complete. The current project you are estimating is similar, and the same people are available to work on this one. Based on that information, you might use the same estimate on the new project. Order of magnitude estimates can vary greatly in the range they cover. A typical order of magnitude estimate can fall between–25% and +75% of the actual cost of the project.

Budget estimates   Are created during the Cost Budgeting process, which is done during the Planning portion of a project. Budget estimates should cover all of the costs of a project. Budget estimates should cover all personnel, equipment, and materials needed for the project. Budget estimating should be done prior to the budget being set for the project. You'll need to work with management to make sure that budgets are set after budget estimates are done. A budget estimate should be more precise than an order of magnitude estimate, falling in the range of –10% to +25% of the actual cost of the project.

Definitive estimates   Will be the most detailed and therefore the most precise estimate of the three types. A definitive estimate is usually derived from an expert or project team looking at a specific task and determining how long it will take to complete the work. When you add up all of the task estimates, you will have a total project estimate that should fall in the range of –5% to +10% of the actual cost of the project. Like budget estimates, definitive estimates are also created in the Planning portion of a project.

Getting clear about the type of estimates you are creating will make it easier on your team to create the right estimate at the right time.

Recommended Reading: Chapter 5, pp. 172–175, *PMP Project Management Professional Study Guide.*

Scenario

TPMP has just placed you at the Pinnacle Candy Company as a temporary project manager. You have been assigned the EspressoFix Bar project. This project is going to create a new candy that will satisfy every coffee addict's need for coffee all wrapped up in a candy bar. The management at Pinnacle only wants to see if this new candy bar is marketable. Production of the finished product will be another project initiated later. You have been asked to estimate your project. You are very interested in making sure the estimates are done well because you are going to be held accountable for the costs of the project.

Types of Cost Estimates

Using the information provided for the EspressoFix Bar project, answer the following questions about types of cost estimates.

1. What are the three types of estimates?

_____

_____

2. Which estimate should be in the –5% to +10% range of the total cost of the project?

_____

_____

3. Which estimate is sometimes created in the Initiation phase?

_____

_____

4. The Pinnacle Candy Company has asked for you to create an order of magnitude estimate for the project. You have learned that the last time they looked at creating a new product and its marketability, they spent $500,000 on the project. What should your estimate range be?

_____

_____

5. What is the most precise type of estimate? Why?

_____

_____

_____

6. You have decided to create a definitive estimate for your project. Your team has created the following effort estimate. What will be the total cost of the project?

_____

_____

Task	Effort	Cost per Task Resources
Market surveys	18 days	$28,800
Legal clearance on name	15 days	$18,000
Create recipe	10 days	$4,000
Create product	7 days	$2,800
Internal taste testing	1 days	$2,000
Focus group taste testing	5 days	$250,000
Marketing plan	20 days	$64,000
Ad campaign	20 days	$32,000
Ad campaign	5 days	$4,000

Exercise 3.3: Cost Estimating

The objectives for Exercise 3.3 are:

- Describe the three ways to create a cost estimate.
- Describe the three steps in creating estimates.

Background

Now that you know about order of magnitude, definitive, and budget Cost Estimating types, it's time to turn your focus on the three steps for creating estimates. First, you need to choose one of the various methods used for Cost Estimating. Next, you will need to determine the unit of measure for the estimates, and finally you will actually create the estimates here in this section.

Determining the Estimating Method

Your first step in creating a cost estimate is to pick a method. There are actually five tools and techniques used in the Cost Estimating process. Here we cover the three most commonly used techniques: analogous estimating, parametric modeling, and bottom-up estimating.

Analogous estimating   This technique uses expert judgment and information from previous projects to create the estimate. The previous projects you use must be very similar to the project you are trying to estimate. Your expert judgment helps you determine whether you will use the previous project's costs as is or extrapolate different portions of information to determine your own estimates. This technique is also sometimes called top-down estimating and is used to create an order of magnitude estimate. Because analogous estimating can be very subjective, it is usually not very accurate.

Parametric modeling   In this method of estimating, you determine what elements should be placed in a mathematical model to help you predict costs. Parametric modeling can be used to create any of the three types of estimates.

Bottom-up Estimating   This method is the most precise method because it requires estimating each individual task separately. These estimates look at the effort required to complete a task, not the duration. Effort can be described as the time it takes to complete a task with no breaks or interruptions. Bottom-up estimating is to create definitive estimates.

Determining the Unit of Measure

Your next task, when you are creating estimates, is to determine the unit of measure the entire team will use. You want all of your estimates in similar time increments (i.e., hours, days, weeks, etc.).

Creating the Estimate

Finally, once you determine the technique to use in creating your estimates, it is time to actually create them. In this step, you will pull together your project team and ask them to determine the estimate. There are times when this might feel like an episode of "Name That Tune," but you need to provide as much precision as possible. You can apply more precision to your estimates by doing the following:

- Have the person doing the work create the estimate.
- Use task information from other projects.
- Use the PERT technique (described in Exercise 2.5).

Be sure to estimate all tasks for all resources: people, equipment, and materials.

Recommended Reading: Chapter 5, pp. 172–175, *PMP Project Management Professional Study Guide.*

Scenario

TPMP has just placed you at the Pinnacle Candy Company as a temporary project manager. You have been assigned the EspressoFix Bar project. This project is going to create a new candy that will satisfy every coffee addict's need for coffee all wrapped up in a candy bar. The management at Pinnacle only wants to see if this new candy bar is marketable. Production of the finished product will be another project initiated later. You have been asked to estimate your project. You are very interested in making sure the estimates are done well because you are going to be held accountable for the costs of the project. Your team has already created the WBS with duration estimates illustrated in Figure 3.3. They have also provided the resource pool located in Table 3.4.

FIGURE 3.3   EspressoFix WBS with duration estimates

TABLE 3.4 Resource Pool for the EspressoFix Project

Resource Type	Name	Number
Skilled resources	Marketing	5
	Advertising	4
	Legal	2
	Chefs	2
	Employees	35
	Vendor—Focused Marketing, Inc.	Unlimited
Equipment	Test kitchen	1

Cost Estimating

Using the information provided for the EspressoFix Bar project, answer the following questions about Cost Estimating.

1. What are the three most commonly used estimating techniques?

_____

_____

_____

_____

2. Top-down estimating is also known as?

_____

_____

3. Which estimating technique requires that you use a mathematical model?

_____

_____

4. Since you are going to be held accountable for the costs of the project, you have decided to create the most precise estimates possible. Which estimating technique will produce the most precise results?

_____

_____

5. What unit of measure will you use to estimate this project?

_____

6. You have decided to ask the people performing the work to create the estimates. Who should create the estimate for the internal taste testing?

_____

_____

7. What are the three types of resources?

_____

_____

Exercise 3.4: Creating a Budget and Cost Baseline

The objectives for Exercise 3.4 are:

- Describe the three inputs in the Cost Budgeting process.
- Describe the steps in creating a budget.
- Describe the concept of a cost baseline.

Background

Chances are that sometime in your career you started planning a project and someone handed you the budget before you had completed the planning. You probably learned the hard way that you should be given a budget after the planning process and that the project manager is the person who should request the amount. The budgeting process outlined in PMI's _Guide to the Project Management Body of Knowledge_ is the means you should use to create your project budget. In PMI's process, you use the cost estimates you created in Exercise 3.3, the WBS created in Exercise 2.1, and the project schedule created in the Schedule Development process. Then, using Cost Estimating tools and techniques, you create the project budget. We'll walk you through this process here.

Inputs to Cost Budgeting

There are three major inputs for the Cost Budgeting process. The first is cost estimates. Depending on what Cost Estimating technique you used—analogous estimating, parametric modeling, or bottom-up estimating—your estimate may be very general or very specific. Regardless of the technique, you should have a list of the estimates for your project. Table 3.5 shows an example list of estimates for a project using the bottom-up estimating technique.

TABLE 3.5 Sample Estimates

Task	Resource	Effort Estimate
A	Resource 1	8 hours
B	Resource 16	4 hours
C	Resource 7	6 hours
D	Resource 9	10 hours
	Resource 10	9 hours
	Resource 11	12 hours

The second input of the Cost Budgeting process is the WBS. The WBS is used to determine which tasks will have costs associated with them. You can use a traditional WBS diagram as shown in Figure 3.4 or you can translate the WBS into a table format like the one in Table 3.5.

FIGURE 3.4 Traditional WBS with duration estimates

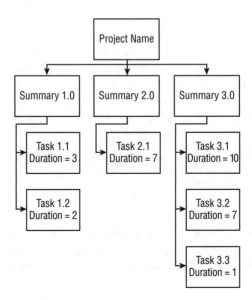

The last input used to create a project budget is the project schedule. The project schedule is created in the Schedule Development process. It provides the element of time to your budget—what monies need to be spent at what time. In the example shown in Figure 3.5, you have already calculated the critical path and know that the project is 19 days in length.

FIGURE 3.5   Project schedule

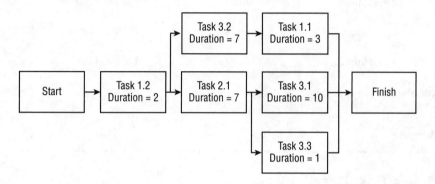

Determining the Budget

Using the Cost Estimating techniques described in Exercise 3.3 (analogous, parametric modeling, and bottom-up estimating), you will determine your cost budget. Remember to include all resource costs, not just human resources. You also need to include the costs for material and equipment resources.

At this point in the budget process, it's imperative that we introduce a term called managerial reserves. Managerial reserves are additional monies put away to cover situations that are impossible to predict. You can add this pot of money to your budget during the Cost Budgeting process. Managerial reserves are usually controlled by upper management but are available to the project manager if the need arises. These monies are not used to fund bad cost estimates. You will need to determine whether you will add these funds to your budget request based on the risks associated with your project.

The result of your work at this point is the total project budget. In Table 3.6, managerial reserves are a part of the budget.

TABLE 3.6   The Total Project Budget

Task	Resource	Effort Estimate	Rate	Cost
A	Resource 1	8 hours	$25 per hour	$200
B	Resource 16	4 hours	$100 per hour	$400

TABLE 3.6 The Total Project Budget *(continued)*

Task	Resource	Effort Estimate	Rate	Cost
C	Resource 7	6 hours	$75 per hour	$450
D	Resource 9	10 hours	$30 per hour	$300
	Resource 10	9 hours	$175 per hour	$1,575
	Resource 11	12 hours	$25 per hour	$300
Managerial Reserve				$500
Total Budget				$3,725

Creating a Cost Baseline

Just as you created a schedule baseline in Exercise 2.8, you also will create a cost baseline. A cost baseline is a copy of the budget prior to work beginning on your project. It is kept for comparison, analysis, and future forecasts. It is also called the planned value (PV). It does *not* include the managerial reserve or any fees that need to be paid on your project. Table 3.7 shows a sample cost baseline.

TABLE 3.7 Sample Cost Baseline

Task	Resource	Effort Estimate	Rate	Cost
A	Resource 1	8 hours	$25 per hour	$200
B	Resource 16	4 hours	$100 per hour	$400
C	Resource 7	6 hours	$75 per hour	$450
D	Resource 9	10 hours	$30 per hour	$300
	Resource 10	9 hours	$175 per hour	$1,575
	Resource 11	12 hours	$25 per hour	$300
Cost Baseline or Planned Value				$3,225

Recommended Reading: Chapter 7, pp. 264–266, *PMP Project Management Professional Study Guide*.

Scenario

TPMP has just placed you at the Pinnacle Candy Company as a temporary project manager. You have been assigned the EspressoFix Bar project. This project is going to create a new candy that will satisfy every coffee addict's need for coffee all wrapped up in a candy bar. The management at Pinnacle only wants to see if this new candy bar is marketable. Production of the finished product will be another project initiated later. The budget of $100,000 was established before you started work on the project. You are just about done with the project planning and wonder whether $100,000 will be enough money to cover the project. Your team has already created the WBS with duration estimates illustrated in Figure 3.6, the network diagram shown in Figure 3.7, and effort estimates shown in Table 3.8.

TABLE 3.8   Effort Estimates for the EspressoFix Project

Task	Resource	Effort Estimate	Rate
Market surveys	Marketing	20 days	$1,200 per day
Marketing plan	Marketing	25 days	$1,200 per day
Ad campaign	Advertising	10 days	$1,000 per day
Legal clearance on the name	Legal	10 days	$1,600 per day
Create recipe	Chef	7 days	$800 per day
	Test kitchen	15 days	$1,000 per day
Create product	Chef	6 days	$800 per day
	Test kitchen	10 days	$1,000 per day
Internal taste testing	Employees on break	0	
	Employee cafeteria	0	
Focus group taste testing		Firm fixed price contract	$50,000

FIGURE 3.6 WBS with duration estimates

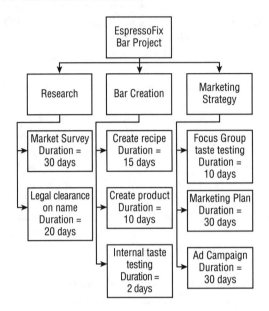

FIGURE 3.7 Network diagram

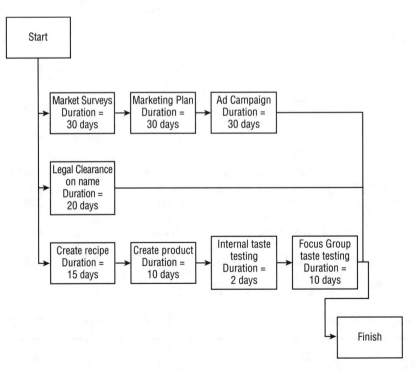

Creating a Budget and Cost Baseline

Use the information provided for the EspressoFix Bar project and answer the following questions about creating a budget and cost baseline.

1. What are three inputs into the Cost Budgeting process?

_____

_____

2. What are three common techniques used to create cost estimates and cost budgets?

_____

_____

3. What are managerial reserves?

_____

_____

_____

_____

4. A cost baseline is a copy of the budget prior to work beginning on your project. Why do you keep a cost baseline?

_____

_____

5. A cost baseline does not include

_____

_____

6. A cost baseline is also known as

_____

_____

7. How long is this project?

_____

_____

8. You have decided to not apply any managerial reserves to this project. What is the total budget? Why?

_____

_____

9. What is the cost baseline? Why?

_____

_____

Exercise 3.5: Controlling Cost Changes

The objectives for Exercise 3.5 are:

- Describe the similarities in cost and schedule change control processes.
- Describe the three most popular EAC formulas.

Background

The project planning is done and you have been executing your project for over a month. It's time to manage the costs of your project using the Cost Control process. The Cost Control process is very similar to the Schedule Control process that was discussed in Exercise 2.8. Both processes use the same inputs of performance reports and change requests. Both processes use tools and techniques like change control systems and performance measurements to control the changes. Both processes produce outputs like revised estimates and updates, in this case budget updates. The one thing that differentiates these two processes is an output called estimate at completion (EAC). EAC is a calculation done at any point in the project that forecasts the likely final costs of the project. There are three different ways to calculate estimate at completion. We'll spend some time on each.

EAC = AC + ETC   This calculation for EAC is used if your original estimates were flawed. You must first determine the estimate to completion (ETC). The ETC is the amount of money you'll need to complete the project. You add the ETC to what has actually been spent or the actual cost (AC) to determine the estimate at completion. Here's an example. Your project is 50 percent complete and it is running over budget. The original budget is $15,000. At this point you should have spent $7,500. Based on the performance reports that you have received, you know you need $7,500 more to complete the project (ETC). When you review the budget reports, you know you have spent $9,000 so far (AC).

EAC	=	AC + ETC
$16,500	=	$9,000 + $7,500

The estimate at completion is $16,500.

EAC = (AC + BAC) – EV   This formula is used when the current variances are not typical and are not expected to continue. In this calculation, you take the total budget for the project (BAC) and add it to the actual cost (AC). You then subtract the work accomplished and the authorized budget for the work (EV), giving you the estimate at completion. Your project is 60 percent complete. You have spent $10,000 (AC) so far. The total budget for the project was $25,000 (BAC). Based on the performance reports, you know you have an earned value (EV) of $18,000.

EAC	=	(AC + BAC) – EV
$17,000	=	($10,000 + $25,000) – $18,000

The estimate at completion is $17,000.

EAC = (AC + (BAC – EV) ÷ CPI)   This calculation is used when the variances you are seeing are typical and you expect them to continue. In this calculation, you take the work accomplished and the authorized budget for the work (EV) and subtract them by the total budgets for the project (BAC). Add that figure to the actual monies spent to date (AC). Then divide that figure by the cost performance index (CPI). Your project is 33 percent complete and the total budget for the project was $17,000 (BAC). Based on the performance reports, you know that you have an earned value of $5,000 (EV). The actual costs of the project to date are $7,000 (AC). The cost performance index is 1.10 (CPI).

EAC   =   (AC + (BAC – EV) ÷ CPI)

$17,273   =   ($7,000 + ($17,000 – $5,000) ÷ 1.10)

The estimate at completion is $17,273.

   You are probably wondering what the estimate to completion is on your Pinnacle Candy Company project. You will get a chance now to calculate the estimate to completion.

    Recommended Reading: Chapter 9, p. 348, and Chapter 10, pp. 376–378, *PMP Project Management Professional Study Guide.*

Scenario

TPMP has just placed you at the Pinnacle Candy Company as a temporary project manager. You have been assigned the EspressoFix Bar project. This project is going to create a new candy that will satisfy every coffee addict's need for coffee all wrapped up in a candy bar. The management at Pinnacle only wants to see if this new candy bar is marketable. Production of the finished product will be another project initiated later. The budget of $100,000 was established before you started work on the project. You have completed the planning and have spent 19 days executing the project. You have had some problems with the test kitchen and the chef creating the recipe and the product. Your earned value reports show an earned value of $40,000 and the actual costs of the project are $65,000. You have done the calculation for the cost performance index. The CPI is .6.

Controlling Cost Changes

Using the information provided for the EspressoFix Bar project, answer the following questions about Cost Control.

1.   What are the two tools and techniques that are used in the Schedule and Cost Control processes?

_____

_____

2. What are the two outputs that are produced in both the Schedule Control and Cost Control processes?

   _____

   _____

3. What is the EAC calculation used if your original estimates were flawed?

   _____

   _____

4. What is the EAC calculation used when the current variances are not typical and are not expected to continue?

   _____

   _____

5. What is the calculation used when the variances you are seeing are typical and you expect them to continue?

   _____

   _____

6. You have decided that the problems with the chef are a fluke and you don't foresee any additional variances. What is your estimate at completion?

   _____

   _____

   _____

   _____

7. You have decided that the original estimates on the Pinnacle Candy Company project were flawed. Your ETC is $50,000. What is your estimate at completion?

   _____

   _____

   _____

   _____

8. You have realized that you did not use the right resources to estimate the costs of the EspressoFix Bar project. The variances you are seeing are typical and you expect the rest of the project to go as poorly. What is your estimate at completion?

   _____

   _____

   _____

   _____

Answers to Exercise Questions

Answers to Exercise 3.1

1. Resource Planning is the first step in the Cost Management process.
2. The three types of resources are people, equipment, and materials.
3. Some examples of material resources include water or electrical power.
4. The three primary inputs used in Resource Planning include scope statement, WBS, and resource pool.
5. Resource requirements are the outputs of Resource Planning.
6. Your answer should be similar to the following:

Task	Resource	Number of Resources
Market surveys	Marketing	2
Legal clearance on name	Legal	1
Create recipe	Chef	1
Create product	Chef	1
Internal taste testing	Employees	10
Focus croup taste testing	Focused Marketing, Inc.	50
Marketing plan	Marketing	4
Ad campaign	Advertising	2
	Marketing	1

Answers to Exercise 3.2

1. The three types of estimates are order of magnitude, definitive, and budget.
2. A definitive estimate should be in the –5% to +10% range of the total cost of the project.
3. An order of magnitude estimate is sometimes created in the Initiation phase.
4. You have learned that the last time they looked at creating a new product and its marketability, they spent $500,000 on the project. Since a typical order of magnitude estimate will fall between –25% and +75% of the actual cost of the project, your estimate range should be $375,000 to $875,000.

5. A definitive estimate is the most precise type of estimate, because it is usually derived by an expert or the project team looking at a specific task and determining how long it will take to complete the work.

6. Given the provided effort estimate, the total cost of the project will be $405,600.

Answers to Exercise 3.3

1. Analogous estimating, parametric modeling, and bottom-up estimating are the three most commonly used estimating techniques.

2. Top-down estimating is also known as analogous estimating.

3. The parametric estimating technique requires that you use a mathematical model.

4. Since you are going to be held accountable for the costs of the project, you create the most precise estimates possible by using the bottom-up estimating technique.

5. You should use hours as your measure for this project.

6. The chef would be the mostly likely candidate to create the estimate for the internal taste testing since she has done this type of work before.

7. The three types of resources are people, equipment, and materials.

Answers to Exercise 3.4

1. Cost estimates, WBS, and project schedule are three inputs into the Cost Budgeting process.

2. Analogous estimating, parametric modeling, and bottom-up estimating are three common techniques that are used to create cost estimates and cost budgets.

3. Managerial reserves are additional monies put away to cover situations that are impossible to predict. These funds are usually controlled by upper management but are available to the project manager if the need arises. These monies are not used to fund bad cost estimates.

4. One reason you should keep a cost baseline is for comparison purposes. You may also use it later for analysis and future forecasts.

5. A cost baseline does not include managerial reserves and fees.

6. A cost baseline is also known as planned value (PV).

7. This is a 90-day project.

8. You create the total budget by adding all of the definitive estimates. Since no managerial reserves have been applied to the project, the total budget is $165,400.

9. The cost baseline is the total project budget minus the managerial reserve. Since this project does not have a managerial reserve, the cost baseline is $165,400.

Answers to Exercise 3.5

1. Change control systems and performance measurements are the two tools and techniques that are used in the Schedule and Cost Control processes.

2. Revised estimates and updates are the two outputs that are produced in both the Schedule Control and Cost Control processes.

3. EAC = AC + ETC is the EAC calculation used if your original estimates were flawed.

4. EAC = (AC + BAC) – EV is the EAC calculation used when the current variances are not typical and are not expected to continue.

5. EAC = (AC + (BAC – EV) ÷ CPI) is the calculation used when the variances you are seeing are typical and you expect them to continue.

6. Your estimate at completion should be:

EAC	=	(AC + BAC) – EV
$125,000	=	($65,000 + $100,000) – $40,000
EAC	=	$125,000

7. If your ETC was $50,000, your estimate at completion should be:

EAC	=	AC + ETC
$115,000	=	$65,000 + $50,000
EAC	=	$115,000

8. If the variances you are seeing are typical and you expect the rest of the project to go as poorly, your estimate at completion should be:

EAC	=	(AC + (BAC - EV) ÷ CPI)
$208,333	=	($65,000 + ($100,000 - $40,000) ÷ .6)
EAC	=	$208,333

Chapter

4

Quality Management

THE EXERCISES PRESENTED IN THIS CHAPTER INCLUDE:

This chapter covers Quality Management, one of the knowledge areas found in PMI's *Guide to the Project Management Body of Knowledge*. This chapter sets the foundation for creating and controlling the quality of the project. It starts with the quality planning process. After that we will spend time on each of the quality planning tools as well as the cost of quality. Then, we cover Quality Assurance and close with Quality Control.

Terrific Project Management Partners has a new challenge for you, this time at USRemotes, Inc. You will be doing all of the exercises on this one project. Quality Management is part of the Planning, Executing, and Controlling objectives for the PMP exam.

Exercise 4.1: Planning for Quality

The objectives for Exercise 4.1 are:

- Describe the four major inputs into quality planning.
- Describe the only output of the quality planning process.

Background

You have probably heard of the triple constraints of project management—time, cost, and quality. These three major areas require constant trade-offs to achieve a project's objectives. The planning process for quality can be just as tricky as schedule or cost planning. In this exercise, we will talk about the inputs to quality planning as well as the output of quality planning—the quality management plan.

Quality Planning Inputs

There are four major inputs in the quality planning process:

Quality policy   A quality policy is a statement (usually provided by top management) regarding the company's beliefs around quality. Your company may have a set quality statement that you can use for your project. If none exists, you will need to create one. This policy will be a guiding light for the people working on the project. If they are in doubt about a quality decision, they can look to the statement to answer their question. A quality policy might look something like this: "Quality will be emphasized in the early stages and throughout the project. It will be planned into the project as work begins, and it will be a part of the fiber of the entire project. We will design quality checkpoints and determine if quality standards have been met."

Scope statement   This is the same scope statement that was created in Chapter 1. You use the scope statement to verify project deliverables. The scope statement may also spell out quality attributes as part of the objectives of the project.

Product description   It is very important for you to understand the product of the project. The product description may contain information about the desired level of quality, which may assist you in your quality management planning.

Standards and regulations   The rules that apply to the creation of your product must also be considered in quality planning. You will want to look for any standards and regulations that may apply. For example, if you are building a shed in your backyard, you would check on standards like homeowner association rules, city and county permits, or easements.

Quality Planning Output

There is only one major quality planning output. It is the quality management plan. The project manager and the project team create the quality management plan. It should detail all quality planning activities and who will perform them. The essence of this plan is how quality will be ensured and how the quality policy will be followed.

TPMP has a new assignment for you. In it, you'll get a chance to begin planning the quality activities for the project.

Recommended Reading: Chapter 6, pp. 192–194, *PMP Project Management Professional Study Guide.*

Scenario

TPMP has just placed you at USRemotes, the largest distributor of remote control devices in the United States. USRemotes has launched a project to redesign the warehouse and shipping areas and processes—the WSAP project. You've been assigned as the temporary project manager.

You have started putting the project schedule and costs together and you know it is time to start working on planning the quality attributes of the project.

Planning for Quality

Using the information provided for the WSAP project, answer the following questions about quality planning.

1.   What are the four major inputs into the quality management process?

_____

_____

_____

_____

2.   Who should create a quality policy?

_____

_____

3.   Why is the product description important to quality planning?

_____

_____

4.   What is the major output of the quality planning process?

_____

_____

5.   You have checked throughout USRemotes and cannot find a quality policy statement. Write a short quality policy statement for the WSAP project.

_____

_____

_____

_____

Exercise 4.2: Quality Planning Tools

The objectives for Exercise 4.2 are:

- Describe the three commonly used quality planning tools.
- Describe the appropriate time to use each quality planning tool.

Background

Many quality gurus like Juran, Crosby, and Deming advocate that quality is planned in, not inspected in. In order to plan in quality, you must use a set of commonly known tools. We are going to review these quality planning tools in this exercise. The three most commonly used tools are benchmarking, cost benefit analysis, and flowcharting.

Benchmarking   Benchmarking is the process of analyzing similar activities as a means of comparison. Say you are able to walk a mile in 20 minutes, and you want to walk faster. You would set the benchmark at 20 minutes. The next time that you walk a mile, you would time yourself and compare your new time to the benchmark of 20 minutes. Benchmarking is a very effective tool to use when you are working on a project that is improving or changing the way a business currently operates. You can set a benchmark where the company is currently performing and compare the new work environment with the old to see if you are improving.

Cost benefit analysis   When you look at the trade-offs of whether or not an activity should be done, you're probably talking about a cost benefit analysis. Let's go back to our previous example of the 20-minute-mile walker. This walker is trying to burn the most calories or get the maximum benefit from walking. She may want to look at walking faster or perhaps walking on a hilly terrain. These options may burn more calories, but there is a price to be paid in the form of sorer muscles or aching feet. She may need to analyze which approach will provide more calories burned and less wear and tear on her body. In quality planning, the same technique is used to determine which quality activities will provide more quality with less cost.

Flowcharting   Flowcharting is a way of depicting the way work flows. This technique is used in quality planning to show the interrelationship of a series of activities, thus giving the project team information about where quality activities should be planned. Figure 4.1 shows a simple flowchart for building a shed in your backyard.

FIGURE 4.1   Simple flowchart

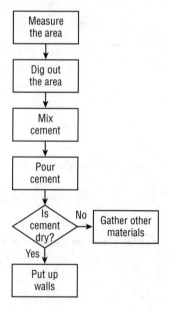

Recommended Reading: Chapter 6, pp. 196–198, *PMP Project Management Professional Study Guide.*

Scenario

TPMP has just placed you at USRemotes, the largest distributor of remote control devices in the United States. USRemotes has launched a project to redesign the warehouse and shipping areas and processes—the WSAP project. You have been assigned as the temporary project manager.

You have started putting the project schedule and costs together and now you know it is time to start planning the quality attributes of the project.

Quality Planning Tools

Using the information provided for the WSAP project, answer the following questions about quality planning tools.

1. What is benchmarking?

   _____

   _____

2. What are the three most commonly used tools of quality planning?

   _____

   _____

   _____

   _____

3. What is cost benefit analysis?

   _____

   _____

4. Since you are new to USRemotes, it would be a good idea to use what quality planning tool to understand the work?

   _____

   _____

5. The reason that USRemotes is redesigning the warehouse and shipping areas and processes is to improve its shipping time to customers. What quality planning tool would be good to use for this project? Why?

   _____

   _____

   _____

   _____

6. What is flowcharting?

_____

_____

7. You have just about completed your quality planning. The team has determined that there are three quality activities to consider for the project. You only have time to perform one of those activities. How will you decide?

_____

_____

Exercise 4.3: Calculating the Cost of Quality

The objectives for Exercise 4.3 are:

- Define the cost of quality.
- Describe the three types of costs associated with the cost of quality.
- Describe the elements that make up each type of cost.

Background

The cost of quality is a quality planning tool that deserves its own exercise. It is imperative that you understand the components of the cost of quality as well as how it is calculated. The definition of the cost of quality is the total amount of money required to ensure quality. It is composed of three different types of costs—prevention costs, appraisal costs, and failure costs. It is sometimes easier to think of these costs as the costs of conformance and nonconformance, with prevention and appraisal as conformance costs and failure as nonconformance. When project managers speak of conformance, they are talking about conforming to the customer's requirements for the product. Let's spend some time on each of the different costs of quality.

Prevention   Prevention costs cover all activities that must be done to keep errors out of the process of creating the product. These, of course, are preventative activities. These costs should include all quality planning activities, any training that must be done to keep errors out of the process, product validation activities, and process validation activities.

Appraisal   Appraisal costs cover all activities that must be done to keep errors out of the customer's hands. These are the end of the line activities that check the product one more time before the product goes to the customer. These costs should include quality audits, evaluations, calibration, inspections, and field testing.

Failure   Failure costs include all of the costs that are incurred due to the failure of the product both internal to the company and external to the company. Internal failures include the costs for rework, repairs to the product before the project is completed, scrap, and additional inventory that had to be purchased because of the failure.

External failures are those that happen after the product leaves the organization. These costs include warranties, complaint handling, product recalls, legal suits, and harm done to the company's reputation.

Computing the cost of quality is as simple as adding the work effort estimate for each activity that is preventative or appraisal in nature to the costs that are incurred because of any type of failure, whether internal or external. The first calculation for cost of quality can be determined during the planning phase. It can also be calculated again during the executing phase when failures occur. The cost of quality can also be calculated after the project is completed when failures finally hit the customer's hands.

 Recommended Reading: Chapter 6, p. 198, *PMP Project Management Professional Study Guide.*

Scenario

TPMP has just placed you at USRemotes, the largest distributor of remote control devices in the United States. USRemotes has launched a project to redesign the warehouse and shipping areas and processes—the WSAP project. You have been assigned as the temporary project manager. You have just completed the project planning phase.

USRemotes is very interested in quality and is planning to gain some type of quality certification. Company executives have asked you to calculate the cost of quality for the WSAP project. The network diagram you have completed is depicted in Figure 4.2.

FIGURE 4.2   WSAP network diagram

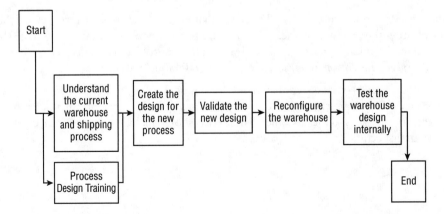

Calculating the Cost of Quality

Using the information provided for the WSAP project, answer the following questions about calculating the cost of quality.

1. What are the three types of costs associated with the cost of quality?

_____

_____

_____

_____

2. What type of cost is associated with nonconformance?

_____

_____

3. What is the definition for the cost of quality?

_____

_____

4. What tasks on Figure 4.2 should be included in the preventative cost of quality?

_____

_____

_____

_____

5. What tasks on Figure 4.2 should be included in the appraisal cost of quality?

_____

_____

_____

_____

6. While the warehouse was being reconfigured, you found out that the new shelving units did not fit the warehouse structure. These shelving units had to be scrapped and new ones purchased. The cost of the shelving units should be included in what cost of quality type?

_____

_____

7. It is a year after the WSAP project completed. You have heard through the grapevine that USRemotes has had to hire several customer service representatives to handle the complaints due to mis-shipped items. These costs are part of what cost of quality type?

_____

_____

Exercise 4.4: Quality Assurance

The objectives for Exercise 4.4 are:

- Describe the tools and techniques used in Quality Assurance.
- Describe the components of a quality audit.

Background

A lot of work goes into the planning of a project. You have done extensive work in planning the quality components of the project as demonstrated in Exercises 4.2 and 4.3. How will you guarantee that the quality will be as good as what you planned? This is where the quality assurance process comes in. Quality Assurance is the process that focuses on making certain the planned quality will be met. Think of Quality Assurance as a managerial process that is concerned with the process of quality. It assures that the quality system you have planned will work.

Two sets of tools and techniques are used in quality assurance process. The first set of tools and techniques are called quality planning tools. These tools were covered in Exercises 4.2 and 4.3. They are benchmarking, cost benefit analysis, flowcharting, design of experiments, and the cost of quality. Even though we talked about using these tools in the planning process, they can also be used while the project is being executed to assure that the quality plans are being met.

The second tool and technique used in Quality Assurance is called a quality audit. A quality audit is a review of the quality management activities that are being performed on the project. This in-depth review will produce findings that should identify lessons learned that can improve project performance. A quality baseline is set when a quality audit is performed after quality planning is completed and before the project begins execution. A quality baseline is used to compare what has been done to what was planned with respect to project quality. Let's look at the components of a quality audit.

Components of a Quality Audit

Determine the auditor   Some companies will hire a highly skilled specialist to perform an audit. Other companies will look for an internal resource to perform the audit to save money. Regardless of whether you use internal or external resources, the auditor must have certain qualities to effectively conduct a quality audit. An individual needs to be assigned who is independent of the day-to-day project activities. They need to be familiar with the business and the processes used but should be able to take a broad perspective of the project's processes. They should be skilled in project management and know what to look for in a well-managed project.

Time frames to audit   There are three parts to the time frames to audit: initial assessment, quality progress review, and quality completion review.

Initial assessment   This first audit should be conducted at the end of the planning process and before the project begins execution. The focus of this review is to evaluate the quality assurance work that is planned. This review also creates a quality baseline for what is planned to be done on the project. This step also familiarizes the auditor on what to look for in subsequent audits.

Quality progress review   This audit should be planned at regular intervals or at key milestones during the execution of the project. The reviewer will be evaluating whether the quality activities that were outlined are being performed. They will also inspect the quality processes of the project and determine if they are sound. The output of the audit is a lessons-learned document that is used for continuous improvement.

Quality completion review   This audit is done at the end of the project and should recap the quality assurance effectiveness in light of final project results. The output of this audit is also a lessons-learned document that is used to continuously improve the quality assurance processes at the company for the next set of projects.

Quality audit process   The quality audit process should include a review log that identifies those points that will be reviewed during the audit. The reviewer should receive relevant materials (e.g., product description, quality policy, project plan, project schedule, status reports, etc.) prior to the review so that questions and suggestions for improvement can be prepared in advance. The review should result in suggested actions for the project manager to enhance the quality of the product. The project manager should follow up on actions with the reviewer according to a schedule established during the audit.

Recommended Reading: Chapter 9, pp. 339–342, *PMP Project Management Professional Study Guide.*

Scenario

TPMP has just placed you at USRemotes, the largest distributor of remote control devices in the United States. USRemotes has launched a project to redesign the warehouse and shipping areas and processes—the WSAP project. You have been assigned as the temporary project manager. You have just completed the project planning phase.

USRemotes is very interested in quality and is planning to gain some type of quality certification. Quality is also very important to you. You have been thinking about what you will need to do to assure the quality of the project.

Quality Assurance

Using the information provided for the WSAP project, answer the following questions about Quality Assurance.

1.   What are the two tools and techniques of Quality Assurance?

_____

_____

2. Why would you do a quality audit at the end of the planning phase?

    _____

    _____

    _____

    _____

3. Why would you do a quality audit at the end of the project?

    _____

    _____

4. Why would you do a quality audit at a key milestone?

    _____

    _____

5. Name three quality planning tools.

    _____

    _____

    _____

    _____

6. What is a quality baseline used for?

    _____

    _____

Exercise 4.5: Quality Control

The objectives for Exercise 4.5 are:
- Define Quality Control.
- Describe the tools and techniques used in Quality Control.

Background

The quality management process contains one controlling process called Quality Control. This process establishes the framework to monitor project results to guarantee that the project will achieve the desired quality. Where Quality Assurance is a management process, Quality Control is a technical process that is concerned with the quality of the product. In this process you measure the performance of the project by collecting data.

Six tools and techniques are used in Quality Control. We will spend time on each of them.

Inspection   Inspections are used to review or verify the quality of the product you are creating in your project. Inspections can be done on a single component or part of the product or it can be done on the entire finished product. For example, when you buy a new piece of clothing, you usually look the garment over carefully. You look at the seams, buttons, and button holes to make sure the garment is well constructed. This type of review is also known as an inspection.

Control chart   A control chart is a graphic display that shows measurements of a specific process over time. This type of chart creates an upper control limit—a boundary that shows when a product is made with very few defects and therefore more expensive than the manufacturer wants to create. It also shows a lower control limit—a boundary that shows that the product has too many defects and will probably not be accepted by the consumer. The middle line on a control chart shows the mean or area where the best product should be created. The diagram in Figure 4.3 shows a control chart for a tire manufacturing process. The third batch created would probably be melted and manufactured again because the quality is not within the accepted parameters.

FIGURE 4.3   Tire manufacturing control chart

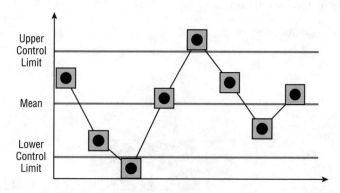

Pareto diagram   A Pareto diagram is used to rank order problems from larger to smallest. A Pareto diagram is also known as a histogram. The concept of a Pareto diagram is based on the Pareto Principle, which says that the majority of defects are caused by a few problems (the 80/20 rule). This diagram is useful in Quality Control in determining where the most problems lie, therefore rank ordering what step of the process should be fixed first. Figure 4.4 shows a typical Pareto diagram.

FIGURE 4.4   Pareto diagram

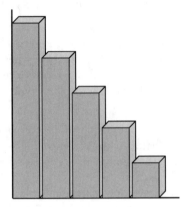

Statistical sampling   If you have many products to inspect as part of your project and you have very little time, you might decide to use statistical sampling. Statistical sampling involves gathering a subset of the total set of units and randomly selecting items to be inspected or reviewed. This method can be very cost effective. In Figure 4.5, you'll see a pie chart that can be used to depict the results of a statistical sampling.

FIGURE 4.5   Statistical sampling

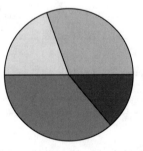

Flowcharting   We talked about flowcharting in Exercise 4.2. Flowcharting can also be used in Quality Control as a way to determine how problems occur. Figure 4.6 shows a simple flowchart for building a shed in your backyard.

FIGURE 4.6   Simple flowchart

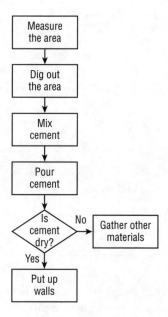

Trend analysis   Trend analysis is a set of mathematical computations that allow you to determine what the future outcome will be for a product you are creating. In simple terms, if you have a process that is creating 100 defects per 10 products and you do nothing to correct the defects, you will have a trend of 100 defects per 10 products. If you have a process that is creating 100 defects per 10 products in March, you fix some process problems, and then have 85 defects per 10 products in April, you know the trend is improving.

Recommended Reading: Chapter 10, pp. 379–387, *PMP Project Management Professional Study Guide.*

Scenario

TPMP has just placed you at USRemotes, the largest distributor of remote control devices in the United States. USRemotes has launched a project to redesign the warehouse and shipping areas and processes—the WSAP project. You have been assigned as the temporary project manager. You have just completed the project planning phase.

USRemotes is very interested in quality and is planning to gain some type of quality certification. Quality is also very important to you. You have been thinking about what data you will need to gather to control the quality of the project.

Quality Control

Using the information provided for the WSAP project, answer the following questions about quality control.

1. What is the definition of Quality Control?

   _____

   _____

2. List the six quality control tools and techniques.

   _____

   _____

   _____

   _____

3. You have determined that the most cost-effective timetable for shipping products from USRemotes is 24 hours. It is too expensive to ship earlier than 12 hours, and customers call to complain after 36 hours. What tool and technique of Quality Control would you use to measure the shipping times? Why?

   _____

   _____

   _____

   _____

4. A Pareto diagram is based on what rule?

   _____

   _____

5. What is a cost-effective tool and technique of Quality Control?

   _____

   _____

   _____

Answers to Exercise Questions

Answers to Exercise 4.1

1. The four major inputs into the quality management process are quality policy, scope statement, product description, and standards and regulations.

2. The quality policy should come from the leadership of the company. If none exists, the project manager should create one.

3. The product description is important to quality planning because it may contain information about the desired level of quality.

4. The major output of the quality planning process is a quality management plan.

5. Your quality policy statement for the WSAP project might be: Quality will be emphasized in the early stages and throughout the project. It will be planned into the project as work begins and it will be a part of the fiber of the entire project. We will design quality checkpoints and determine if quality standards have been met.

Answers to Exercise 4.2

1. Benchmarking is the process of analyzing similar activities as a means of comparison.

2. The three most commonly used tools of quality planning are benchmarking, cost benefit analysis, and flowcharting.

3. A cost benefit analysis is looking at the trade-offs of whether or not an activity should be done.

4. A flowchart would be a good quality planning tool to use if you are new to the company.

5. You would use the benchmarking quality planning tool for projects where you are improving or changing the way a business currently operates.

6. Flowcharting is a way of depicting the way work flows.

7. A cost benefit analysis would be a good quality planning tool to use to determine what quality activity will provide the most benefit for the least cost.

Answers to Exercise 4.3

1. The three types of costs of quality are prevention, appraisal, and failure.

2. A failure is the type of cost associated with nonconformance.

3. The definition of the cost of quality is the total amount of money required to ensure quality.

4. Process design training is an activity that should be included in the preventative cost of quality.

5. Validating the new design and testing the warehouse design internally are activities that should be included in the appraisal cost of quality.

6. The cost of scrapping the shelving units should be included in the internal failure cost of quality figures.

7. The cost of the additional customer service representatives should be included in the external failure cost of quality figures.

Answers to Exercise 4.4

1. The two tools and techniques of Quality Assurance are quality planning tools and quality audits.

2. You would do a quality audit at the end of the planning phase of the project to set a quality baseline for what you planned to do in regard to quality.

3. You would do a quality audit at the end of the project to create a quality lessons-learned document for future projects.

4. Quality audits are done at key milestones to assure the quality of the project. Doing an audit at this time gives you a chance to correct problems prior to the product being completed.

5. The quality planning tools are benchmarking, cost benefit analysis, flowcharting, design of experiments, and the cost of quality.

6. A quality baseline is used to compare what has been done to what was planned with respect to project quality.

Answers to Exercise 4.5

1. Quality Control monitors project results to guarantee that the project will achieve the desired quality.

2. The six quality control tools and techniques are trend analysis, flowcharting, statistical sampling, Pareto diagrams, control charts, and inspection.

3. A control chart would be a good tool and technique to use for this measurement because it allows you to set an upper and lower control limit as well as a mean. Since you have these parameters, determining whether the process is in control or out of control could be measured with this tool.

4. The Pareto diagram is based on the 80/20 rule.

5. A cost-effective tool and technique of Quality Control is statistical sampling.

Chapter

5

Human Resource Management

THE EXERCISES PRESENTED IN THIS CHAPTER INCLUDE:

- ✓ Exercise 5.1: Creating a Staffing Management Plan
- ✓ Exercise 5.2: Creating a Responsibility Assignment Matrix (RAM)
- ✓ Exercise 5.3: Acquiring Staff
- ✓ Exercise 5.4: Team Development

This chapter covers human resource management, one of the knowledge areas found in PMI's *Guide to the Project Management Body of Knowledge*. Project managers must have myriad management skills to manage projects effectively. One of these critical skills is managing human resources on a project. This chapter starts with planning processes of creating a staffing management plan, a responsibility assignment matrix, and acquiring staff, and ends by exploring the process of team development.

In this chapter, you will face new challenges in regards to your fictional company: Terrific Project Management Partners (TPMP). Since the processes of human resource management build on each other, we use the same scenario throughout this chapter and ask you to build on each step of the human resource management process. Human resources management is covered in the Planning and Executing process group objectives of the PMP exams.

Exercise 5.1: Creating a Staffing Management Plan

The objectives for Exercise 5.1 are:

- Describe a staffing management plan.
- Describe the inputs for a staffing management plan.
- Describe contents of a staffing management plan.

Background

The staffing management plan documents for the project team exactly how the human resources will be assigned to a project, what they will work on, and when they will depart from the project. This plan is the foundation for how human resources will be managed during the project. A staffing management plan can be general or very detailed. Regardless of the approach that you take, you will need to work through how this plan is created. In this exercise, we will examine the inputs to creating a staffing management plan as well as the thought process for creating it. Let's start with the inputs.

Inputs for a Staffing Management Plan

There are three pieces of information that the project manager needs to have at their fingertips in order to create a staffing management plan. These inputs are project interfaces, staffing requirements, and constraints. We will cover each of them here.

Project interfaces   As you think through the staffing management plan, you will need to understand the interfaces that affect your project. Interfaces can be organizational, technical, or interpersonal. Organizational interfaces deal with coordinating project work across multiple vendors, departments, or both. Technical interfaces deal with the way the work of the project must be done. And, finally, interpersonal interfaces deal with the reporting relationships among all of the project's personnel. You will want to document the types of interfaces and how you will mange each of them for your staffing management plan.

Staffing requirements   In Exercise 3.1 we spent a lot of time discussing resource planning. In resource planning you determined what types of resources should be used on which tasks of your project. Staff requirements are a subset of the resource plans that you created. This subset describes the types of competencies that are required for each resource type.

Constraints   "Constraints" is usually a generic term that is used throughout project management process descriptions. In a staffing management plan, constraints are used to describe the factors that limit the team's ability to use resources the way that the project manager desires. Constraints can be things like organizational rules, the preferences of the team, organizational structures, union agreements, or even the competencies of the people working on the project.

Contents of a Staffing Management Plan

Once you have your inputs together, it is time to construct your staffing management plan. These plans can be as individual as your organization or your project. Here are some ideas of sections that might be included in a staffing management plan.

Organization charts   An organization chart is a graphical depiction of the hierarchy of the project team. It is used to depict the reporting relationships of the team members to the project manager. Figure 5.1 shows a sample organization chart.

FIGURE 5.1   Sample organization chart

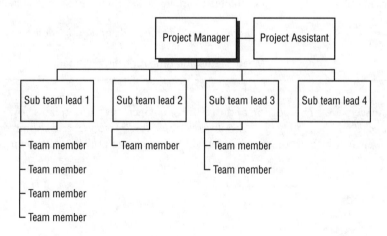

Resource assignment matrix (RAM)   A resource assignment matrix is a diagram that merges an organization breakdown structure and the work breakdown structure. We dedicate an entire exercise to the RAM in Exercise 5.2.

How assignments are made   A section on assignments includes your methodology for assigning team members to specific tasks.

Roles and responsibilities   A roles and responsibilities matrix would include each team member or resource grouping and a list of their responsibilities. This matrix makes it clear who is accountable for what on the project. In Table 5.1 general responsibilities are noted.

TABLE 5.1   Roles and Responsibilities Matrix

Role	Responsibility
Executive Sponsor	Chairs the steering committee
	Champions the project
	Resolves issues escalated from the steering committee
Project Manager	Organizes the team structure
	Manages the project
	Tracks progress
	Creates project plan
Project Team Member	Completes assigned tasks and their associated deliverables
	Adheres to project standards and methodology
	Meets status and time reporting obligations

Attrition management   This portion of the staffing management plan explains how all types of project vacancies will be managed. It should cover how key personnel and team members are replaced as well as how all project personnel will be reassigned at the end of the project.

Recommended Reading: Chapter 5, p. 161, *PMP Project Management Professional Study Guide.*

Scenario

TPMP has just placed you at Affordable Sweeping, Inc., an up-and-coming property maintenance company. Affordable Sweeping has just been awarded the contract to get the local NFL stadium ready for the current football season. Affordable Sweeping named the project Operation:NFL and has hired you to project manage. You will have over 100 people working on the project: team leads and sub team leads who are employees of Affordable Sweeping and many subcontractors.

Creating a Staffing Management Plan

Using information provided for the Operation:NFL project, answer the following questions about creating a staffing management plan.

1. What is the definition of a staffing management plan?

    _____

    _____

2. What are the three types of project interfaces?

    _____

    _____

3. What are the three inputs into a staffing management plan?

    _____

    _____

4. Why would you include an organization chart in a staffing management plan?

    _____

    _____

5. Why would you include a roles and responsibilities matrix in a staffing management plan?

    _____

    _____

Exercise 5.2: Creating a Responsibility Assignment Matrix (RAM)

The objectives for Exercise 5.2 are:

- Describe a responsibility assignment matrix.
- Describe the components of a RAM.

Background

Project planning requires the integration of many different types of information to plan the project effectively. The responsibility assignment matrix (RAM) is an example of merging two different knowledge areas, integrated to create a planning output. The RAM combines an organization chart with project tasks and creates a planning tool that describes who will accomplish what on a project. These components are an organizational breakdown structure and the work breakdown structure. Let's examine the two components more closely.

Organization breakdown structure   An organizational breakdown structure is really nothing more than a project organization chart. It needs to depict who is working on the project and the departments they represent. Figure 5.2 shows a typical organization breakdown structure.

FIGURE 5.2   Sample organization breakdown structure

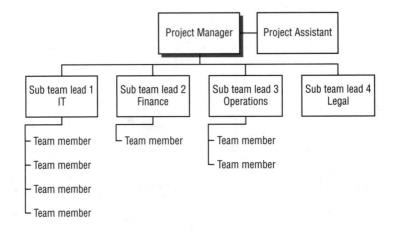

Work breakdown structure   A work breakdown structure is a tool and technique that is utilized to decompose project scope components into smaller and more manageable components or work packages. The project manager creates it with project team members. We covered work breakdown structures in Exercise 2.1. Figure 5.3 shows a typical work breakdown structure.

FIGURE 5.3   Typical work breakdown structure

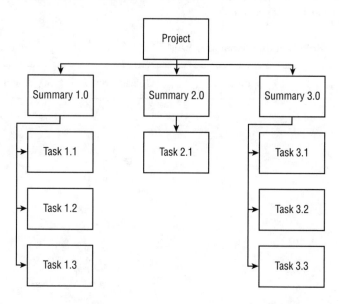

These two charts now come together to create the RAM. Table 5.2 shows a RAM based on Figures 5.2 and 5.3.

TABLE 5.2   Responsibility Assignment Matrix

	IT	Finance	Operations	Legal
Task 1.1	x		x	
Task 1.2	x	x		
Task 1.3				x
Task 2.1			x	
Task 3.1	x			
Task 3.2	x	x	x	x
Task 3.3	x			

You can now see that the RAM explains who will work on what task of the project.

RAMs can also be used to describe the responsibilities of team members on specific tasks. Creating a legend and applying it to the RAM allows team members to understand their roles on the same task. In Table 5.3 we have added the legend of a = accountable, c = creator, u = updater, r = reviewer to our previous table.

TABLE 5.3   Roles and Responsibility RAM

	IT	Finance	Operations	Legal
Task 1.1	a		r	
Task 1.2	c	a		
Task 1.3				a
Task 2.1			a	
Task 3.1	a			
Task 3.2	r	r	c	a
Task 3.3	a			

Recommended Reading: Chapter 5, p. 160, *PMP Project Management Professional Study Guide.*

Scenario

TPMP has just placed you at Affordable Sweeping, Inc., an up-and-coming property maintenance company. Affordable Sweeping has just been awarded the contract to get the local NFL stadium ready for the current football season. Affordable Sweeping named the project Operation:NFL and has hired you to project manage. You will have over 100 people working on the project: team leads and sub team leads who are employees of Affordable Sweeping and many subcontractors.

Creating a Responsibility Assignment Matrix (RAM)

Using the information provided for the Operation:NFL project, answer the following questions about creating a RAM.

1. What does the acronym RAM mean?

_____

_____

2. What is a RAM?

_____

_____

3. What two components make a RAM?

_____

_____

4. Why might you use a legend in creating a RAM?

_____

_____

Exercise 5.3: Acquiring Staff

The objectives for Exercise 5.3 are:

- Describe the three inputs of staff acquisition.
- Describe the three tools and techniques of staff acquisition.
- Describe the steps of negotiating for project staff.

Background

Staff acquisition is a key planning process for completing the human resource management processes. In staff acquisition, the project manager gathers inputs of the staffing management plan, staffing pool descriptions, and the organization's recruitment practices and uses three tools and techniques to put the project staff into place. Those three staff acquisition tools and techniques are negotiations, pre-assignment, and procurement. We examine each of these in this exercise.

Negotiations

One of the necessary skills a project manager must have is negotiating. This skill is highly utilized during the staff acquisition process.

In order to get the right people on your project, you will need to have a negotiating strategy. Here are the steps to effective staff negotiations:

1. Identify your target team.   If you could have the best people for your project, who would they be? Step through your WBS and examine the staffing requirements outlined in your staffing management plan. Determine the right person for each task. Have a fallback plan by identifying one or two people who also could do the task yet may not be as desirable as your first choice.

2. Identify potential barriers to getting your target team.   You will need to understand why you may not be able to get the right people for your project. Examine the following possibilities:

- Availability of the people you want—Jose is your top candidate for Task 62. Jose is constantly sought after for projects because of his expertise and work ethic. What strategy will you use if Jose is not available when you need him?

- Your relationship with the functional manager—You have found Jose's boss Mary to be difficult to work with. How will you work with her to come to a win-win solution that will benefit your project and her?

- Your authority as a project manager—Organizations give project managers different levels of authority to run their projects. What is your authority to staff your project? How strong are your influencing skills?

- Your organization structure—Organizations can be established as functional or as projectized, with many variations in between. Functional organizations have clear reporting relationships, where a subordinate usually has one supervisor. Projectized organizations are created to support project work and most of the people are doing project work. Projectized organizations tend to provide more authority to project managers by the very nature of the organization. (An exercise on project organizations is in Exercise 9.4.) What is your organization structure? How will that structure help or hinder your ability to get the right resources?

3. Build your negotiation strategy.   Spend a little time building your negotiating strategy. Determine your requests and your fallback strategy if you can not get your requests filled. Understand enough about your barriers to know what will help or hinder your position. Determine the best approach to negotiate your position.

4. Negotiate for your project team.   Start negotiating for the most critical staff first. If you are able to get them assigned to your project, you may not need your first choice candidate for other, less important positions. Work your way negotiating through your dream list until all of your positions are filled.

Pre-assignment

The second tool and technique of the staff acquisition process is pre-assignment. Pre-assignment is described as a situation where a project has certain positions filled as the project is initiated. This can happen when:

- There is only one resource available who can fill a specific position.
- Projects are "sold" with staff predefined.
- Projects where the staff is defined in the charter.

Procurement

The last tool and technique of staff acquisition is procurement. We will not spend any time on this subject here. Procurement will be extensively covered in Chapter 8, "Contracts and Procurement Management."

Recommended Reading: Chapter 5, pp. 162–163, *PMP Project Management Professional Study Guide.*

Scenario

TPMP has just placed you at Affordable Sweeping, Inc., an up-and-coming property maintenance company. Affordable Sweeping has just been awarded the contract to get the local NFL stadium ready for the current football season. Affordable Sweeping named the project Operation:NFL and has hired you to project manage. You will have over 100 people working on the project: team leads and sub team leads who are employees of Affordable Sweeping and many subcontractors.

You are ready to start staffing the project. You have some concerns about getting the right people for the project. Affordable Sweeping has many contracts, and most of the people you need are already assigned to other projects.

Acquiring Staff

Using the information provided for the Operation:NFL project, answer the following questions about staff acquisition.

1. What are the three inputs to the staff acquisition process?

    _____

    _____

2. What are the three tools and techniques of staff acquisition?

   _____

   _____

3. Name the four steps to negotiating staff.

   _____

   _____

4. When the contract for Operation:NFL was signed, Bill was named as the lead of the outside maintenance team. This is an example of what tool and technique of staff acquisition?

   _____

   _____

5. Why would your organization structure influence your ability to acquire staff?

   _____

   _____

Exercise 5.4: Team Development

The objectives for Exercise 5.4 are:

- Describe the team development process.
- Describe the four primary tools and techniques of team development.
- Describe when team development techniques should be utilized.

Background

Team development is the only human resource management process that is performed in the executing portion of a project. Team development deals with how a project team performs together to create the project deliverables. There are four primary tools and techniques of the team development process. They are team-building activities, reward and recognition systems, collocation, and training. We will discuss each of these tools and techniques, as well as how to decide when each should be used.

Team-Building Activities

Team-building activities are any type of planned activities that increase the comfort level of the team in working with each other. There is a substantial body of literature published on this subject. Project managers need to be well aware of the types of activities that are available through this literature. Team-building activities can be as simple as a group lunch or as complex as day-long facilitated sessions. Project managers should use team-building sessions at three different points in the team development process.

Initiation   As soon as the project team is assembled, team-building activities should begin. Sufficient time should be devoted to the team-building work at this stage. These activities will serve as a foundation to move the team through progressing stages of development.

New team members   Anytime a new team member joins a project, the dynamics of the team will change. Project managers need to be aware of the effects of adding new staff. It may be necessary to incorporate team-building activities back into the work plan.

Conflict   Conflict is normal and desirable on projects. It allows the team to resolve problems and find the right solutions for successful project completion. There are times though when conflict lasts longer than necessary and is a detriment to project completion. This may be a time to use team-building techniques to resolve the conflict and bind the team into a better performing group.

Reward and Recognition Systems

The second primary tool and technique of the team development process is reward and recognition systems. This technique describes what you will use to incentivize the team to outstanding performance. You will need to design your rewards and recognition systems at the beginning of the project. Communicate the plan to the team members so they understand "what is in it for them" to complete the project successfully. The key to a rewards and recognition system is doing what you promised. If you have promised a day off for extra work, be sure to let the person have the day off. The first time you do not reward as you said, the system will be destroyed because trust in the system will now be lacking. You would then need to redesign and reapply a new system.

Collocation

Another primary tool and technique of team development is collocation. Collocation is simply moving the project team next to each other to facilitate team development. If it is impossible to move the team together, the project manager needs to find other ways for team interaction. Collocation should be established at the beginning of the project. Replacement collocation activities must be ongoing through the project's execution.

Training

The last tool and technique of team development is training. Training is used to enhance the team's management or technical skills. If team members are allowed to attend training together, it can be used as another type of team-building activity. Training should be completed at the beginning of the project where core competencies are missing. Training can be utilized later in the project when specific needs arise.

Recommended Reading: Chapter 8, pp. 294–307, *PMP Project Management Professional Study Guide.*

Scenario

TPMP has just placed you at Affordable Sweeping, Inc., an up-and-coming property maintenance company. Affordable Sweeping has just been awarded the contract to get the local NFL
stadium ready for the current football season. Affordable Sweeping named the project Opera-
tion:NFL and has hired you to project manage. You will have over 100 people working on the
project: team leads and sub team leads who are employees of Affordable Sweeping and many
subcontractors.

  The staffing is complete and you have heard a lot about team development techniques. You
are wondering what techniques you should utilize and when you should use them.

Team Development

Using the information provided for the Operation:NFL project, answer the following questions
about team development.

1. Team development is performed during what phase of a project?

    _____

    _____

2. What are the four primary tools and techniques of team development?

    _____

    _____

    _____

3. Affordable Sweeping has several offices throughout the city. You have acquired the staff
    and now you are moving them all into the same office. This is an example of which primary
    tool and technique of team development?

    _____

    _____

    _____

4. When the staff acquisition for Operation:NFL was completed, you took the entire team on
    a tour of the stadium and later to lunch. At lunch you had team members introduce them-
    selves and explain their role on the project. This is an example of which primary tool and
    technique of team development?

    _____

    _____

    _____

5. You have been working on Operation:NFL for several months. You have found that the groundskeepers and turf preparation teams are constantly fighting and are running behind schedule. What tool and technique of team development would you use now? Why?

_____

_____

_____

_____

Answers to Exercise Questions

Answers to Exercise 5.1

1. The staffing management plan documents for the project team exactly how the human resources will be assigned to a project, what they will work on, and when they will depart from the project.
2. Project interfaces can be organizational, technical, or interpersonal.
3. The three inputs into a staffing management plan are project interfaces, staffing requirements, and constraints.
4. You would include an organization chart in a staffing management plan so the project team understands the reporting relationships on the project.
5. You would include a roles and responsibilities matrix in a staffing management plan to make it clear who is accountable for what on the project.

Answers to Exercise 5.2

1. The acronym RAM stands for responsibility assignment matrix.
2. The RAM is the integration of an organization chart and project tasks that creates a planning tool that describes who will accomplish what on a project.
3. A RAM is created by merging an organization breakdown structure with a work breakdown structure.
4. A legend can be used in a RAM to describe project team roles.

Answers to Exercise 5.3

1. The three inputs of the staff acquisition process are the staffing management plan, staffing pool descriptions, and the organization's recruitment practices.
2. The three staff acquisition tools and techniques are negotiation, pre-assignment, and procurement.

3. The four steps to negotiating staff are (1) identifying your target team, (2) identifying potential barriers to getting your target team, (3) building your negotiation strategy, and (4) negotiating for your project team.

4. When the contract for Operation:NFL was signed, Bill was named as the lead of the outside maintenance team. This is an example of the pre-assignment tool and technique of staff acquisition.

5. The organization structure of your company can influence your ability to acquire staff because projectized organizations are built for executing projects. Project managers should have more power and influence in this type of structure.

Answers to Exercise 5.4

1. Team development is the only human resource management process that is performed in the executing portion of a project.

2. The four primary tools and techniques of team development are team-building activities, reward and recognition systems, collocation, and training.

3. Moving staff into the same office is an example of the team development technique called collocation.

4. Taking the entire team on a tour of the stadium, having members introduce themselves, and talk about their role on the project is an example of the team-building activities tool and technique of team development.

5. You would use team-building activities to shore up the relationship between the groundskeepers and turf prep team. These teams do not need additional training; they just need to complete the project on time.

Chapter

6

Communication Management

THE EXERCISES COVERED IN THIS CHAPTER INCLUDE:

- ✓ Exercise 6.1: Understanding Your Stakeholders
- ✓ Exercise 6.2: Communicating with the Team
- ✓ Exercise 6.3: Deciding on Information Distribution
- ✓ Exercise 6.4: Creating a Communications Plan
- ✓ Exercise 6.5: Performance Reporting, Including Earned Value Analysis
- ✓ Exercise 6.6: Closing a Project or phase

This chapter covers Communication Management, one of the knowledge areas found in PMI's *Guide to the Project Management Body of Knowledge*. Communication Management involves understanding to whom you need to communicate, in what forms, and how often.

First, you need to identify and analyze all of your stakeholders. Knowing your stakeholders helps you think about their needs and expectations, which is important so that you can figure out what kind of communication you need to have with them and how often you need to communicate. Next, you need to decide how you will communicate with your team. You will also decide on how you distribute the information (for instance, on what kind of media will the information be distributed). You need to create a communications plan detailing how and when you will communicate with your stakeholders. This plan includes a communication matrix that you will use to organize your communication with your team and stakeholders. You need to decide how you are going to report on your project's continued performance. Performance reporting will focus on earned value, an important measurement process in project management. Finally, in the last exercise highlighting closing processes recommended by PMI, you will learn about project closeout.

Communication Management is covered in the Planning, Executing, Controlling, and Closing objectives of the PMP exam.

Exercise 6.1: Understanding Your Stakeholders

The objectives for Exercise 6.1 are:

- Identify project stakeholders.
- Learn how to think about the needs of project stakeholders.
- Analyze the needs and expectations of stakeholders.
- Create a stakeholder analysis tool.

Background

Communication Management means knowing your stakeholders and communicating with them about their needs and expectations regularly. A project stakeholder is anyone positively or negatively impacted by your project—including project team members. Stakeholders are individuals and organizations, and you will want to identify both kinds to thoroughly identify all needs and expectations. Stakeholders may include the following people or organizations: the project manager, sponsor, team members, customers, the organization performing the work, functional managers providing team members, operations, and many others. You also need to think about stakeholders external and internal to the organization, such as contractors, the government, your community, team member or company families, and the media.

Recommended Reading: Chapter 1, pp. 4–5, and Chapter 12, pp. 441–443, *PMP Project Management Professional Study Guide.*

Stakeholder Analysis

Once you identify all the stakeholders (and this could be quite a list, depending on the complexity of the project), you need to identify their driving needs and expectations. Some may only need to know about what's going on with the project, whereas others will be decision makers or influence project direction or outcome even if they do not have decision-making power on the project. It's important to understand these needs and expectations early in the project and how they might change over the course of the project. Some people may have different expectations in the planning phase than in the controlling phase of the project. If you do this identification and analysis upfront, you will not be as easily swayed or pulled in different directions as the project progresses. Defining stakeholders, depending on the sensitivity of the data gathered, may be a tool only you would use to help define your communication plan (described in a later exercise). You will also find that you need to update your analysis throughout the project as the stakeholders change or you get to know them better. Some expectations or needs to consider are:

- How important is cost and profit to the stakeholder?

- What kind of information will they require?

- How important is the schedule to the stakeholder?

- Is quality important to the stakeholder?

- Will the project threaten or enhance his or her position or organization in any way?

- Is the stakeholder a major player in scope change?

- Does he or she care more for results or more for how people are affected?

- What are the major issues or risks at stake for this stakeholder?

- How much influence does the stakeholder have? Can he or she threaten the success of your project?

- Is the stakeholder a performer, influencer, decision maker, technical or subject matter expert, or nonessential to the project but interested in it?

- How often do they need information about your project?

- When do they need to be included in the project or when are they most impacted during the project?

You may want to keep your stakeholder analysis to yourself and your sponsor. For instance, someone might think he or she is a decision maker on the project, but really is nonessential. For such stakeholders, they may look at the project as something that will enhance their position if they look like they are involved in it. Letting them see a list where they are categorized as "nonessential" might be counterproductive.

Creating a Stakeholder Needs Matrix

Now that you know some of the criteria behind stakeholder analysis, you can create a stakeholder needs matrix. To do so, follow these steps:

1. Identify criteria as needs and expectations for your stakeholders. Items may be:

-   Does he or she care about quality over everything else?

-   Does he or she care more about results than other aspects of the project?

-   Does he or she care more about technology than other aspects of the project?

-   Does he or she have the ability to impact the project positively or negatively?

-   Does he or she care about its cost or profit-making potential?

-   Does he or she require special care? (You might need to indicate that this person might need some special care to help achieve success on the project.)

-   Does he or she care more about the project making its scheduled date above all else?

-   Does he or she deal well with change? (If not, you may need to build in some special steps to help him or her with the change.)

-   Does he or she have scope approval or influence?

-   Does he or she need special recognition during the course of the project to feel more valued?

-   Is he or she an influencer, decision maker, performer, expert, or nonessential who needs information only?

-   Does he or she demonstrate the ability and desire to help solve problems (this means you might have someone to call on to help when you need to solve a problem)?

-   Is he or she people-oriented?

-   Does he or she need one-on-one meetings to help motivate or clarify project goals and tasks?

2. Decide on ratings (high/medium/low or 1 through 10) for each of the criteria so you can rate its importance to the stakeholder.

3. Identify each and every individual and organizational stakeholder that you and your team can think of. Don't forget to include people who are external to the organization such as

the government or media. Include a brief description for each person or organization with this list.

4. Interview as many stakeholders as you can, and find out their expectations and needs for the project. Using a questionnaire with the criteria will help—you may also find you need some additional criteria as you talk with stakeholders.

5. Create a matrix for your stakeholders so you understand their needs better and are able to understand the influence they will have on your project. This matrix will help you make better decisions about how to communicate with them.

Scenario

TPMP is working with an independent, not-for-profit organization, Health America (HA), that is creating reports for the status and quality of hospital health care in the United States based on goals created by the president of the United States. Health America is implementing project management processes and TPMP is helping them. This project is a highly visible program in the government, and it entails working with the major hospitals within major U.S. cities, and rating the hospitals' achievement of specific goals as identified by the president's program. Research and reporting started about two years ago.

You are helping the project manager, Bill Smith, identify stakeholders and their expectations so that he can analyze their needs and expectations, and thus have a better communications plan. Bill works for Karen Palmer, and she wants to make sure that project management methodologies are applied to this project. Jeremy Checks, a peer of Karen's, thinks that project management is a waste of time and is hoping the project will turn sour and that project management will be the cause. Bill Smith will have several team members, including Kate Sullivan and Edward Salazar who are researchers on the project. Because this project is so visible at Health America, Edward is hoping his excellent work on this project will help promote him to manager of research one day. Once the research is completed, and the program is implemented by all of the hospitals, Fran Freeling will be taking on incidental research and follow-up for the project. You will help Bill create a matrix analysis so he can understand the issues he may have on his project. Some of the people interested in your project are the media, so they can report on the goals being met or not met; the Health and Welfare branch of the government, who is monitoring the project for the president and who is paying for the program; the hospitals throughout the United States; and the public, who needs to understand how this program is helping them.

Understanding Your Stakeholders

1. What criteria do you want to include to help identify stakeholder expectations and needs?

_____

_____

_____

_____

2.   List the stakeholders. Don't hesitate to list any that might not be mentioned in the setup for this exercise.

_____

_____

_____

_____

3.   Rate the importance of each criterion for each of the stakeholders.

_____

_____

_____

_____

4.   Based on your analysis, how often do you need to communicate with the Department of Health and Welfare and what would you communicate?

_____

_____

_____

_____

5.   Based on your analysis, is there someone who can adversely affect the program?

_____

_____

_____

_____

6.   How often does the public need to be updated about this program?

_____

_____

_____

_____

Exercise 6.2: Communicating with the Team

The objectives for Exercise 6.2 are:

- Use the lines of communication to understand communication complexity.
- Identify communication forms and listening skills.
- Learn and practice some conflict resolution methods.

Background

As the project manager, one of your most important jobs will be to effectively communicate with the team so your team members understand their particular contributions to the project and you can keep them focused on the goals of the project. You need to understand the complexity of communication and how you use various forms of communication, including listening, to provide information to and receive information from your team. Finally, you need to help your team resolve differences using various conflict resolution methods.

Recommended Reading: Chapter 8, pp. 307–313, *PMP Project Management Professional Study Guide.*

Lines of Communication

Communication is a very complex activity, often taken for granted. The following formula illustrates the lines of communication (also called communication channels) that can exist based on the number of people involved on a project:

$[n \times (n - 1)] \div 2$

where "n" is the number of people on the team who will be communicating.

This means if you have five people on your project, there are 10 lines of communication. Team members on the project don't just communicate to the project manager, but also with each other. When they communicate with each other, the chances for miscommunication and distortion increase. If you have 20 people on the project, then there are 190 lines of communication—quite an increase for only 10 more people. These lines of communication keep growing exponentially and could become very difficult to manage if you don't have a plan and a consistent method of managing the communication.

In Exercise 6.4, we will describe how to create a communications plan that will help you keep your communication consistent.

Feedback

There is a basic model of communication based on a sender encoding a message and receivers decoding the message. Perhaps the most important aspect of this model is that there needs to be feedback: You can't expect to just send information out and that everyone will understand. And the receiver has some responsibility in understanding the message. The receiver needs to do something to confirm he or she understands the communication as you intended. So, using the terms of the model, the sender formats the message to be sent (encoding it in a way that can be decoded by the receiver). The receiver, or in this case, your team member, might "filter" the information to perceive the message according to his or her mindset as learned by culture, language, or emotions. But it is their duty to try to describe what they perceived so you can confirm the communication as you intended it. Important items need to be communicated often, too.

People usually don't get the message once. That's why commercials play over and over again—the media has figured out that messages aren't received the first time. You as a project manager need to remember it too: important information needs to be repeated. You will need to repeat important information like milestones, quality expectations, changes, the project goals, or job expectations.

You also need to understand the forms of communication—whether they are formal or informal—so you can use them in the appropriate situations: you will make decisions on whether your communication should be verbal, nonverbal (pictures or gestures), or written, depending on the situation. Become aware of your communication habits. You may frown a lot while you listen and folks may interpret this as disapproval, while you may be just listening hard—you may need to change that habit to have a more open look on your face. And as a project manager you will need to tune your listening skills: you will need to practice active listening (keep an open mind while listening—don't formulate responses in your head), eye contact, gestures showing interest (like nodding), recapping what was said, and not allowing interruptions.

Conflict Resolution

As a project manager, you will also get the chance to practice conflict resolution. Most people have some natural reactions to conflict, but as project managers, you need to actively use problem solving as much as possible. The following five terms describe possible conflict resolution methods you may choose to apply.

Forcing   One person tries to force their point of view to solve a problem on another. The opinion is usually imposed by someone with authority. It solves the conflict temporarily, but your team or the person who is on the receiving end continues to harbor issues.

Smoothing   Emphasizes agreement, choosing to ignore the disagreement. Again, this is a temporary solution, because you or your team have not worked through the disagreement and solved the issue more thoroughly. The issue may resurface again.

Compromise   Allows those who disagree to come to some kind of satisfaction when each party gives something up. This method provides for a grudging agreement, and although this may be a permanent solution because everyone makes a commitment to it, there might have been a better solution.

Withdrawal   One of the parties avoids conflict by leaving or avoiding it so the conflict doesn't get resolved. The project manager needs to look out for this kind of situation: you might need to have more discussions with the team to keep working on the issue. This is one of the worst forms of resolution, because no one wins and the problem will continue.

Problem solving (Confrontation)   Getting to the bottom of the issue and resolving it to everyone's satisfaction. Usually, you use the problem solving techniques of analysis, alternatives review, recommendations, and finally coming up with the best solution based on fact. This is the best way to solve conflict.

By looking for the various forms of conflict, and attempting to facilitate the team to solve the issue through problem solving, you will be performing one of your most important roles as a project manager.

Planning and Managing Team Communications

Knowing that communication, feedback, and conflict resolution are such an important part of maintaining an effective project team, you should keep the following considerations in mind when planning and managing your team and its activities:

1. Estimate the number of communication channels on your team. This will help you better define how complex your communications will be and how consistent and organized you must be.

2. Take an inventory of your communication skills, and develop your listening skills. Practice active listening regularly.

3. Think about the types of communication you will use and decide on how you will use them. You will probably want to use verbal communication in status meetings as you discuss issues informally, but to record the decisions, you will want to write them down in some kind of weekly report.

4. Study and understand the methods of resolving conflict. When you resolve an issue with a method other than problem solving, ensure you understand why, and the possible consequences.

5. Practice conflict resolution using the problem-solving method as much as possible.

Scenario

TPMP is working with an independent, non-profit organization, Health America, who is creating reports for the status and quality of hospital health care in the United States based on goals created by the President of the United States. Health America is implementing project management processes and TPMP is helping them. This is a highly visible program in the government, and it entails working with the major hospitals within the major cities of America, and rating if they are achieving specific goals as identified by the President's program. The research and reporting started about 2 years ago. You are helping the project manager, Bill Smith, discover some communication methods and techniques he can employ as he manages this very complex project. Bill works for Karen Palmer, and she wants to make sure that project management methodologies are applied to this project. Jeremy Checks, a peer of Karen's, thinks that project management is a waste of time and is hoping the project will turn sour and that project management will be the cause. Bill Smith will have several team members, including Kate Sullivan and Edward Salazar who think project management will get in the way of getting their work done. Bill will be introducing several project management techniques and methods during the course of the project.

Communicating with the Team

1. Bill has 17 people on his immediate project team. How many lines of communication does he have? He has around 85 stakeholders he has determined he needs to communicate with or who might communicate with each other. What is the potential number of lines of communication on the entire project?

    _____

    _____

    _____

    _____

2. What kinds of information should Bill communicate formally?

    _____

    _____

    _____

    _____

3. Bill is sending an e-mail to his project team telling them that there will be a review of the latest research findings next Monday at 10:00 AM. Identify each of the following: Who is the sender? What is the message? What is being encoded? Who is the receiver? What is being decoded? What are some of the filters the team members might have about this message?

    _____

    _____

    _____

    _____

4. Kate Sullivan has been researching the quality of pre-op procedures in the various hospitals, and she needs help in resolving an issue in the information she has found. She comes to Bill to tell him her problems because she does not think she can produce a report with what she's finding. What are some of the listening techniques Bill could use to help her out?

    _____

    _____

    _____

    _____

5. Jeremy Checks has come to Bill to complain. He found out that some of his employees, who are members of Bill's team, will be spending a couple of days on project management training. He doesn't like it all—none of the time will help them get their work done. He said the

team members are complaining to him already. Which conflict resolution method should Bill use to help solve the issue with Jeremy and why?

_____

_____

_____

_____

6. Kate and Edward are arguing about the best research method for collecting data about each hospital's use of peer reviews for complex operations on patients. They need to collect this data for one of their reports. Kate feels the Internet will work, whereas Edward knows that at least 20 percent of the hospital staff will only respond to traditional mail. They need to come up with the best method to get this data. What conflict resolution method should Bill use to help facilitate this issue?

_____

_____

_____

_____

Exercise 6.3: Deciding on Information Distribution

The objectives for Exercise 6.3 are:

- Identify the forms of information.
- Identify information retrieval systems.
- Identify the ways that information can be distributed.
- Decide on information distribution for your project.

Background

Once you know who you need to communicate to and something about their needs, you need to decide on what you will distribute and how you will distribute the information. You might take an inventory of what forms of information you can create and the methods your organization has (or which you can obtain) for distributing information.

First, what kinds of information will you distribute? The list could be almost endless and could include some of the following information: status/progress; escalations; issues; risks and risk response plans; quality standards; project processes and standards; contracts; change requests; scope statements; team directory; work breakdown structure; schedule or budget and their variances; requirements; specifications; user guides; test plans; reports; project charter; responsibility and organization charts; and a project plan.

Second, you will then decide on how the information will be distributed, such as e-mails, written memos, formal or informal meetings, presentations (including charts and graphs), conference or video calls, websites, instant messaging, videos, TV, press releases, faxes, voicemail, articles, brochures, announcements, phone calls, and speeches.

Not only do you need to think about how you push information to your team or other stakeholders, you also need to consider the way your team or stakeholders will pull information when they need to get to it. Do you store all your information on a website or in an electronic database? Or do you store it in a project management software files, or in an electronic directory, or in hard copy via a file cabinet or notebook? Some of these decisions might be based on the need for archiving files or corporate policies.

The decisions about what and how information is distributed may be based on how often and how formal the information needs are, your organization's capabilities, or your people's skills, and confidentiality and need to know. Do people need information updated frequently, or can people wait for a week? If your team is not trained in reading and using a project schedule, you may need to find a simpler form for communicating status and progress rather than using a Gantt chart. Or you may need to find project management training for the team.

What's more, you need to match the right kind of information, with the right kind of audience, at the right time. For instance, although you may create a status report, you may find you need to design two kinds of status reports: a detailed status report for the team involving the status of each of the team's deliverables for the week and an overview of major deliverables, budget, and escalations for executives. The format for each may also be entirely different so that the team sees the detailed schedule and executives see only a high-level milestone report.

Last but not least, you need to decide how you can get information to people when they request it outside of the regularly scheduled times or stakeholders have special requests for information you don't normally provide. In other words, you need to create an information distribution strategy. Following are some guidelines on how to create an information distribution strategy:

1. Decide on your major forms of communication for the various types of information you will be creating. For instance you might have a written status via presentations for executives; and meetings, issues, and updated schedules for your team meetings.

2. Decide on the technology or method you will use to distribute the information: e-mail, Internet, written memos, or a directory structure on the network.

3. Decide how often you will distribute your different forms of information. You might start forming a matrix for this kind of information that will eventually be complete in a communications plan (discussed in the next exercise).

4. Let the team members know where all the information is, where they can put their information, and how they can get information when it's needed.

Recommended Reading: Chapter 8, pp. 313–315, *PMP Project Management Professional Study Guide.*

Scenario

TPMP is working with an independent, non-profit organization, Health America, who is creating reports for the status and quality of hospital health care in the United States based on goals created by the President of the United States. Health America is implementing project management processes and TPMP is helping them. This is a highly visible program in the government, and it entails working with the major hospitals within the major cities of America, and rating if they are achieving specific goals as identified by the President's program. The research and reporting started about 2 years ago. The Health and Welfare department is your client and needs to keep up on budget and status of the reports you are creating. You are helping the project manager, Bill Smith decide on his information distribution strategy so he is more consistent in communicating with the team. In preparation for creating the communications plan, he is thinking about all of the kinds information he has been creating and the technologies the organization has. Bill has the extra charge of communicating how the project management techniques are working as well. The Health and Welfare department is the customer and needs to keep up on budget. Health America relies on e-mail for communication, uses the Web to gather information, and has a shared network drive to store and share files. Karen Palmer, Bill's boss at Health America, and her peer, Jeremy Checks, are very interested in the project management processes being implemented, even though Jeremy is skeptical of project management processes. Bill has a team doing research and creating the reports. In working with his team, Bill realizes several of his teammates use e-mail daily, and some check it every now and then. Bill has also been receiving some calls from some national news agencies asking about the new program.

Deciding on Information Distribution

1. What kinds of information would you recommend that Bill Smith distribute?

    _____

    _____

    _____

    _____

2. What are some methods you would recommend that Bill use to distribute information at Health America?

   _____

   _____

   _____

   _____

3. After consulting with you, Bill has decided to distribute a status report to the team, to Health America executives, and to the Health and Welfare department. He will also create press releases and provide status on an external website that only hospitals can access. How often do you think he should issue or update each of these and why?

   _____

   _____

   _____

   _____

4. When someone needs information in between statuses, how would you recommend that Bill set up the information for them to get it?

   _____

   _____

   _____

   _____

5. Bill will be training the team next week about how often to expect information and where to store project information. Will this training be enough for the team? What should Bill do to follow up this training?

   _____

   _____

   _____

   _____

Exercise 6.4: Creating a Communications Plan

The objectives for Exercise 6.4 are:

- Understand how a plan can help you organize your communications.
- Create a detailed communication management plan.
- Create a communication matrix.

Background

The best way to communicate consistently and in an organized form is to write down your communications plan. First, you need to create a plan describing the types of communication you will distribute and the methods by which you will distribute them. You will need to describe the strategy and tactics you are using for communication in this plan. If your project is complex, and you have many stakeholders, your strategy and tactics for communicating will need to be far more formal and organized than if your project is small and you have few stakeholders. You will also create a communication matrix as part of this plan, which will list all of your communication methods and the stakeholders who will receive the communication. You will describe the communication forms and when they will receive their information.

Components of a Communication Management Plan

A thorough communications management plan incorporates many details. First, you need to determine how and where you will store your project information. You need to decide the structure of the filing methods you will be using: electronic or hard copy. This plan will be published to team members so they know how to get information, and where they should store the project information they create. Your plan for storage should also include procedures for documentation and communication management.

Your communications plan should include a communication matrix explaining who receives information, what the information is, when it will be distributed, and how it will be distributed. Also, you need to provide your team members with a description of the format and content for each of the kinds of information that will be distributed. For instance, if you listed status report for one of the information types, you would describe the data that will be captured in the status report. This matrix makes you pre-plan all of the formats you will use. You may also include a schedule for each type of information so it's clear when it will be produced.

Your team will need procedures for getting information between regularly scheduled communications, and you need to provide the methods for updating the communications plan itself as the project proceeds.

Creating a Communication Management Plan

Creating a communications plan is absolutely essential on a medium or large-sized project, and by sticking to it you'll prove to your organization that you are consistent and in control of the communication and, by implication, the project itself. Following are the steps you should take to create a communication management plan:

1. Decide on an overall strategy for your communication. You will need to describe how you are going to handle communication and why. For instance, you might state that you are going to manage communication on a very formal basis, with meetings and follow-up documents at all times, because you have a large project. You might state that you will require a part-time communication manager on your project because of its complexity, or that you may need help from the public relations staff because you will publish information to the media.

2. Describe how you will store information and how your team will retrieve information. For instance, you might state that you will keep all documents on the network drive and provide the directory name and file structure for all the project information. This policy will

keep the directory from becoming unusable because people put documents wherever they think they should. You should also provide procedures as to how the team or stakeholders should use this structure.

3.   Create a communication matrix. Make sure you create it thoroughly, by answering the basic questions of who, what, where, when, why, and how. You might consider including the following information: what is the information (such as status report), who will use the information (per stakeholder groups), when will it be published (such as weekly, as needed, or daily), and how the stakeholders will receive it (such as via e-mail attachments, presentation, or meeting). You will have an example form to use for your exercise. You might even think about creating the matrix for each phase of the project (concept, design, execution, finish) because the information needs and frequency may change.

4.   Create a form and example content for each type of information listed in the matrix above, or refer to where the form can be found. For instance, create a status report form. Show all of the fields of data you want to be included, such as dates covered, objectives and accomplishments for the status time frame, hot topics, issues, or action items. Make sure you describe what would go into each field.

5.   Describe procedures for how your team and stakeholders will request and obtain information outside of normal distribution times. For instance, by detailing that the media must contact the PR department first if they have a question, everyone on the project will know what to tell the media if they should get a call from a reporter.

6.   Describe in the communication management plan how changes will be made and approved for the plan itself. If you have found you need another form of communication as you move into the execution stage, you will need to write a procedure to ensure your team knows about the new communication form, and that you add the information to the plan itself.

Recommended Reading: Chapter 4, pp. 137–138, and Chapter 8, pp. 313–315, *PMP Project Management Professional Study Guide.*

Scenario

TPMP is working with an independent, non-profit organization, Health America, who is creating reports for the status and quality of hospital health care in the United States based on goals created by the President of the United States. Health America is implementing project management processes and TPMP is helping them. This is a highly visible program in the government, and it entails working with the major hospitals within the major cities of America, and rating if they are achieving specific goals as identified by the President's program. The research and reporting started about 2 years ago. You are helping the project manager, Bill Smith, create a communication management plan, including a communication matrix. Your team is made up of researchers, analysts, and writers who will produce the hospital quality report for the Health and Welfare department. Some of the people interested in your project are the media, so they can report on the goals being met/not met; the Health and Welfare branch of the government, who is monitoring the project for the president and who is paying for the program; the hospitals throughout the United States; and the public, who needs to understand how this program is helping them.

Creating a Communications Plan

Complete the following matrix to help you answer the questions. When you complete the "Who" column, describe groups, not individuals.

What	Why (Purpose)	Who	When	How	Where (Storage)	Inputs

1. What should Bill's strategy be for communication on this project? Should it be formal or informal, mostly written or verbal? How much time should he spend on communication?

   _____

   _____

   _____

   _____

2. Will there be issues if Bill does not receive status updates from his team regularly? Why or why not?

   _____

   _____

   _____

   _____

3. Should Bill share the executive and client status reports with his team? Why or why not?

   _____

   _____

   _____

   _____

4. What is the purpose of the communication matrix?

   _____

   _____

   _____

   _____

5. Will meetings and written status be enough communication for your team members? Why or why not?

   _____

   _____

   _____

   _____

6. What kind of data would you include on your status report form? Why is it important to create a form?

   _____

   _____

   _____

   _____

Exercise 6.5: Performance Reporting, Including Earned Value Analysis

The objectives for Exercise 6.5 are:

- Understand the importance of performance reporting.
- Decide on the best methods for performance reporting.
- Understand earned value analysis.
- Practice earned value analysis.

Background

Once your project gets underway, you need to communicate where it stands and how it is progressing to your sponsor and other executives on your project. It's important to provide the executives objective measurements. You need to measure progress objectively based on the major elements of the project: cost, schedule, and quality (performance) within the current scope. You may also report on procurement and risk. You might have regularly scheduled performance reviews showing progress with reports, graphs, and charts.

Performance Reporting

There are various forms of Performance Reporting to choose from, including:

- Performance reviews
- Variance analysis
- Trend analysis
- Earned value analysis

We will briefly discuss performance reviews, variance analysis, and trend analysis in this section; however, in this exercise, we will stress earned value analysis as the primary performance reporting method. We will discuss earned value analysis in detail separately.

One form of Performance Reporting that you might consider during a performance review is to show schedule progress via a milestone report. This report will help show graphically if your project is on track, provided you show the original, baseline targets. Figure 6.1 illustrates a milestone report chart. The project was originally baselined to complete on March 7, but now shows a finish date of March 12. You can look at the individual tasks that have made the project move out.

FIGURE 6.1 Milestone chart

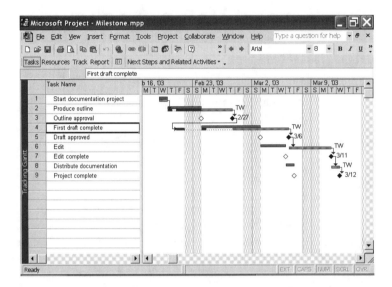

The project illustrated in Figure 6.1 is behind schedule. As you can see, extra days have been added to the original end date for creating the outline (maybe someone left something out of the scope). The performance reviewers might ask the tech writer to work overtime, or maybe the performance reviewers accepted the changed dates because making sure everything is in the document is more important than getting the manual produced on time.

Besides the milestone report, you might have a budget report. You might show how much you've spent in relation to the total budget and gauge if you have spent too much in relation to how much more work you have to complete.

During performance reviews you might use variance analysis reports to show you are ahead, behind, or on target for scheduled end date or budget. Figure 6.2 shows a schedule variance report for the documentation project. This report shows you overall variance for completing the project is +3.1 days over the original target.

You might use trend analysis (possibly using scatter diagrams) to show quality (number of defects) and progress toward reducing them or schedule or budget trends.

FIGURE 6.2 Variance analysis report

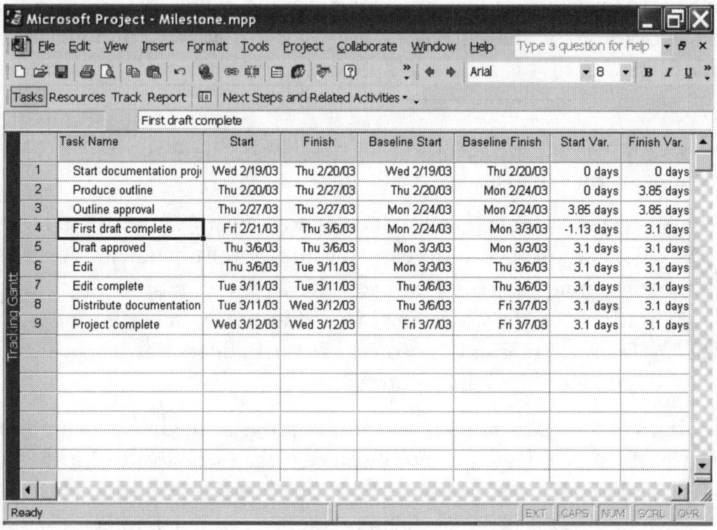

	Task Name	Start	Finish	Baseline Start	Baseline Finish	Start Var.	Finish Var.
1	Start documentation proj	Wed 2/19/03	Thu 2/20/03	Wed 2/19/03	Thu 2/20/03	0 days	0 days
2	Produce outline	Thu 2/20/03	Thu 2/27/03	Thu 2/20/03	Mon 2/24/03	0 days	3.85 days
3	Outline approval	Thu 2/27/03	Thu 2/27/03	Mon 2/24/03	Mon 2/24/03	3.85 days	3.85 days
4	First draft complete	Fri 2/21/03	Thu 3/6/03	Mon 2/24/03	Mon 3/3/03	-1.13 days	3.1 days
5	Draft approved	Thu 3/6/03	Thu 3/6/03	Mon 3/3/03	Mon 3/3/03	3.1 days	3.1 days
6	Edit	Thu 3/6/03	Tue 3/11/03	Mon 3/3/03	Thu 3/6/03	3.1 days	3.1 days
7	Edit complete	Tue 3/11/03	Tue 3/11/03	Thu 3/6/03	Thu 3/6/03	3.1 days	3.1 days
8	Distribute documentation	Tue 3/11/03	Wed 3/12/03	Thu 3/6/03	Fri 3/7/03	3.1 days	3.1 days
9	Project complete	Wed 3/12/03	Wed 3/12/03	Fri 3/7/03	Fri 3/7/03	3.1 days	3.1 days

Earned Value Analysis

If you use earned value analysis, then you show variance and trends at the same time, and it is especially powerful if displayed graphically. Earned value analysis is one of the best ways to provide performance reporting, and PMI emphasizes it as the primary performance reporting methodology for project management.

There are many terms and formulas you need to learn to be able to describe and use earned value analysis.

Planned value (PV, also known as BCWS) Budgeted cost of work scheduled. This is what most of us understand as our budget. It is the estimated cost of what you thought it would take to get the task or project done. This may be reported on the task itself or for the entire project.

Actual cost (AC, also known as ACWP) Actual cost of work performed. This is what most of us think of as actuals. It is the cost incurred up to a particular point in time of the project. You capture this from labor performed, and include expenses if they have been applied. Again, you can report this on the task or project level.

Earned value (EV, also known as BCWP) This is the value of a task or project applied at a particular time. The work accomplished is worth something even if it is not completely done. Note that you have to initially establish how you are going to measure earned value. Some organizations decide work does not have a value until it is 20 or 50 percent done and it would have an earned value of zero until it is at least 20 percent or 50 percent done. Some have decided it needs to be 100 percent done before value can be applied.

The following formulas are what you will use to calculate variances and forecast completions using planned value, actual cost, and earned value.

Cost variance (CV) This formula tells you if costs are higher or lower than budgeted. The formula is CV = EV – AC. For instance, if the earned value for the documentation project is $1,605 (the outline and some writing have some earned value as of the status date), and the actual costs are $2,120 on the status date, the CV is <$515>. If the cost variance is a negative number (as shown with the angle brackets <>), the project is over budget. If it is a positive number, the project is under budget. Zero is right on target.

Schedule variance (SV) This formula tells us if the project schedule is behind or ahead of its estimate. The formula is SV = EV – PV. For instance if the earned value for the documentation project is $1,605, and the planned value is $1,550, the SV is $55. If the schedule variance is a negative number, the project is behind schedule. If it is a positive number, the project is ahead of schedule. Zero is right on target.

There are some basic truths about looking at these variances in concert:

- If CV is positive and SV is positive, the project is under budget and ahead of schedule.
- If CV is negative and SV is negative, the project costs are over budget and the schedule is slipping.
- If CV is positive and SV is negative, some project tasks may not have started or they've started, but not enough resources have been assigned to them.
- If CV is negative and SV is positive, then extra money may have been spent to shorten (crash) the schedule.

Performance index (CPI and SPI) The cost performance index formula is CPI = EV ÷ AC. If this calculation comes out higher than 1, your cost performance is great. If it is less than 1, your cost performance is poor. If it is zero you are on target. This is a ratio that can tell you how well you are doing. Using the documentation project (EV = 1,605 and AC = 2,120), CPI = 1,605 ÷ 2,120 = .76. Our performance index is .76 (less than 1) and indicates that we have a cost overrun. You could take the original budget calculation (in this case, $8,800) and divide it by .76, and the forecasted budget is now $11,579.

The formula for schedule performance index is SPI = EV ÷ PV. If this calculation comes out higher than 1, your schedule performance is great. If it is less than 1, your schedule performance is poor. If it is zero you are on target. Again, using the documentation project (EV = 1,605 and PV = 1,550), SPI = 1,605 ÷ 1,550 = 1.04. Our performance index is showing 1.04, which means we are about .04 days ahead of schedule at the point of time for this measurement. You can use this to show trends over time each time you take this measurement.

Figure 6.3 shows an earned value chart taken for our documentation project, showing various earned value calculations.

FIGURE 6.3   Earned value chart

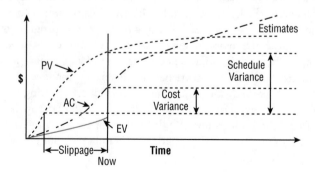

	Task Name	BCWS	BCWP	ACWP	SV	CV	EAC	BAC	VAC
0	⊟ earned va	$1,550.00	$1,605.50	$2,120.00	$55.50	($514.50)	$8,800.00	$4,400.00	($1,410.03)
1	Start docu	$0.00	$0.00	$0.00	$0.00	$0.00	$0.00	$0.00	$0.00
2	Produce o	$800.00	$640.00	$1,120.00	($160.00)	($480.00)	$1,600.00	$800.00	($600.00)
3	Outline ap	$0.00	$0.00	$0.00	$0.00	$0.00	$0.00	$0.00	$0.00
4	First draft	$750.00	$965.50	$1,000.00	$215.50	($34.50)	$4,000.00	$2,000.00	($71.47)
5	Draft appr	$0.00	$0.00	$0.00	$0.00	$0.00	$0.00	$0.00	$0.00
6	Edit	$0.00	$0.00	$0.00	$0.00	$0.00	$2,400.00	$1,200.00	($1,200.00)
7	Edit comp	$0.00	$0.00	$0.00	$0.00	$0.00	$0.00	$0.00	$0.00
8	Distribute	$0.00	$0.00	$0.00	$0.00	$0.00	$800.00	$400.00	($400.00)
9	Project co	$0.00	$0.00	$0.00	$0.00	$0.00	$0.00	$0.00	$0.00

You will also see the terms estimate at completion (EAC), budgeted at completion (BAC), variance at completion (VAC), and estimate to completion (ETC), which you should learn, but which will not be covered in this exercise.

One of the best ways to show earned value variances and trends is to use a cumulative cost curve, illustrated in Figure 6.4, and continue to measure it over the life of your project. Depending on how long your project is, you might measure it weekly, biweekly, or monthly.

FIGURE 6.4   Cumulative cost curve

Once you take these measurements and report them, you may discuss how you are taking corrective action with the team. The executive team may also help you take some kind of corrective action if you still need help. For instance, with the documentation project, the review team might ask you to reduce the scope of the documentation to help reduce the budget and time to complete the work.

Recommended Reading: Chapter 9, pp. 343–350, *PMP Project Management Professional Study Guide*.

Creating a Performance Report

Now that you know the types of performance reports and what goes into them, you can use the following list to create a performance report.

1. Decide on information that needs to be communicated: schedule, budget, quality, risk, procurement activities, or scope changes.

2. Decide on the kinds of measurements and when you will take them. You will need to make sure you baseline your schedule.

3. If using earned value, use tools that will help you generate the data regularly. Find a scheduling tool with an earned value reporting capability to capture earned value regularly.

4. Decide on the best form to communicate the information based on the needs of the audience. You will probably want to create a combination of status report, text, and charts or graphs. Executives usually prefer charts and graphs, so you would want to create a standard chart/graph for you performance reports.

5. Schedule performance review meetings regularly, discuss the variances, and decide on corrective action if it is required.

Scenario

TPMP is working with an independent, non-profit organization, Health America, who is creating reports for the status and quality of hospital health care in the United States based on goals created by the President of the United States. Health America is implementing project management processes and TPMP is helping them. This is a highly visible program in the government, and it entails working with the major hospitals within the major cities of America, and rating if they are achieving specific goals as identified by the President's program. The research and reporting started about 2 years ago. You are helping the project manager, Bill Smith, set up performance reporting using earned value and other performance reporting methods. The performance reports will go to HA executives and the Health and Welfare department. Bill is reporting earned value performance to both groups of stakeholders for the first time. You have determined that earned value for the current reporting period is $1.9 million. Your planned value is $2.5 million. Your actual costs are $1.8 million.

Performance Reporting, Including Earned Value Analysis

1. What are SV and CV for this project? What do the results mean?

_____

_____

_____

_____

2. What are SPI and CPI for this project? What do the results mean?

_____

_____

_____

_____

3. If Bill wanted to show quality improvements over time for the hospitals, what kind of performance reporting might he use?

_____

_____

_____

_____

4. Why is Performance Reporting important?

_____

_____

_____

_____

5. What are some of the kinds of Performance Reporting that Bill could choose from?

_____

_____

_____

_____

Exercise 6.6: Closing a Project or Phase

The objectives for Exercise 6.6 are:

- Understand why project close and phase close is important.
- Describe project and phase close tools.
- Practice creating lessons learned for a project.

Background

Closing is one of the most neglected activities in project management. Project managers are often assigned the next project or ready to move to the next phase of a project and just can't take the time to properly verify all the activities of the phase or do everything to close down the phase or project. So it is important to actually plan closing into your project schedule, and set up the verification and measurement deliverables around the closing activities. Closing means closing a phase or a project, not just closing the project down. In this exercise, we will explore closing for both processes.

Closing a Phase

First, for closing of project phases, a closing process ensures you have performed all activities for the phase. You might pass through a phase gate, a stage gate, or a kill point according to your industry practices. After the work of the phase is complete, and measurements have been reviewed, a group of decision makers decides to move on to the next phase, possibly make some corrections to the current phase, and sometimes, cancel the project entirely if warranted. You may have moved onto the next phase already, because the team needed to get started on the next phase, but you still need to close out this phase. At this point, you might also conduct a lessons learned to explore what you could have done better. This information can be used for another project going through the same type of project phase. Completing one phase of a project is also a good place to celebrate with the team. Here are some specific steps you can take to close a phase in a project:

1. Make sure you understand all of the deliverables and quality audits that must be passed to move out of a phase. The deliverables should be in your project plan.

2. Gather measurements and reports that describe project or phase performance.

3. Create a checklist based on the deliverables and associated measurements completed showing their success. Prove completion or provide justification why the deliverable was not needed.

4. Receive approval from the customer or sponsor for the end of the phase and to move on to the next phase.

5. Store the documents from the phase in your project files. If they are to be changed, make sure you have a good process and justification for the changes.

6. Hold lessons learned as soon after the phase completion as possible. Try to get participation from as many stakeholders as possible.

7. Document the lessons learned in a nonjudgmental way, and share with the rest of your organization. Try and implement as many improvements in other projects as possible.

Closing a Project

There are two kinds of project closings: when the project is terminated before completing all work and when all the work of the project completes. In the project closing process, you will verify that all the work has completed that needed to be completed according to the project's requirements. You will archive the project's data, receive formal acceptance for the project, perform a project lessons learned, and release the resources on the project (including the project manager!). You do this even when a project has terminated early—the process establishes a record of where it ended and if by some chance it gets picked up again (yes, it can happen), then it will be much easier to restart. If the project is terminated early, it is especially important to perform a lessons learned.

You can use the following steps to close a project:

1. Review the project plan to ensure that all phases have been completed to satisfaction. You might also conduct an independent audit for the project.

2. Gather measurements and reports that describe project performance.

3. Prove project completion or provide justification why the deliverable was not needed or the phase did not complete with all expected deliverables.

4. Receive approval from the customer or sponsor for project closure.

5. Archive the project files.

6. Hold lessons learned as soon as possible near project close. Try to get participation from as many stakeholders as possible. You might have to request time from team members who may have already been reassigned to another project.

7. Document the lessons learned in a nonjudgmental way, and share the information with the rest of your organization. Try to implement as many improvements in other projects as possible. If you found tasks or processes that should be added to other projects, think about including those tasks or processes to project schedule templates or project plans.

Contract closeout is part of Procurement Management but it is closely related to project closing, and is probably worth talking about here. You would perform many of the same functions to close the contract as the project itself, but you would ensure the terms of the contract are completed, including ensuring final payment and written approval. You will make sure you keep a contract file (especially if there could be legal repercussions at some point), and you might perform a procurement audit to create a lessons learned on the contract and to help rate the vendor for future considerations. Contract closeout would be performed prior to the full project closure and maybe one of the inputs to it.

Lessons Learned

Perhaps the most important part of closure is lessons learned. This process should occur throughout the project at important junctures and if something in particular goes very wrong. But it is best performed at the end of a phase or project and as soon as possible after the phase or project ends, so ideas are fresh and the project stakeholders are available to participate. One of the most important aspects of a lessons learned is that it be conducted in an atmosphere that does not place blame. The project manager or an independent facilitator should create an atmosphere in which the team approaches it as, "If we had it all to do again, what would we do better"—not, "what did we do wrong." You can't change the past, but you can do better in the future. Your team should look at lessons learned as an opportunity to take the improvements into the next project. This attitude toward improvement is critical to ensure the best lessons learned. Depending on the make-up of your team, you may hold one lessons learned with as many stakeholders participating as possible. You may also need to consider holding several sessions. For instance, team members might be more likely to bring up improvements with other team members, but not in front of the customer because it looks like admitting mistakes or problems.

You also need to capture the right data for lessons learned. You can cover both product processes or project processes. You might include the following in your lessons learned:

- A brief description of something discrete that could be improved. If possible, make this description positive. For instance, instead of saying, "Reports were incomplete" you might state, "Add more relevant data to reports." Then you can actually state what the data should be.

- Analysis of the lesson (perhaps root cause or some reason why the issue occurred).

- Recommendations (sometimes this happens without the analysis because a team member has already figured out the solution).

- Make sure you record who originated the lessons learned in case you need to get clarification later.

- How you might implement the improvement in a future project or future phase.

    In Exercise 6.6, you'll explore some important processes you should consider for closing and practice some of the elements of lessons learned as TPMP helps one of its clients implement improved project management processes.

Recommended Reading: Chapter 11, pp. 402–415, *PMP Project Management Professional Study Guide.*

Scenario

TPMPs is working with an independent, non-profit organization, Health America, who is creating reports for the status and quality of hospital health care in the United States based on goals created by the President of the United States. Health America is implementing project management processes and TPMP is helping them. This is a highly visible program in the government, and it entails working with the major hospitals within the major cities of America, and rating if they are achieving specific goals as identified by the President's program. The design phase for how the reports will be created is coming to a close soon. You are helping the project manager, Bill Smith, set up closing processes for his project. These processes may be used for future projects. During the design phase, the budget was exceeded by about 15 percent; he lost several team members to promotions, which disrupted the project; and the scope of the design changed several times. His team feels like the design phase went on for too long, and some team members have already started many implementation tasks. The team wants to move on quickly. Many of his team members have told Bill they can make design changes anyway as they start implementing the project.

Closing a Project or Phase

1. What closing processes will you suggest that Bill create for the end of his design phase?

_____

_____

_____

_____

2. What are some lessons learned that the team might come up with? Remember to keep the descriptions positive.

_____

_____

_____

_____

3. Bill had a contractor design the report format that would be used in his project for the government. What will Bill need to do to close the contract?

_____

_____

_____

_____

4. What deliverables or milestones should Bill add to his project schedule for the closing processes?

_____

_____

_____

_____

5. Are closing processes important? Why or why not?

_____

_____

_____

_____

Answers to Exercise Questions

Answers to Exercise 6.1

To complete the questions in Exercise 6.1, it might help to create a matrix such as the following to determine the interests and qualifications of your stakeholders. Remember, your answers may be different, depending on how you see the needs of these people or groups.

Stakeholder	Type	When	Concerns	Change	Special Care
Fran Freeling	I	E, CL, O	P = l C = l S = h Q = h	L	Fran's group must accept turnover when project is complete.
Health and Welfare	C, D	A	P = l C = h S = h Q = m	L	Must know all changes to cost and schedule. They will fund a second phase, so need to impress them with Health America.
Hospitals	I, E	E	P = l C = l S = h Q = h	M	They do not want their hospital to look bad. A bad report will mean explaining to the public and to their management.
Jeremy Checks	N	A	P = l C = l S = l Q = l	L	Must keep him informed, and slowly win him over to project management. He could be a problem to success of PM methodologies in project.
State government	I	E,C,CL	P = m C = h S = l Q = l	l	Could enact local legislation to support or block the program.

Stakeholder	Type	When	Concerns	Change	Special Care
Health America	D, P, E, I	A	P = h C = h S = h Q = m	l	This is a very high visibility and prestigious project. It could lead to more and bigger projects. It is also important to prove project management methodologies for other projects.
The public	I	E	P = l C = m S = l Q = l	l	Public is not very aware of program. Will need clear, concise data and information needs to be compelling.

The following key explains each header in the above table:

Type   The kind of stakeholder: C = customer, D = decision maker, I = influencer, P = performer, E = expert, N = nonessential

When   When in the project they might be affected most: P = planning, E = execution, C = controlling, CL = closing, O = operating A=equally in all phases

Concerns   The major concerns the person has, with each rated according to their view (h = high, m = medium, l = low): P = how the project will affect the project team and people at Health America, C = cost, Q = quality, S = schedule

Change   A rating as to how well this stakeholder deals with change. (H = able to deal with change easily, M = has some ability to deal with change, L = does not deal with change well)

Special care   A column to enter text to describe special needs or expectations the stakeholder might have.

1. To help identify stakeholder expectations and needs, you could include the criteria as listed in the top row of the table. Other criteria you might include is how much the stakeholder cares about improved health care or financial hardship on the hospitals trying to implement the improvements.

2. Stakeholders are listed in the matrix above. Note that state government has been added as it might support or block the program based on local legislation.

3. The importance of each criterion for each of the stakeholders is documented in the matrix above. Note that not all criteria have ratings. For instance, "Type" is a designation, and should not include a rating.

4. The Department of Health and Welfare is the main customer of this project and the funder. It would need a report frequently, at least every two weeks. Bill would need to provide a status report on progress emphasizing schedule and cost, and perhaps using earned value performance reporting (see Exercise 6.5).

5. There are many people who could adversely affect the project: Since Jeremy Checks is more interested in the project management failing, he could start emphasizing issues with project management that could jeopardize the project itself. Edward Salazar could possibly take some action to bring attention to himself, but harm the project. The hospitals, if not kept informed of their status, could get very angry if they are blindsided by any of the data reported in the research. And the media could report too early or present false information, if they are given inaccurate reports at inappropriate times in the project. Based on this analysis, you can plan ways to provide each stakeholder the best information and involve them at the right time to help reduce the risk of a stakeholder adversely affecting the project.

6. The public needs to be updated about this project at key milestones and after the more influential stakeholders have been informed. Possible milestones include when the planning is completed, several times during execution to understand progress, and at the end when the final report is issued. The Department of Health and Welfare may provide advice as to when the public should be informed. Bill may also want to direct team members to perform regular research about any local legislation that may be related to the program: Bill may need to communicate the project's intent and progress during those times to garner support from the public for the project.

Answers to Exercise 6.2

1. Using the formula, $[n(n-1)] \div 2$, Bill has 136 lines of communication as seen in the computation below:

$[17 \times (17-1)] \div 2 = [17 \times 16] \div 2 = 272 \div 2 = 136$

Bill has 3,570 potential lines of communication on the entire project as seen in the computation below.

$[85 \times (85-1)] \div 2 = [85 \times 84] \div 2 = 7,140 \div 2 = 3,570$

2. Bill will need to formally communicate the progress of the project and he will need to do it regularly so that people don't wonder if the project is on track. He will need to communicate that major deliverables have been completed, such as when a major piece of research is completed, or a report is issued. He needs to communicate changes in the makeup of the team, or any changes in what is being delivered, or when it will be delivered. If people expect a major report to be completed on Wednesday, and it will be completed on Friday, Bill will need to proactively communicate the date change. He needs to communicate the status of the project budget to executives and the client regularly. Your answer may contain other items Bill should report formally.

3. When Bill sends an e-mail to his project team telling them that there will be a review of the latest research findings next Monday at 10:00 AM, the sender is clearly Bill. The message is that there will be a review on Monday at 10:00 AM. The message is being encoded. Bill encodes the message according to the way he is accustomed to communicating. He needs to make his messages as clear as possible. To ensure the team understands the message, he

might want to add more information, perhaps create an agenda that describes why they are meeting, the expected outcome, how long the meeting will be, and who is expected to be there. The receiver is everyone on the team to whom Bill sent the message, including Kate Sullivan and Edward Salazar. The message is being decoded by each team member using their personal or cultural filters. For instance, Kate might think this is just another way to take up her valuable time and Bill is trying to unjustly impose his project management authority on her. Edward might think this is a great idea: they never review the research to make sure they are on the right track, and this will help the team see what each other is doing to achieve better results.

4. There are many things Bill could do to help Kate out. Bill may not know much about the kind of research that Kate does, but he can help her resolve her issue by listening well. Some techniques he can use: eye contact and nodding to show he is listening and appears interested, not interrupting as she speaks, and not allowing interruptions from the telephone or other people. At appropriate pauses, Bill can restate what he thought he heard Kate say and make sure she confirms he heard her correctly. He's got to concentrate on the moment, and not let other internal thoughts distract him from what Kate has to say.

5. Bill has a few options to help resolve the argument with Jeremy. Bill may try problem solving. Bill needs to use his listening techniques to account for all of Jeremy's issues and needs. But this may be a situation in which the "status quo" works for Jeremy, and there may be no way to convince him that project management will be effective without showing him. So this may be a situation in which forcing is used to resolve the conflict. Bill may go to his boss, Karen, and ask for help to make sure he gets management support to reiterate the importance of project management to help achieve greater efficiencies. Bill may also remind Jeremy that Bill's project plan calls for the team to be trained in some portions of project management and that it his plan's budget and time that is being used, not Jeremy's.

6. Bill has a few options to help resolve the disagreement between Edward and Kate. The best conflict resolution method will be problem solving in this case. Since these team members will continue to work together, and perhaps have similar issues, it will be important to come to a final resolution where both team members agree. Bill should start by having them analyze the best way to get the most responses (via research into marketing surveys or other objective measurements). He should have them choose some alternatives as to how they could solve the issues and have them resolve the issue together by selecting the most objective method.

Answers to Exercise 6.3

1. This project has many communication requirements, based on the number of stakeholders. Information that Bill needs to think about distributing are press releases to the media, a regular budget and milestone report to the Health and Welfare department, and meeting minutes after team meetings. Due to the fact that he also needs to communicate status about the project management processes being implemented, he also might create a small team

that meets regularly to discuss those processes, how they are working, and create improvements based on team feedback. You might also recommend that he informally meet with Jeremy Checks and Karen Palmer now and then to get some feedback of their impressions about the project management processes being implemented.

2. Bill might use e-mail regularly, although, because some of his team members do not check it regularly, he will need to train the team to use e-mail as a form of team communication. For important or timely information, he may need to leave voicemail for the team, or have regular meetings where attendance is required. Since the team members regularly research using the Web, Bill might create a website with the latest status, issues, and project schedule to help keep them informed. He might also store the information on the network directory since the company uses that method for storing information.

3. Bill should distribute the status report to the team weekly and it will be the basis for team status meetings. This method will keep the team up-to-date and focused on the project's progress. He will distribute a status biweekly to the executives. Since the project is research-oriented and deliverables have long time frames, the executives don't need to know the status more often. The status for the Health and Welfare department will be monthly and might include a meeting. This method lets the department understand progress on deliverables often enough, but not too often, since they have many other projects to monitor. Bill might distribute press releases at important milestones he identifies in this project schedule, rather than based on a regular calendar time. This way the press gets major information in a timely fashion. He should update the website when he receives new research for the hospitals so that they see that the data they provided is actually being used.

4. Bill's project website can provide the information for anyone to pull if needed. If someone needs information other than what is on the website (which executives always seem to need!), Bill could create a form or checklist to help him qualify the request. This practice will help Bill put the information together faster, and may even reveal that the information already exists and just needs to be put in a different format. Here are some ideas for the questions Bill should ask—you may think of more.

    - Who is the audience?
    - Why do they need the information?
    - How current does the data have to be?
    - What format does it need to be in?
    - What specific kind of information is needed?
    - Will this information need to be produced again?

5. Bill needs to follow up at least two more times to train the folks on the communication methods of the project. During the meeting, he needs to provide written information on the communication they can expect, and what is expected of them. After the meeting, he might follow up a week later in an e-mail, reminding everyone of the communication methods. Then, two weeks later, he might call another meeting to reiterate the methods, and request any feedback on how it is working. Although it might seem that Bill should only have to communicate the

distribution methods once, people need to be reminded several times and rewarded for supporting the methods before the information is integrated into team behavior.

Answers to Exercise 6.4

To complete some of these questions, it might help to create a matrix such as the following example. Remember, your answers may be very different, depending on how you see the needs of these stakeholder groups.

What	Why (purpose)	Who	When	How	Where (Storage)	Inputs
Executive status	To gather and check progress and discuss corrective actions.	Heath America (HA) executives and lead functional managers	Biweekly	Meetings and written communication	Website and network drive under Status/Executive	Team status
Team status	Same as Executive Status but at detailed level.	Team	Weekly	Meetings and written communication	Website and network drive under Status/Team	Team member updates
Status—escalations	To communicate critical status changes and to get help with corrective actions outside of normal status time frame.	HA executives	As needed	Via e-mail with follow-up voicemail if needed; enter on escalation log. Might need special meetings.	Website and network drive under Status/Executive/Escalations	Team status and ad hoc communication
Client status	Same as escalation status but emphasize budget and schedule.	Health and Welfare department	Monthly	Meetings and written communication	Network drive under Status/Client	Executive and team status
Press	To send information to news agencies	Print media	As needed	Written in press release format	Website and network drive under Press Releases	Newspapers, radio and TV media

What	Why (purpose)	Who	When	How	Where (Storage)	Inputs
Change request	To communicate changes.	Team change board	Weekly	Written, reviewed in meetings, enter in change log	Website and network drive under Change Requests	Anyone filling out a change request form
Project processes and standards	To ensure consistent and organized PM processes.	Team and stakeholders	Initially, and when updates are made	Written, e-mail, changes via log	Website, log, and network drive under Project Standards	Tech writer updates
Hospital quality reports	To provide status to Health and Welfare department of hospital improvements based on team research.	Health and Welfare department	Quarterly	Written	Website for hospitals only; network drive under Quarterly Reports	Research by team members

1. Bill's strategy, due to the high visibility, should support a very formal and well-documented communication methodology. He will need to allot quite a bit of his time to communication. This does not mean that he needs to do it himself. He might hire a communication manager, or delegate or distribute some of the work. Bill might indicate the percentage of time he will spend on communication, such as 85 percent. He should also state that he will need some help from the PR or media relations department regularly.

2. Status to the Health and Welfare department and to the HA executives depends on regular and accurate updates from the project team. Bill must be sure he has team updates prior to the status he must provide to the executives and Health and Welfare department. Also, Bill does not want to be rushing around trying to get status just before the high-level statuses. If he does not get regular status from his team, he may miss issues or escalations that his executives may need to help him overcome project roadblocks. If he reinforces behavior that requires updated status from his team members and sets up a status form, he probably will just need to plug in the information regularly.

3. Yes, Bill should share the status reports with his team. If his team members see this information, they will understand the importance of their updates for their project manager and also know the level of information that their executives want. They may also be able to see issues that the executives care about and communicate them more efficiently. Bill might even want to review the executive and client status format with the team to make sure team members understand it so they can help improve their input.

4. The communication matrix helps the project manager and his team understand what must be communicated in a standardized, consistent form according to regularly scheduled communication. The matrix helps systemize communication, so that the project manager can focus on issues and exceptions rather than gathering the information each time someone asks for it. It will help the project manager see dependencies of the communication, so he or she can plan when information should be collected so it can be fed into follow-up processes and communications.

5. Meetings and written status will probably not be enough communication for your team members. Team members will also need one-on-one time to understand your project status needs as well as communicate possible project issues. Some people will not feel comfortable communicating issues in a public forum. So besides the formal, regularly scheduled communication in group meetings, you will need to schedule regular one-on-one meetings with your team members. You will also probably receive and need to send e-mails and make phone calls to team members.

6. The information you might include on a status report: date range of status, overall project schedule status (on time, behind schedule, ahead of schedule), upcoming milestone (deliverable) completion progress and accomplishments, issues and progress on solving them, budget status and projections, and accepted changes to the project and how they are being integrated into the project. It is important to create a form so that you collect all the status you need and make sure you get updates consistently. Without it, you may miss important items from status to status.

Answers to Exercise 6.5

1. For the Health and Welfare department project, SV = EV – PV. SV = 1.9M – 2.5M = <.6M> This means you are behind schedule. The CV = EV – AC. CV = 1.9M – 1.8M = .1M. This means your costs are lower than expected. Looking at these variances together, this might mean Bill did not apply enough resources to the project, and that's why it's behind. However, because it is behind, the team may decide applying some extra resources for a short time will get it back on track.

2. For the Health and Welfare department project the SPI = EV ÷ PV. SPI = 1.9M ÷ 2.5M = .76. This means the project is behind schedule. The CPI = EV ÷ AC. CPI = 1.9M ÷ 1.8M = 1.05. This means the project is below expected cost. Although Bill has just started using this index, he can start showing a trend, and at this point it means the project is about 76 percent of where the schedule needs to be. He is underrunning costs by about 5 percent. To change this trend, he will have to make some major changes on the project.

3. If Bill wanted to show quality improvements over time for the hospitals, he might he use trend analysis to show improvement for the hospital quality reports. He could show the number of errors/problems via a scatter diagram.

4. Performance reporting is important to provide objective measurements to a project's executives, sponsors, or customers to provide project progress, variances, and trends. Objective measurements allow the project manager and the reviewers to discuss corrective actions.

5. Bill could choose from performance reviews, variance analysis, trend analysis, or earned value analysis.

Answers to Exercise 6.6

1. Bill should complete all processes for design: Don't give into the team's desire to skip any design deliverables, although it might be fine to move onto steps in the next phase. File design documents, take time for lessons learned, and get acceptance of the design phase. Schedule a go/no go meeting for next phase. Have a design closeout party.

2. Some lessons learned might be: Report on budget progress weekly to make adjustments sooner so the team won't go over budget quite as much. Bill or other project managers might consider building a team of both junior and senior folks so that promotions won't disrupt the team as much. Also, project managers might consider ensuring that the important tasks have team members trained as backups. Because the budget went over, all project managers want to make sure they have a good scope change control process. In the future, the schedule might include some checkpoints. At the checkpoints, the team can determine whether they are on track for completing the phase and discuss corrections to the work of the project if it is going on for too long.

3. Bill will need to review the contract terms and, in written format, approve that all deliverables and expectations have been met. Bill might use one of the organization's lawyers to help with that task. Bill will need to ensure final payment is made to the contractor. Bill should also have lessons learned with the team and the contractor and perform a procurement audit. He will then need to file the contract documents according to company standards. TPMP would advise that Bill make sure that in the future, all of these tasks are included in future project schedules and plans.

4. Bill needs to add the following regular tasks to the end of each phase: review and approvals, gathering and filing of the documents approved during the phase, lessons learned sessions, procurement audits (optional), and team celebration.

5. Although you could possibly have success without great closing processes, by having them, you will ensure you've done everything required on the project. You make sure you cover everything the customer wanted. It is also an excellent way to show completions to the team throughout the project—you need incremental success points to motivate the team. Most important, though, you can help future projects. Most project management process improvements have come from other project managers sharing their knowledge with others and making consistent and standardized processes so everyone has a chance for even greater success on their next project.

Chapter

7

Risk Management

THE EXERCISES PRESENTED IN THIS CHAPTER INCLUDE:

- ✓ Exercise 7.1: Creating your Risk Management Plan
- ✓ Exercise 7.2: Identifying Risks
- ✓ Exercise 7.3: Qualitative Risk Analysis
- ✓ Exercise 7.4: Quantitative Analysis Methods
- ✓ Exercise 7.5: Quantitative Risk Analysis—Risk Impact/ Probability Matrix
- ✓ Exercise 7.6: Type of Risk Responses
- ✓ Exercise 7.7: Creating a Risk Response Plan

Risk management is a project management process that helps fend off potential damaging events. It might also identify opportunities for your project. In order to manage risks for your project, you need to create a plan that describes your team's risk strategies. Then, you choose a method to identify and analyze potential risks of your project. You use qualitative and quantitative analyses to measure the probability of each risk occurring and the impact each risk would have on your project if it were to occur. Once you've analyzed and rated your risks via a risk probability matrix, you will decide how to respond to the risks, choosing various risk response types. You implement risk response plans to help your project avert risks before they occur, or react quickly if they do occur. Risk management is mostly a Planning process and putting time into it up front will save your project time and money later.

Risk management is covered in the Planning and Controlling process groups objectives of the PMP exam.

Exercise 7.1: Creating Your Risk Management Plan

The objectives for Exercise 7.1 are:

- Introduce risk management.
- Understand what a risk management plan (RMP) does.
- Describe the elements of the RMP.
- Practice building parts of an RMP.

Background

Risk management is a project management process that helps defend against the potential damaging events. Risk management also helps you identify opportunities for your project. This aspect is an important one in risk planning since a lot of people focus on the negative aspects of risks. Although doing something innovative or new with your project could be a risk if it doesn't work properly, your organization may ultimately revolutionize technology that leads to far more profit or opportunity than expected. In order to manage risk management activities, you need to create a plan. This plan describes the strategy you will use for your project in relation to risk. It describes how much time you will spend, how your team will work on risk, the measurements you will use to describe risk, and why you are taking the time to manage risk.

The major steps of risk management are:

- Creating a risk management plan (RMP).
- Identifying risks.
- Analyzing risks.
- Creating a risk response plan.
- Monitoring and controlling risks throughout the project.

Elements of the RMP

An RMP should contain at least the following eight elements that will help your project team members understand how they need to manage risk.

Methodology   Describes how you will manage risk management. Your team and stakeholders need to understand the purpose and objectives of the risk management strategy. What are the processes the team will follow to perform risk management? What kind of analysis will you use for your risks? Will you hire consultants? Will you use expert judgment, or will you use sensitivity analysis? Will you keep it simple, or due to the complexity of your project, will you need to put a lot of time and expertise into managing risk, including bringing in outside consultants or the organization's risk management experts? In this section, you will describe in detail how you are going to manage risk and why.

Roles and responsibilities   Describes who will be in charge of the risk management plan, and who will be in charge of risk management responses. This step identifies the overall management team (such as the project manager or independent facilitator being the lead), and who will analyze the risks and implement risk response plans if a negative or positive risk event occurs. This responsible party is often a functional manager, or someone who understands the risk well, who has the subject matter expertise, or who has the authority to be able to gather the resources to analyze and respond appropriately and quickly.

Budgeting   Describes how much the risk management process costs. If you are going to hire a risk management expert and have her or him manage the process and have meetings every two weeks, that will cost something toward project management processes. The project may simply by complex enough to warrant a larger budget. In small projects, the risk process might be a part of the weekly status meeting, and the project manager ensures that risk discussions continue regularly in the project team meetings. The budget would be small, but appropriately relative to the complexity of the project.

Timing   Describe how often the risk management processes will occur on the project. This may also reflect different timing for different phases in the project. For instance, you might meet once a week during the concept phase, once a week during the design phase, and twice a week during the implementation phase. You might also plan some kind of independent Risk Identification to be performed early in the design phase.

Scoring and interpretation   How will you rate and react to risks you identify? You will come up with a method to rate the probability of a risk occurring, and the impact it will have on the project. This process has to be done before you actually start identifying and rating the risks on your project. Completing this step ensures that your team has a consistent understanding so when the rating processes occurs you are not debating how you will score risks while you are in the midst of the process itself.

Describe thresholds   Defines which risks will be addressed. You could have a big list of risks. You cannot work on all of them, or your budget would be astronomical. This process describes the thresholds of risks you will work on. For instance, you might work on all risks that have a greater than 50 percent probability of occurring. Or ones that have a combined probability and impact of greater than .25 rating. You would possibly base this on your organization or stakeholder tolerance for risk.

Reporting formats   Describes your Risk Identification and response reporting and how you will communicate risk processes and results to your stakeholders. You will see more about formats in Exercise 7.7 when you create a risk response plan. This step might also include describing risk performance reporting and its processes for your executives. You may have one format for your team, and another format for executives.

Tracking   Describes the process for how you will track your project's risks. You might describe your risk management database that will store and track risks. You will also record the benefit of risk management results for lessons learned.

Once you understand the components of a risk management plan, you should be ready to learn the steps involved with creating a risk management plan.

Creating a Risk Management Plan (RMP)

In risk management, you will hear the term "risk response plan," which is how you plan to actually respond to particular risks. However, a risk management plan is a road map for how you and your team will deal with risk processes and how you plan to analyze and manage risks. The two are vastly different kinds of plans but both are important outputs of the risk management process. Following are the steps you'll need to take to create a risk management plan.

1.   Decide on and document your processes and strategy for risk management based on the following questions. Is it new technology? Is it extremely difficult or financially risky? Is it a large project? Is the customer extremely "finicky?" Create a methodology around risk to match the complexity of the project. Don't forget to see if your organization already has risk management processes, guidelines, or expertise.

2.   Create a risk management team.

3.   Get input from the team and stakeholders and other risk management experts about best practices and how they would like to see risk managed on the project.

4.   Assign risk management roles and responsibilities. You will select leads for each risk, and it is often best to pick a functional manager, or someone with expertise that could help

analyze a risk, then put a plan in place to take care of the risk. Create a roles and responsibilities matrix for risk and include it in the plan. The following table provides an example of a risk roles and responsibilities matrix.

Risk Type	Owner	Who	Responsibility
Overall	Risk manager	Myrna Floyd	Ensures overall risk management processes are identified and followed throughout the project lifecycle.
Documentation	Documentation lead	Ted Dimino	Identifies risks, analyzes risks, implements changes in documentation plan, or creates contingencies.
Project Processes	Project manager	Myrna Floyd	Implements changes in project plan and project schedule.
Operational	Operations manager	Thomas Sing	Identifies risk, analyzes risks, and implements changes in operational processes or systems.
HR system software	HR system manager	Lee Neely	Implements risk response plans or contingencies.

5. Determine the budget for the risk process based on all the work you must do. Include this in the schedule and costs of the project. Describe and justify the budget in the plan.

6. Decide how often you will have risk management meetings and work on risk for the project. PMI recommends that you have risk as an agenda item at every project meeting. Describe this under the heading of risk timing in the plan.

7. Determine the risk rating approach (scoring and interpretation). Create a matrix of how you will rate risks. Also create as detailed a definition of probability and impact as possible. An impact of medium might mean that the project will go on, but will be slowed significantly with over $10,000 being spent to deal with the problem. Write these discrete definitions in the plan, and make sure your team understands them. Exercise 7.5 will describe this matrix in more detail.

8. Describe in the plan the thresholds for determining risk. For instance, you might say you will create plans for only half of the risks, or those with a high impact and high probability only.

9. Create reporting formats for risk (forms that describe all the data you want to collect and record about risk) and tracking methods so you and your team can easily and consistently manage Risk Identification and responses.

10. Publish the plan to your team and stakeholders, get approval, and make sure everyone understands it through review and training.

11. Review the plan throughout the project to see whether you must make updates to the plan.

In Exercise 7.1, you will learn about the elements of the risk management plan and help a telecommunications company implementing a large and complex project decide on the important elements of the plan.

Recommended Reading: Chapter 6, pp.201–203, *PMP Project Management Professional Study Guide.*

Scenario

TPMP is helping Mountain Communications (MC), a well-established telecommunications company, create risk management processes. One of your first assignments is to create risk planning for a project that is replacing two old systems with newer systems to reflect modern technological advances. The old systems will need to continue functioning while data is converted. The new systems are provided by a vendor who is asking MC to be one of the first companies to implement them. The MC company has decided to use a gateway program, which will convert the old data into the formats of the new systems. The company has decided to create this program itself, although several are available on the market. The program is critical to both conversion efforts, and a plan has been created for a phased conversion—the data will not be converted all at once—MC has been able to segment the data to be converted over the next couple of years. The project has around 100 people working on the conversion and implementation of the new systems. Some of the team members are the program manager, Tasha Smith (whom you are advising to establish the risk management processes); the production manager who is responsible for the current systems and will take over the new systems; a development manager responsible for the gateway program; another development manager responsible for implementing the new systems and managing the conversion plan; the client who will need to maintain current service while the new systems are converted; and the vendor who is helping to implement both systems.

Creating Your Risk Management Plan

1. Why should Tasha create a risk management plan?

    _____

    _____

    _____

    _____

2. Describe elements of the methodology you will suggest Tasha use for this project.

    _____

    _____

    _____

    _____

3. Describe what Tasha should do to justify a budget for risk management on the project.

    _____

    _____

    _____

    _____

4. Describe the risk management processes you would recommend that Tasha implement and describe how often they should be performed.

    _____

    _____

    _____

    _____

5. Describe the roles and responsibilities of the stakeholders participating in the risk management process.

    _____

    _____

    _____

    _____

6. What is the difference between a risk management plan and a risk response plan? Will Tasha need to make sure both are created?

    _____

    _____

    _____

Exercise 7.2: Identifying Risks

The objectives for Exercise 7.2 are:

- Understand risk categories.
- Learn how to identify risks.
- Practice identifying risks on a project.

Background

After you have created a plan for managing risk, the next step in risk management is to identify the risks on your project. This step can be done in many ways: You can brainstorm with your team to identify everything you can think of. You can review your documentation to help you think of risks. You can get survey and interview experts to discover risk based on their experience (using the Delphi technique). You can look at previous projects that were similar to yours to capture some of their risks. You can look at industry publications to see if they have identified and classified typical risks. This might include finding risk checklists for the industry. You might perform assumptions analysis or use diagramming techniques to identify risks. The main output from this step is to document all the risks you identify and make sure you describe them and their characteristics well. This exercise will explore some of the various ways you can categorize and identify risk.

To help you identify risks, and also organize them in similar groupings for more efficient risk response plans, you can use risk categories (also called risk sources). You may find these categories from your project's particular application or industry. Look in industry or application publications for a list of categories (which often have actual risks identified with them). Based on each of these categories, your team, executives or sponsors, outside experts, customers, or other stakeholders can start identifying risks. You may also use these categories to identify who should own the risk for analysis and possible risk response. Some major risk categories are:

Technical, quality, or performance   Sources of risk can come from major technical complexity or new technology. If your project is counting on a new technology, it could be seriously jeopardized if the technology fails or is delayed in some way. Risk can come from low quality standards, or even high ones. For instance, for high quality standards, the time and effort to include the steps for quality can create risk for the schedule, especially if something is found to be wrong. Eventually, however, that risk may be better than releasing an inferior product. Performance goals may also cause risk—for instance, the sponsor may have an unrealistic expectation of the product's performance that cannot be met with the expected schedule or budget.

Project management   There may be risks associated with an undeveloped project management methodology, an inexperienced project manager, or lack of training. Also, the organization may not support project management, or give the project manager enough authority to manage the project as needed. For instance, if the project is to provide a complex medical application, using a junior project manager could be very risky.

Organizational   Many of us realize that many of the greatest risks on a project are based on the organization: frequent changes in an organization's management, a culture that does not support the project, downsizing, or a project that does not fit into the overall strategy can cause many risks. For instance, the project may be moved around to two managerial groups within three months, based on an organizational shake-up. The project team has to re-educate each manager, and discuss how it affects their roles and jobs during this time. Productivity could plummet, and the project could go off schedule.

External   Projects often overlook examining external risks: those caused by legal changes, government regulations, market changes, or changes in political influences. They are outside of the influence of the project manager, and often of the organization. For instance, if your project's product launch was based on the assumption that your market's niche would continue expanding, what would the risk be if you started seeing a downward trend?

Besides identifying risks, you will want to identify triggers for each risk. If a piece of equipment is not delivered on time, could that be a trigger for a possible schedule delay?

1. Gather a group of people to identify risks. You may have several groups or iterations to complete this process. Having different perspectives can help you get a much more exhaustive list that will cover all aspects s of your project. This step might include management, process, methodology, quality, or technical perspectives.

2. Choose a method or methods that you would like to use to identify risks. You might want to use a few techniques to make sure you identify as many risks as you can or to make your team as comfortable as possible with the process.

3. Review industry or application area publications and create the categories you would use to identify and organize your risks.

4. List the risks and describe them as clearly as possible.

5. Describe the trigger for each risk if you can identify it.

6. Categorize your risks.

7. While you and your team are identifying risks, you may identify further actions, some possible responses, or issues with the risks you identify. Perhaps you realize you don't have enough information about a particular risk, and you realize you need to research it. However, keep an open mind, and try to keep from jumping to conclusions too fast about how you would respond to this risk. The next step is analysis, and you might find more information during that process.

8. Document the risks, triggers, and categories and further action using a matrix or database. The following table illustrates a matrix you might use to document risks, triggers, categories, and further action.

Risk	Category	Trigger	Further Action or Comments

In Exercise 7.2, you will learn how to identify risks by helping a telecommunications company examine the risks in a large and complex project converting two old systems to two new systems.

 Recommended Reading: Chapter 6, pp.203–208, *PMP Project Management Professional Study Guide.*

Scenario

TPMP is helping Mountain Communications (MC), a well-established telecommunications company, create risk management processes. One of your first assignments is to create a risk management process for a project that is replacing two old systems with two newer systems to reflect modern information technological advances. The systems depend on one another and will have telephone and location information for MC's customers. The old systems will need to continue functioning while data is converted. The new systems are provided by a vendor who is asking MC to be one of the first companies to implement them. The company has decided to use a gateway program, which will convert the old data into the formats of the new systems. The company has decided to create the gateway program itself though several are available on the market. The program is critical to both conversion efforts and a plan has been created for a phased conversion—the data will not be converted all at once—MC has been able to segment the data to be converted over the next couple of years. The project has around 100 people working on the conversion and implementation of the new systems. Some of the team members are the program manager, Tasha Smith (whom you are advising to establish the risk management processes); the production manager who is responsible for the current systems and will take over the new systems; a development manager responsible for the gateway program; another development manager responsible for implementing the new systems and managing the conversion plan; the client who will need to maintain current service while the new systems are converted; and the vendor who is helping to implement both systems.

Identifying Risks

1. What are some of the categories Tasha might use to identify risks and why?

    _____

    _____

    _____

    _____

2. Who should be on the risk identification team, and why?

    _____

    _____

    _____

    _____

3. What are the risk identification methods Tasha could use for this project?

    _____

    _____

    _____

    _____

4. What are some of the risks that Tasha and the team might identify? Use the risk identification table below to complete the exercise.

Risk	Category	Trigger

Exercise 7.3: Qualitative Risk Analysis

The objectives for Exercise 7.3 are:

- Understand Qualitative Risk Analysis.
- Learn to analyze risks via a rating matrix and decide which risks to perform quantitative analysis on.
- Practice rating risks via qualitative analysis.
- Practice ranking risks.

Background

Qualitative Risk Analysis is the next step in risk management. It is a process in which you and your risk team determine, through subjective analysis, the probability of your identified risk occurring and the impact if it occurs. Again, this step can be done in many ways, including using some of the same methodologies as Risk Identification and may be done at the same time you identify risks. Although a quantitative analysis step follows this step, you might actually decide to stop your risk management analysis process after qualitative analysis based on the thresholds you have decided on based on cost, priorties, risk tolerance, low probability or low impact.

Risk Probability

To decide the probability of whether the risk will occur, you can use a scale of high/medium/low, 0 to100 percent, 1 through 10, or whatever scale you think is appropriate. The team will decide on the scale and define the gradations when you set up your risk management plan, as defined in Exercise 7.1. You might define that a one in two chance is high, but a one in a million chance is low depending on what you are measuring.

For instance, you have identified a risk on a construction project—that the dump truck you need on March 15 won't be delivered on time. Your team has determined that the equipment company is very reliable. You have used it for all major equipment rentals, and of the 35 times you have rented from the company, it has been able to deliver the equipment on time all but two times. So you might rate the chance of the equipment not being delivered on time as low. If you can get this accurate of probability data, that is terrific. But, usually, this data is based on the experience and feelings of the team. That is okay in qualitative analysis.

Risk Impact

Next, you need to decide on the impact of each risk. You can use a scale of high/medium/low, 1 through 10, or some other kind of scale that ranks the impact. Again, you will need to have set this up prior to the actual impact rating, and it should be defined in your risk management plan. You might define a high impact as one in which the budget will go over 15 percent or the schedule will be delayed by more than two weeks. You might define it as affecting the quality or disappointing the customer so it jeopardizes the project.

To continue with the previous example, let's say your team is trying to rate the impact of the dump truck not being delivered on time. Your team members do this independently of the probability rating they give the risk. Your team decides the impact would be high. The entire project would be delayed based on the delivery being delayed, even by one day.

Risk Rating Matrix and Risk Ranking

Based on these two factors, impact and probability, you create a ranking for the risks. For instance, risks with low probability and low impact would be rated low risk events. But how would you rank something with low probability but high impact? Should you do something specific about it and rate it a high risk event? And what about a high probability but low impact? That sounds like it might be a lower rated risk event, because if it happens, the actual impact to the project is not so important. So when you look at both factors together, you need to figure out how you want to rate the event. So you might come up with a graph to plot the ratings, or you choose the rankings like those displayed in Table 7.1.

TABLE 7.1   Risk Ranking Table

Probability/Impact	Risk Rating
Low/Low	Low
Low/Medium	Low
Low/High	Medium
Medium/Low	Low

TABLE 7.1 Risk Ranking Table *(continued)*

Probability/Impact	Risk Rating
Medium/Medium	Medium
Medium/High	High
High/Low	Medium
High/Medium	High
High/High	High

In this case, you may work on all risks that have a rating of medium and high and just monitor those that are rated low.

Performing Qualitative Risk Analysis

You and your project team will want to perform Qualitative Risk Analysis to document the probability and impact of the risk. You will perform the following steps to analyze your risks.

1. Gather your risk team.

2. Make sure you have a standard definition of probability and impact.

3. List all the risks previously identified and rank the probability of each occurring.

4. Separately, rank the impact if it were to occur.

5. Enter the findings in the risk matrix. You may use a table like the following to create this matrix.

Risk	Probability	Impact	Score

6. Rank those with a high score, then rearrange the tasks from top rated to low rated.

7. Decide on which risks you would like to continue to perform analysis on by moving onto the next step of risk quantification.

In Exercise 7.3, you will learn how to create a risk rating matrix based on qualitative analysis and help the MC company develop its own risk matrix.

Recommended Reading: Chapter 6, pp. 208–215, *PMP Project Management Professional Study Guide.*

Scenario

TPMP is helping Mountain Communications (MC), a well-established telecommunications company, create risk management processes. One of your first assignments is to create a risk management process for a project that is replacing two old systems with newer systems to reflect modern technological advances. The old systems will need to continue functioning while data is converted. The new systems are provided by a vendor who is asking MC to be one of the first companies to implement them. The company has decided to use a gateway program, which will convert the old data into the formats of the new systems. The company has decided to create this program itself although several are available on the market. The program is critical to both conversion efforts and a plan has been created for a phased conversion—the data will not be converted all at once—MC has been able to segment the data to be converted over the next couple of years. The project has around 100 people working on the conversion and implementation of the new systems. Tasha's team has identified 10 possible risks on the project. They are:

- The gateway program will not convert some of the data in time for the new system to go live on the conversion days.
- The new system will not perform a function the old system performed.
- Upon going live, the new system does not work properly, and end customer orders start backing up.
- The order takers cannot properly work the new system.
- The data gets converted but is wrong upon going live.
- The new system is slow.
- The vendor can't fix a system bug in time for the next scheduled conversion.
- The MC sponsor for the project is promoted to another division.
- Another company hires Tasha away from MC.
- The customer is dissatisfied with the performance of the new systems with a few of the conversions completed.

Qualitative Risk Analysis

For each risk laid out in the Scenario, use the following table to enter your answers.

Risk	Probability	Impact	Score

1. For each risk, help Tasha and her team determine the probability. Use a high/medium/low rating scheme. Do this first, without rating the impact.

2. For each risk, help Tasha and her team determine the impact. Use a high/medium/low rating scheme.

3. Use Table 7.1, Risk Ranking Table, to score the risks.

4. Which risks should Tasha work on first and which ones might her team just monitor?

_____

_____

_____

_____

Exercise 7.4: Quantitative Analysis Methods

The objectives for Exercise 7.4 are:

- Understand the difference between qualitative and quantitative risk analysis.
- Learn about particular quantitative risk analysis methods.
- Practice using a quantitative risk method using expected value and decision tree analysis.

Background

Quantitative Risk Analysis, the next step in risk management, uses several methods to numerically analyze the probability and impact of your risks. The methods are more detailed and objective than the methodology you used in Qualitative Risk Analysis. If you decided to perform this analysis based on impact or probability thresholds you established in your risk management plan, you must have planned this work into your schedule because it will take up a lot of your team's time. You may even need to hire someone with expertise in performing this analysis if you or your team does not have it.

Some of the methods you might use for Quantitative Risk Analysis are:

- Interviewing (including PERT analysis and probability distributions)
- Sensitivity analysis
- Simulation
- Decision tree analysis and expected value

Interviewing

This process is similar to the methods in which you bring a team together to brainstorm the risks. But in this case, you may be asking particular subject matter experts to determine the probability and consequences of risks on project objectives. The sessions or questions you ask depend on the kind of information you are trying to retrieve for analysis. One particular interviewing session can lead to PERT analysis when you ask your subject matter experts to provide their pessimistic, most likely, and optimistic estimates for how long it will take to perform a particular task. Exercise 2.5 described this method for analyzing risk.

Sensitivity Analysis

This form of quantification can help you determine which events have the most impact on a project and how the risk can be changed by varying one item if everything else is kept equal. You may have used sensitivity analysis to a certain extent when you used a computer scheduling tool and added a task to the project schedule to see how it would affect the end date or cost of the project.

Simulation

This method of quantitative analysis (also known as Monte Carlo Analysis) runs a model over and over again with different variables to see how it might change the overall project and its risks. Many software programs can be added to a computer scheduling application to run this simulation process automatically.

Decision Tree Analysis and Expected Value

Decision tree analysis is a form of quantitative analysis that represents the decisions that can be made on a graphical "tree." It is often used with expected value to determine the various monetary impacts for the decisions you might make on your project. It multiplies probability times impact to create expected value. This exercise will focus on this form of quantitative analysis. The following formula describes expected value:

Risk Probability × Amount at Stake (or Impact) = Expected Value

If you have several possibilities for an outcome, the probability of each of the cases must add up to one. Table 7.2 shows you an expected value table when you have four possible choices in a decision.

TABLE 7.2   Expected Value Table

Probability	Amount at Stake	Expected Value
.3	50,000	15,000
.2	30,000	6,000
.4	(20,000)	(8,000)
.1	75,000	7,500
1	—	20,500

Similarly, you can illustrate expected value for a decision on a decision tree. For instance, you have two choices: You may release your new Easy-Start Snow Blower in January or in March. You know you may have more success of getting all the kinks out of the product in March, whereas you have some doubt you can fix all bugs by January. Your probability of success or failure is calculated on both. If you release in March, the probability of success is .7 with an expected value of $200,000. The expected value of failure is ($30,000). If you release in January, the probability of success is .4 with an expected value of $350,000 (you project more sales in January than March). The expected value of failure is ($75,000). Figure 7.1 illustrates a decision tree for the Easy-Start Snow Blower project.

FIGURE 7.1   Decision tree example

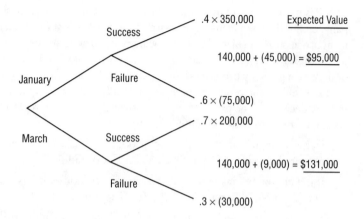

In this case, releasing in March is a better financial projection despite the fact that the sales could be a great deal better in January. If the organization decides to use financial gain as the basis for decisions, then releasing in March is the best decision.

In Exercise 7.4, you will help the MC company use decision tree analysis and expected value to perform quantitative analysis on its new telecommunications system.

Now that you know what a decision tree analysis is and how you can apply expected value, if you need to perform a decision tree analysis, you can follow the steps below:

1. Decide on the risks and decisions you would like to analyze in greater depth based on the work you did in qualitative analysis.

2. Use statistical analysis to determine numerical probability for the decisions. Use market research for possible value/impact for each branch of the decision tree.

3. Create the diagram showing the decision paths with probability and impact.

4. For each branch, multiply probability and impact. Add up the results to achieve expected value for each discrete decision.

5. Review and decide the best path for the decision. Sometimes, risk tolerances for your stakeholders become visible in reviewing this method. For instance, in Figure 7.1, your stakeholders may actually choose to release in January because of the greater opportunity for sales. This decision would indicate they have a high tolerance for risk.

Recommended Reading: Chapter 6, pp.215–218, *PMP Project Management Professional Study Guide.*

Scenario

TPMP is helping Mountain Communications (MC), a well-established telecommunications company, create risk management processes. One of your first assignments is to create a risk management process for a project that is replacing two old systems with newer systems to reflect modern technological advances. The company must make a decision regarding the risks of either buying or making a gateway program that will convert the data from the old systems to the new systems. You are helping the program manager, Tasha Smith, create quantitative analysis processes for making decisions. The project team, with the help of market research and company financial analysts, has come up with the following information:

- If the company buys the gateway product, it has a 70 percent change of success with a potential impact of $250,000. The impact of failure is ($20,000).

- If the company makes the gateway project in-house, it has a 50 percent chance of success with a potential impact of $500,000. The impact of failure is ($150,000).

The project team feels that building the gateway product in-house can be a great opportunity for the company, since it is expecting to upgrade several other systems within the next 10 years. The team members feel they may be able to reuse the product for these efforts and perhaps even sell it to other telecommunications companies if it proves efficient and accurate.

Quantitative Analysis Methods

1. Create the expected value table for the exercise above using the following tables.

For Buy Decision:

Probability	Amount at Stake	Expected Value

For Make Decision:

Probability	Amount at Stake	Expected Value

2.   Create the decision tree for the exercise above.

3.   What is the best decision for making or buying the gateway system based on this analysis and why?

_____

_____

_____

_____

4.   What are the quantitative tools and techniques?

_____

_____

_____

_____

Exercise 7.5: Quantitative Risk Analysis— Risk Impact/Probability Matrix

The objectives for Exercise 7.5 are:

- Understand a quantitative risk impact/probability matrix.
- Practice rating risks via quantitative analysis.

Background

After Qualitative Risk Analysis, the next step in risk management is Quantitative Risk Analysis. It is a process in which you and your risk team determine, through numerical and other objective analysis, the numerical probability of your identified risks occurring and the impact on your project objectives if it occurred. This process can be time consuming and may require the special tools and techniques you learned in Exercise 7.4. You may choose not to perform Quantitative Risk Analysis on all of your risks, but only your most probable or high-impact risks. However, if you do perform this analysis, it will be more precise, and help you determine the true costs of risk response and justify any actions you may take to offset those risks.

Quantitative Risk Probability/Impact

In Exercise 7.3, you learned to create the scales or measurements you will use for probability (such as 0 to 100 percent or high/medium/low) and impact (such as 0 to 10, or high/medium/low). In Quantitative Risk Analysis, you might use the same probability scales, but one of the most effective means of determining impact is putting dollars on the impact. For instance, if a construction team does not receive a bulldozer on time for work to begin, it will cost the wages of everyone on the job not doing anything, and the wages for each day the bulldozer is not on site. Say this is a cost of $1,500 per day. With a probability of 40 percent, this becomes a risk expected value of $600. This tells you much more about the relative cost of the risk occurring (or maybe even the opportunity you could gain), than just rating items high, medium, or low. You can start re-rating the risks with much more substantial emphasis on their real impact to the objectives of the project.

Quantitative Risk Rating Matrix

Create a risk impact/probability matrix for you quantitative ratings. For instance, for the construction project, the team has listed risks and quantified their impact and probability. Table 7.3 shows you the results of the construction team's efforts.

TABLE 7.3   Quantitative Risk Rating Matrix

Risk	Probability	Impact	Value
Bulldozer is not delivered on time	40%	$1,500	$600
Rain stops work on any given day	20%	$6,000	$1,200
Customer disapproves the quality of work when first room is being painted	30%	$15,000	$4,500
Permits are not received on time	50%	$6,000	$3,000
Strike occurs (impact per day)	10%	$7,000	$700

With this data, you can start identifying the most important risks. For instance, for each day of rain, the impact is $1,200. With a few days of rain, this amount can easily become one of the biggest impacts. Thus, the team needs to think of things that can be done to lessen the impact. And with a 50 percent possibility of permits not being received on time, the team needs to look at ways of reducing the probability of that happening. But, most important, it looks like the customer's disapproval of the quality can have a big impact. Perhaps, the team will want to build in a customer quality check into the process way before the rooms get painted. You will look at how a team might come up with risk responses to reduce or mitigate these impacts in Exercises 7.6 and 7.7.

Performing a Quantitative Risk Analysis

If your team decides to perform quantitative analysis, the following steps will help you create a consistent and organized approach to the analysis.

1. Gather your risk team.

2. Make sure you have a standard definition of probability and impact and use any quantitative information you might have gained in expected value, sensitivity analysis, Monte Carlo Analysis, simulation, or decision tree analysis you might have performed (see Exercise 7.4).

3. List all the risks previously identified and rank the probability of each occurring using a numerical equivalent for probability.

4. Separately, rank the impact if it were to occur using a numerical equivalent for impact, such as dollars.

5. Enter the findings in the risk matrix and multiply the information to get the expected value. You may use a table similar to Table 7.3 to create this matrix.

6. Rank those with a high score, then rearrange the tasks from top rated to low rated.

7. Decide on which risks you would like to continue to create responses for.

Recommended Reading: Chapter 6, pp.215–218, *PMP Project Management Professional Study Guide.*

Scenario

TPMP is helping Mountain Communications (MC), a well-established telecommunications company, create risk management processes. One of your first assignments is to help Tasha Smith, the program manager on the project, create a risk management process for replacing two old systems with newer systems to reflect modern technological advances. The old systems will need to continue functioning while data is converted. The new systems are provided by a vendor who is asking MC to be one of the first companies to implement them. The company has decided to use a gateway program, which will convert the old data into the formats of the new systems. The company has decided to create this program itself although several are available on the market. The program is critical to both conversion efforts and a plan has been created for a phased conversion—the data will not be converted all at once—MC has been able to segment the data to be converted over the next couple of years. The project has around 100 people working on the conversion and implementation of the new systems. Tasha's team has identified 10 possible risks on the project. They are listed in a matrix created earlier for the Qualitative Risk Analysis and are repeated in the table below for quantitative analysis. The team has completed some quantitative expected value analysis and has decided on the following probabilities/impact.

Quantitative Risk Analysis—Risk Impact/Probability Matrix

1. Complete the expected value in the following table.

Risk	Probability	Impact	Value
1. The gateway program will not convert some of the data in time for the new system to go live on the conversion days.	40%	50,000	
2. The new system will not perform a function the old system performed.	20%	20,000	
3. Upon going live, the new system does not work properly, and customer orders start backing up.	50%	60,000	
4. The order takers cannot properly work the new system.	60%	100,000	
5. The data gets converted but is wrong upon going live.	10%	250,000	
6. The new system is slow.	15%	25,000	
7. The vendor can't fix a system bug in time for the next scheduled conversion.	45%	12,000	
8. The MC sponsor for the project is promoted to another division.	20%	65,000	
9. Another company hires Tasha away from MC.	25%	50,000	
10. The customer is dissatisfied with the performance of the new systems with a few of the conversions completed.	40%	30,000	

2. What are the top three risks Tasha's team should work on and why?

_____

_____

_____

_____

3. Why is quantitative analysis better than qualitative analysis?

_____

_____

_____

_____

4. Should quantitative analysis always be performed?

_____

_____

_____

_____

Exercise 7.6: Types of Risk Responses

The objectives for Exercise 7.6 are:

- Learn the various risk response types.
- Practice recognizing the risk response types.

Background

Once you have identified your risks and analyzed them, you want to do something about them. In fact, while you analyze them, you might come up with ways to reduce them or avoid them completely. Although you may think of particular ways to respond to risks, they can be categorized in one of the four following categories.

Avoidance   This is a response type where you attempt to overcome the risk event by trying to stray away from or eliminate it altogether. You do something to your plan, so that the risk simply won't occur. For instance, if a construction project has a risk that the dump truck won't be delivered on time and the project could be delayed and money lost, perhaps you would reduce the scope of the project to eliminate the elaborate landscaping part of the project that required the dump truck.

Transference   Most of us understand insurance—you pay someone to protect against the risk of possible losses. Transference is the response type where you transfer the responsibility for the risk to someone else. In project management, insurance is one response using transference, but you might also transfer the risk by hiring a vendor who is more adept at the particular work itself. For instance, in a construction project, a project manager would probably subcontract with an electrical company who can do the building's wiring. This transfers the risk of doing the work to someone else rather than the construction company hiring or training electricians themselves. Transference does not necessarily eliminate the risk—and in fact, the company who takes on the risk should be insured itself, otherwise, your project could still suffer great consequences if the risk occurs.

Mitigation   This risk type is almost like avoidance, but in this case, you may only be able to reduce the probability of the risk or the impact to the project or its objectives. For instance, if the risk of rain would delay your project, you would add extra days into your project schedule, to "pad" it for rain days. Many times, this involves building more budget or adding more tasks to your schedule to reduce your risk. That's why risk management is a planning process—by doing it up front, you can get important items built into your schedule before they become difficult to manage.

Acceptance   There are many risks that are so expensive, that trying to avoid, insure, or mitigate them might be as expensive as the project itself. There may be other risks where the expense is so small, and the risk can be so easily handled, it is not worthwhile making major changes to the project plan or schedule. This response type is called acceptance: you are willing to take the consequences of the risk were it to occur. For instance, it might be possible that you would have the flood of the century that would wipe out your project, and yet you can't get flood insurance in your city. Since you live in a very dry region, with no major floods, your team might decide to accept the risk of flooding and deal with it if it occurs. Your team would do well, though, to create a contingency plan if flooding does occur, which is discussed next.

Contingency planning   Contingency planning is a plan of action if the risk event occurs. You may have created a response type using mitigation for the risk event, but the event could still happen anyway. You might have decided to accept the risk, and you need a plan to deal with it when it happens. Or maybe, even though you transferred the risk, you know that if it occurs, it can still affect other aspects of the project, so you still need to have a plan if the risk occurs. You and your team will create a plan of action to deal with the risk, but only if the event occurs. For instance, on a construction project, perhaps there is a threat of a strike by dump truck drivers during a time when you are expecting to need numerous dump trucks. You might create a contingency plan to hire temporary workers who have experience driving dump trucks. You decide to do nothing proactively to deal with the risk, but if it happens, you have a plan of action to implement immediately.

Understanding the various risk types can help you and your project team create risk responses that can have quite an impact on our project plan. To help you think about what you need to do when creating risk responses, perform the following steps.

1.   After the majority of risk analysis is complete, gather your risk team.

2.   List the risk response types to help you think of possible responses. Start detailing the steps you would take for each response based on the response types you have chosen. You may choose more than one response type and plan for a risk.

3. For each response, also detail the contingency plan(s).

4. Document the response and contingency plans. Exercise 7.7 will describe this documentation in more detail.

In this exercise, you will help the MC company's project team recognize various risk response types as you consult with them on best risk management processes.

Recommended Reading: Chapter 6, pp.218–222, *PMP Project Management Professional Study Guide.*

Scenario

TPMP is helping Mountain Communications (MC), a well-established telecommunications company, create risk management processes. One of your first assignments is to create a risk management process for a project that is replacing two old systems with newer systems to reflect modern technological advances. The old systems will need to continue functioning while data is converted. The new systems are provided by a vendor who is asking MC to be one of the first companies to implement them. The company has decided to use a gateway program, which will convert the old data into the formats of the new systems. The company has decided to create this program itself although several are available on the market. The program is critical to both conversion efforts and a plan has been created for a phased conversion—the data will not be converted all at once—MC has been able to segment the data to be converted over the next couple of years. The project has around 100 people working on the conversion and implementation of the new systems.

Types of Risk Responses

1. What response types does Tasha's team have to choose from?

_____

_____

_____

_____

2. The team has decided that one of the biggest risks for this project is that the in-house gateway program will not work. They have decided that they will create a prototype of the gateway, and test it on data they would convert. What kind of risk response type is this?

    _____

    _____

    _____

3. The team has decided that there is not much it can do if the office is closed down for several days due to a large snowstorm shutting down the city. What kind of risk response strategy is this?

    _____

    _____

    _____

4. The team has decided that it would be a good idea to hire an outsourcing agency to run the operating systems for the new computer systems since the MC company has decided to reduce computer operations personnel. What kind of risk response type is this?

    _____

    _____

    _____

5. The team has decided that although it will accept the risk of the office shutting down for several days, team members could work at home for the days the office is shut down. The team has created steps for taking action if the office does shut down. What kind of response is this?

    _____

    _____

    _____

6. The team has decided that the requirements for the functionality for one of the systems is not very clear. The team has decided to hold another requirements session to eliminate this risk. What type of risk response is this?

    _____

    _____

    _____

7. The team has decided to hire another gateway system from a reputable vendor if the in-house gateway program fails after the first three conversion attempts. This contingency plan will be implemented only after the in-house gateway program fails. Why is contingency planning important, even if the team is able to create plans for mitigating the gateway's failure?

_____

_____

_____

_____

Exercise 7.7: Creating a Risk Response Plan

The objectives for Exercise 7.7 are:

- Understand the purpose of a risk response plan.
- Create a risk response plan.

Background

The most important output of the risk management process is the risk response plan. Once you have identified, analyzed, and rated the risks and decided which ones to work on, you and your team need to set up a documented and living plan for dealing with the risks. Among many possible items you can document on the risk response plan are:

- Risks and their categories
- Owner
- Response types
- Actual response steps you would take and budget for the response
- Contingency plan and possible contingency actions
- Secondary risks which are new risks that might have been identified based on the risk response plans

The owner will be responsible for implementing the response or the contingency. And one of the overlooked processes with the risk response plan is continual review of it by the project team during execution and control of the project. In fact, as the team members continue to review risks, or come up with risk response plans, they may identify new risks for which they need to create risk response plans. For instance, if you decided that you will reduce a risk by creating a prototype system, you may have created a new risk that management will want to use the prototype instead of creating a new system based on the prototype as originally planned.

Creating a documented risk response plan is the most important aspect of risk planning. The following sample table and suggested steps will help you and your team create a plan that you can apply to your project.

1. First, decide on how you will document your risk response plan. You should have done this initially when creating your risk management plan (see Exercise 7.1). The table you create might looks something like the table below:

Risk	Owner	Risk Type	Risk Plan	Plan Budget	Contingency	Contingency Budget	Secondary Risk

2. Make sure the risks and their analysis are documented, and gather the team to review the list.

3. Discuss with the team the various risk responses you could use for the risk. Decide on the best response or responses for each risk.

4. Document each risk response in detail. The risk owner may do this or the team may provide input. Don't forget to create a contingency plan for each risk if it is appropriate.

5. Add appropriate risk responses into the schedule or budget. Change the project plan or other areas of the project as necessary based on the risk response plans.

6. Add any secondary risks and risk responses based on any risk responses your team decides to implement.

7. Review the risk responses and contingency plans and ensure the owner and any other implementer understands it and knows what to do.

8. Review the risk response plan regularly to see if the risk has occurred and if the plans are still applicable.

9. Identify any new risks based on continued risk identification meetings you hold with the project team.

In this exercise, you will help the MC company create a risk response plan for some of the risks it has identified through risk management processes you helped it create.

Recommended Reading: Chapter 6, pp.218–222, *PMP Project Management Professional Study Guide.*

Scenario

TPMP is helping Mountain Communications (MC), a well-established telecommunications company, create risk management processes. One of your first assignments is to create a risk management process for a project that is replacing two old systems with newer systems to reflect more modern technological advances. The old systems will need to continue functioning while data is converted. The new systems are provided by a vendor who is asking MC to be one of the first companies to implement them. The company has decided to use a gateway program, which will convert the old data into the formats of the new systems. The company has decided to create this program itself although several are available on the market. The program is critical to both conversion efforts and a plan has been created for a phased conversion—the data will not be converted all at once—MC has been able to segment the data to be converted over the next couple of years. The project has around 100 people working on the conversion and implementation of the new systems. Some of the team members are the program manager, Tasha Smith (whom you are advising to establish the risk management processes); the production manager who is responsible for the current systems and will take over the new systems; a development manager responsible for the gateway program; another development manager responsible for implementing the new systems and managing the conversion plan; the client who will need to maintain current service while the new systems are converted; and the vendor who is helping to implement both systems.

Creating a Risk Response Plan

1. What are some of the response plans for the risks to Tasha's project? Complete the following table by choosing five of the risks and entering the response type, owner, and a possible response plan for each.

Risk	Owner	Response Type	Plan
The gateway program will not convert some of the data in time for the new system to go live on the conversion days.			
The new system will not perform a function the old system performed.			
Upon going live, the new system does not work properly, and customer orders start backing up.			

Risk	Owner	Response Type	Plan
The order takers cannot properly work the new system.			
The data gets converted but is wrong upon going live.			
The new system is slow.			
The vendor can't fix a system bug in time for the next scheduled conversion.			
The MC sponsor for the project is promoted to another division.			
Another company hires Tasha away from MC.			
The customer is dissatisfied with the performance of the new systems with a few of the conversions completed.			

2. What are some of the contingency plans for Tasha's project? Complete the following table with at least five contingency plans (they do not need be the same ones for which you chose to create responses).

_____

_____

_____

_____

Risk	Contingency Plan
The gateway program will not convert some of the data in time for the new system to go live on the conversion days.	
The new system will not perform a function the old system performed.	
Upon going live, the new system does not work properly, and customer orders start backing up.	
The order takers cannot properly work the new system.	
The data gets converted but is wrong upon going live.	
The new system is slow.	
The vendor can't fix a system bug in time for the next scheduled conversion.	
The MC sponsor for the project is promoted to another division.	
Another company hires Tasha away from MC.	
The customer is dissatisfied with the performance of the new systems with a few of the conversions completed.	

3. When the team creates a response, it creates a new risk. What does the team need to do with the new risk?

    _____

    _____

    _____

    _____

Answers to Exercise Questions

Answers to Exercise 7.1

Your answers may be somewhat different, but the following answers provide a guide.

1. Tasha needs to create a risk management plan in order to help her and the team create a strategy and methodology for dealing with risk on the project. The team members and stakeholders need to have common expectations and objectives for what they will be doing, when they will be doing it, why, and who will be involved. By setting the standards up front, the team won't use precious time later trying to figure out the processes and will understand the rating system to objectively rate risks.

2. Since this is a very complex project, with a number of stakeholders, and dependencies for successful conversions, you recommend she consider a highly organized and regular process for risk management. You suggest that the team consider expert risk management consultation in setting up the processes. You might suggest Tasha consider some outside auditing of the technology and conversion approach to determine risks, analyze them, and determine plans for the risks. You might suggest to Tasha that she ask the vendor to implement risk management processes, as well.

3. To justify a budget for risk management on the project, Tasha will need to create a work breakdown structure of all the deliverables from the risk management process and determine resources needed for the activities. For instance, possible deliverables are a risk management plan, Risk Identification, risk analysis, and a risk response plan. She would need to include the deliverables in the schedule, and estimate the budget based on the resources costs and time. In this case, if she brings in expert help, she will need to include the costs of the vendor or consultants. She needs to consider all the team's time in meetings, analysis, and developing risk responses.

4. You might suggest Tasha explore initial risk management planning and team organization: two hours for three weeks. Initial Risk Identification: once a week for a month (during the planning phase). Analysis of the risks: an average of two hours for each selected risk for analysis. Reviewing the risk list (monitoring and controlling risk): 20 minutes in a weekly status meeting.

5. The following might be the roles and responsibilities.

    - Program manager: risk manager (since the project is complex, you might suggest a separate manager).
    - Production manager: old systems risk analysis and risk response implementer.
    - Vendor: new systems risk analysis and risk response implementer.
    - Gateway manager: gateway risk analysis and risk response implementer.
    - New systems manager and conversion manager: new systems risk analysis and risk response implementer. This particular role is very complex. Tasha might want to look at ensuring this role is broken into two responsibilities: new systems and conversion, with a different analysis and response manager for each.

6.   The difference between a risk management plan and a risk response plan is that the risk response plan is how Tasha and her project managers plan to actually respond to particular risks. The risk management plan is the team's road map for dealing with risk processes and how they plan to analyze and manage risks. Tasha will need to create both. The team needs the RMP to understand why they are doing Risk Management Planning and what their roles and processes will be. The risk response plan describes how the team will react to an actual risk event.

Answers to Exercise 7.2

1.   Tasha might use risk categories based on data she could find in information technology publications. Since this is a major systems project, you would want to use the expertise and experience of others who have managed complex systems projects. You also might suggest she use the technical category, since the entire project is very complex due to new systems and the gateway program. Tasha would want to organize all identified risks into this category, and she would want some of her most senior technical people to manage those risks. Another category you might use is project management risks since the project has several managers ensuring their portions of the project are completed (the development manager, conversion manager, vendor project manager, etc.).

2.   The members of your risk team should include Tasha Smith, the production manager; the gateway development manager; the new systems and conversion development manager; the client; and the vendor. Tasha might also include some technical experts. All of these people need to identify risks that are important to their portions of the project.

3.   Some of the risk identification methods Tasha could use for this project include documentation reviews, brainstorming, surveying and interviewing experts, checklists, assumptions analysis, or diagramming techniques. You might recommend she use a couple of methods to ensure she gets a more exhaustive list than if she uses only one method.

4.   Considering some of the risks that Tasha and the team might identify, your answer should look like the table below.

Risk	Category	Trigger
The new system can't perform the same function as the old system.	Technical	Testing shows a function will not be performed.
The vendor decides to stop supporting one of the systems.	Organization	The vendor starts to "lose interest" in helping with solving issues with the system.
The gateway program does not convert some of the data accurately.	Technical	Testing shows data is not converting properly.

Risk	Category	Trigger
One of the new systems does not allow for data conversion as fast as the other new system.	Technical	Testing shows data cannot be converted as well in one system in the same time frame as the other.
The vendor cannot fix a major bug in one of the systems, which delays the conversion schedule.	Technical	The time frame for a bug to be fixed comes and goes so that the conversion schedule is in jeopardy.

Answers to Exercise 7.3

The following table shows the risk rating matrix that Tasha and her team completed. Your answers should be similar.

Risk	Probability	Impact	Score
The gateway program will not convert some of the data in time for the new system to go live on the conversion days.	Medium	High	High
The new system will not perform a function the old system performed.	Low	Medium	Low
Upon going live, the new system does not work properly, and customer orders start backing up.	Medium	High	High
The order takers cannot properly work the new system.	Medium	High	High
The data gets converted but is wrong upon going live.	Low	High	Medium
The new system is slow.	Low	Medium	Low
The vendor can't fix a system bug in time for the next scheduled conversion.	Medium	Low	Low
The MC sponsor for the project is promoted to another division.	Low	High	Medium
Another company hires Tasha away from MC.	Low	Medium	Low
The customer is dissatisfied with the performance of the new systems with a few of the conversions completed.	Medium	Medium	Medium

1. The table above shows you the probability ratings for each risk Tasha faces.

2. The table above shows you impact ratings determined by Tasha's group.

3. The table above shows you the scores determined by Tasha's group.

4. Tasha and her team might now show the risks according to the order below based on the highest to lowest scores. The team may decide to move on to quantitative analysis for the high and medium risks only. They may monitor the low risks without doing quantitative analysis.

Risk	Probability	Impact	Score
The gateway program will not convert some of the data in time for the new system to go live on the conversion days.	Medium	High	High
Upon going live, the new system does not work properly, and customer orders start backing up.	Medium	High	High
The order takers cannot properly work the new system.	Medium	High	High
The data gets converted but is wrong upon going live.	Low	High	Medium
The MC sponsor for the project is promoted to another division.	Low	High	Medium
The customer is dissatisfied with the performance of the new systems with a few of the conversions completed.	Medium	Medium	Medium
The new system is slow.	Low	Medium	Low
The vendor can't fix a system bug in time for the next scheduled conversion.	Medium	Low	Low
Another company hires Tasha away from MC.	Low	Medium	Low
The new system will not perform a function the old system performed.	Low	Medium	Low

Answers to Exercise 7.4

1. Your answers for creating expected value tables for the make/buy decision for the gateway system should look like the following.

For Buy Decision:

Probability	Amount at Stake	Expected Value
.7	$250,000	$175,000
.3	($20,000)	($6,000)
Total = 1	—	$169,000

For Make Decision:

Probability	Amount at Stake	Expected Value
.5	$500,000	$250,000
.5	($150,000)	($75,000)
Total = 1	—	$175,000

2. Your answer for creating the decision tree analysis for the make/buy decision for the gateway system should look like the following illustration.

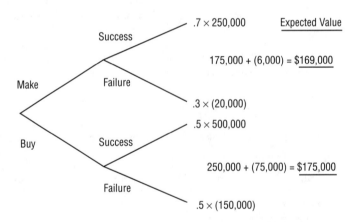

3. The best decision is to make the gateway system for two reasons. First, the expected value is higher for the "make" decision, though not significantly. Second, the loss potential is much higher, but the team has decided that the opportunity for future use of the product if they make it in-house is much greater.

4. Quantitative tools and techniques are interviewing, sensitivity analysis, simulation, and decision tree analysis.

Answers to Exercise 7.5

1. The following table provides the expected value for the risks.

Risk	Probability	Impact	Value
1. The gateway program will not convert some of the data in time for the new system to go live on the conversion days.	40%	50,000	$20,000
2. The new system will not perform a function the old system performed.	20%	20,000	$4,000
3. Upon going live, the new system does not work properly, and customer orders start backing up.	50%	60,000	$30,000
4. The order takers cannot properly work the new system.	60%	100,000	$60,000
5. The data gets converted but is wrong upon going live.	10%	250,000	$25,000
6. The new system is slow.	15%	25,000	$3,750
7. The vendor can't fix a system bug in time for the next scheduled conversion.	45%	12,000	$5,400
8. The MC sponsor for the project is promoted to another division.	20%	65,000	$13,000
9. Another company hires Tasha away from MC.	25%	50,000	$12,500
10. The customer is dissatisfied with the performance of the new systems with a few of the conversions completed	40%	30,000	$12,000

2. Tasha's team should work on risks 3, 4, and 5. They have the highest expected value of all of the risks. In mitigating or reducing these risks, they could save the company $115,000. All the other risks combined would add up to $70,650.

3. Quantitative analysis is better than qualitative analysis because it provides more objective data. The project team can make better decisions and perhaps achieve more support from management in the risk management process they will need to reduce the risks.

4. Quantitative analysis, although more objective than qualitative analysis, does not always need to be performed, although it is recommended for the top risks of your project. It takes a long time to perform quantitative analysis. Sometimes it's important to invest less time and money. So it depends on what your project team has decided to do.

Answers to Exercise 7.6

The answers shown here are by no means the only possible solutions. Your answers, however, should be similar.

1. Tasha's team can choose from avoidance, transference, mitigation, and acceptance. It also should create a contingency plan for each risk it has chosen to deal with.

2. Creating a gateway prototype is a mitigation risk response type. This would help reduce the probability of the gateway's failure. The team would add tasks to the work breakdown structure and the project schedule to create this prototype.

3. If team members have decided they can do little about the office shutting down for several days, they have chosen acceptance as the risk response type.

4. Since team members have decided that it would be a good idea to hire an outsourcing agency to run the hardware for the new computer systems, they have chosen a risk response type of transference because they will transfer the risk of operating the computers to someone else.

5. The team members created a contingency plan as a response when they decided that, although they will accept the risk of the office shutting down for several days, they could work at home for the days the office is shut down.

6. The team has responded with an avoidance risk response type by holding another requirements session to eliminate the risk of the requirements not being clear.

7. Even thought the team members might have created several risk responses that reduce the failure of the gateway system program, it could still fail. So, it was important for the team members to still create a contingency plan in case, after all of their efforts, the in-house system still fails.

Answers to Exercise 7.7

The answers shown here are by no means the only possible solutions. Your answers, however, should be similar.

1. To assign the owner and describe the response type and plan for five of the risks, you might complete the table according to the following answers.

Risk	Owner	Response Type	Plan
The gateway program will not convert some of the data in time for the new system to go live on the conversion days.	Gateway development manager	Mitigation	Add tasks to the project plan to perform test conversions with the data one month prior to conversion date.
The new system will not perform a function the old system performed.	Production manager	Avoidance	Hold a requirements review session to ensure that all functions of the old system will be performed in the new system.

Risk	Owner	Response Type	Plan
Upon going live, the new system does not work properly, and customer orders start backing up.	Client	Acceptance	Use a contingency plan.
The order takers cannot properly work the new system.	Program manager	Transference	Hire a training firm to create a training plan, document, and perform training to help the order takers learn the new system.
The data gets converted but is wrong upon going live.	New systems and conversion manager	Mitigation	Create tasks in the plan to test the first 50 orders, to ensure the data is correct during the weekend before the conversion goes "live." If there are issues, create a rollback plan.
The new system is slow.	New systems and conversion manager	Mitigation	Add tasks to the project plan to create performance testing on the system prior to production.
The vendor can't fix a system bug in time for the next scheduled conversion.	Vendor	Mitigation	Add tasks to the project plan to review test plans early in vendor testing and also schedule a client review for the system functionality testing. Also, create a clause in the contract that penalizes the vendor for delays it causes.
The MC sponsor for the project is promoted to another division.	Program manager	Transference	Create a "contract" with several executives besides the sponsor on the project to help rally support through this second tier of sponsors.

Risk	Owner	Response Type	Plan
Another company hires Tasha away from MC.	MC company management	Acceptance	Create a contingency plan to find a replacement quickly, including identifying some good potential replacements within the company.
The customer is dissatisfied with the performance of the new systems with a few of the conversions completed.	Program manager	Avoidance	Create a change plan and education program to address the concerns of the client prior to conversions.

2. To describe the contingency plan for the five risks you have chosen, you might have completed the table according to the following possible answers.

Risk	Contingency Plan
The gateway program will not convert some of the data in time for the new system to go live on the conversion days.	Make up the time delay by adding the conversions to a future conversion time frame. This will increase the risk for that future conversion, however.
The new system will not perform a function the old system performed.	Create a manual workaround until the function can be added, if the functioning is not delayed significantly. This may also require hiring of retired employees temporarily if this missing function cannot be implemented in a timely fashion. If the function is significant, the conversions will be delayed until the function is added.
Upon going live, the new system does not work properly, and customer orders start backing up.	Set up extra shifts with retired employees temporarily to help reduce the backlog.
The order takers cannot properly work the new system.	Be ready to send an appropriate number of trainers or employees familiar with the systems to the order taker's site to train on the job.
The data gets converted but is wrong upon going live.	Hire extra employees who can review and clean up the data quickly before the order is completed.

Risk	Contingency Plan
The new system is slow.	Implement a customer education campaign to alert the customers that their orders will take longer than usual when the order takers are processing the orders with the customers.
The vendor can't fix a system bug in time for the next scheduled conversion.	Delay the current conversion and roll it into a future one. Implement the contract clause that penalizes the vendor for delays to conversions due to vendor issues.
The MC sponsor for the project is promoted to another division.	Immediately set up a communication campaign to let management know the importance of the project, and start soliciting a new sponsor from previously identified candidates immediately.
Another company hires Tasha away from MC.	Identify good potential replacements within the company, and have management aligned to make the replacement quickly.
The client is dissatisfied with the performance of the new systems with a few of the conversions completed.	Implement a lessons learned session with the client company to understand its issues, and slow down conversions, until issues are addressed.

3. When the team identifies a new risk because of a response created for a previously identified risk, the team needs to go through the entire identification, analysis, and risks response planning process that Risk Management Planning requires. Based on the analysis and ranking, the team decides if it warrants response or not.

Chapter

8

Contracts and Procurement Management

THE EXERCISES PRESENTED IN THIS CHAPTER INCLUDE:

✓ Exercise 8.1: Deciding on Contract Types

✓ Exercise 8.2: Creating a Procurement Management Plan

✓ Exercise 8.3: Creating a Statement of Work (SOW)

✓ Exercise 8.4: Evaluating and Selecting the Vendor

✓ Exercise 8.5: Creating the Contract

Procurement management is a project management process that you perform only if you are procuring services or goods from someone outside of your organization. In such a case, you will first decide on the type of contract you want for your project and make sure you have a plan for procuring and managing your contracts. Once you have a good set of requirements for the work you need done, you will create a statement of work (SOW) so that organizations bidding can understand the work in enough detail to provide good proposals. You will need to document evaluation criteria so you can objectively select your vendors, and then you will create the contract that the vendor and you will use throughout the project to manage status and change and handle disputes. Using procurement management processes is extremely important for cost and organizational efficiency, and good relations between you and your vendors.

Procurement management is covered in the Planning, Executing, and Closing process group objectives of the PMP exam.

Exercise 8.1: Deciding on Contract Types

The objectives for Exercise 8.1 are:

- Introduce contract concepts.
- Understand the most common contract types.
- Practice recognizing contract types.
- Practice applying contract types to different situations.

Background

Often, project teams cannot do all the work that must be performed to accomplish the scope of the work. The project needs someone else to do the work, because it might be more cost effective, the organization lacks a particular expertise, or another organization simply has the goods you need for the product. Whenever you have someone outside of your organization (also known as a vendor, contractor, or supplier) provide goods or services on your project, you will need to create processes to manage them and agreements to set expectations for the work they will provide. When the organization is not a part of your own company, the agreements must be made via a contract. A contract provides an agreement that one party will provide goods or services and the other party will pay for them (in money or some other kind of trade of equal value). It also provides for legal recourse for disputes that may occur between the two parties. Most of us don't really think about contracts as anything but a lot of "legalese," but you can actually choose the type of contract for your project to help create the results you want. Your understanding of the different types may help you create the best contract for your project.

Contracts also have a certain amount of risk associated with them for the contractor or the buyer of the services or goods. That is, based on whether it is fixed fee or cost reimbursable, either the contractor or buyer might have more risk in recouping their costs or making a profit. There are many creative variations of contracts these days, especially if you want to create incentives for your contractors, but most contracts are based on two basic contract types: fixed price (also known as lump sum) or cost reimbursable. Fixed price is one predetermined fee for the goods or services you and the contractor agree on. You can set incentives or penalties in addition to that fixed price. Cost reimbursable is a floating price contract, based on the costs the contractor incurs. Again, you can set up incentives or penalties in addition to the costs. You can also have a time and materials contract, which is a hybrid of the fixed price and cost reimbursable contract types. Each contract type is described below in more detail.

Fixed Price or Lump Sum

The fixed price (also known as fixed fee) or lump sum contract sets a fixed fee for the work the contractor will provide. This means that if the fee is $10,000, the contractor must get all the work done within that amount. If, for some reason, there are delays and the contractor's costs go above $10,000, the contractor loses money. If the contractor's costs go below $10,000, then the contractor makes money. Because of this, most of the risk of the contract is on the contractor. If the kind of work has been done frequently, or the scope of the work is very well understood, this can be a very good contract for the contractor. If the scope of the work is not well defined, or this is a research project, it would be very risky for the contractor to bid using a fixed price. And the seller should be wary of such a bid. This is the most common kind of contract, but again, is used usually for well-defined work.

For this kind of contract, you may add incentives to reward the contractor with earlier delivery or better performance than the agreed-to terms of the contract. You may want the contractor to complete the project sooner, but know it may not be possible under normal circumstances. So you motivate the contractor with a bonus of 10 percent of the contract to finish 10 days early. When you add an incentive, you are taking on more risk than the fixed fee contract, because you may have to pay more (which you are willing to risk), or the work may not be completed when you really hope it will (which you must accept if the contractor cannot make the earlier date). Although not usually a part of a contract type, but often added as a contract clause, you could also add a penalty for the product or service not being delivered on time, or with lower than agreed-to quality.

Cost Reimbursable

The cost reimbursable contract reimburses the contractor for all their costs (direct and indirect, with the indirect costs being figured as a percentage of the direct costs) in producing the goods or services for you. Since you don't know how much the total costs will be, this provides a lot of risk to you and your project, and less risk to the contractor, who can just keep working and charging you for all the work he or she does. You might insert some checkpoints along the way in the contract to audit what is going on—to make sure the project does not keep growing. Although this might seem to be a less than desirable contract type, it is quite necessary for projects with a lot of uncertainty. Good contractors will require a cost reimbursable contract when you require research and development on something never done before, or if the scope of your project is poorly defined. You can also add incentives or awards to cost reimbursable contracts. This often helps reduce the risk to the buyer because it motivates the contractor to get done as soon as possible, depending on how the incentive or award is written in the contract.

Time and Materials

The time and materials contract is a mixture of fixed fee and cost reimbursable. The price of the units is fixed, but the cost is not known when the contract is awarded. Some people use this type to get work started before the contract is awarded since finalizing a contract can take so long, but the work must get started.

In order to create the right kind of contract, you and your organization decide on what you expect of your contractors and decide how much risk you need to take on. The following lists the contract types from highest risk to lowest risk to you.

- Cost (highest risk to you)
- Cost reimbursable plus incentive or award
- Time and materials
- Fixed price plus incentive
- Fixed price (lowest risk to you)

In Exercise 8.1, you will learn about contract types when you help the Creative Cartoon Company decide on the contract types for the products and services it needs to acquire for creating its first full-length feature film.

Recommended Reading: Chapter 6, pp.223–226, *PMP Project Management Professional Study Guide.*

Scenario

Recently, the Creative Cartoon Company (CCC) has obtained enough capital to create its first feature-length animated film based on its most recent short film, which won several major entertainment awards. CCC hired TPMP several months ago to help it improve project management processes, and now, because CCC has to subcontract some of the work to outside organizations in order to complete the film, the company executives are asking you and your company, TPMP, to help them with their procurement management processes. For the new feature film they have decided that they will need outside services for sound production, an overseas cartoon firm to create background artwork, a marketing firm, and an animation software development firm to implement an idea that the producer has for advancing the animation industry to the next level. Marcus Manning is the producer of the film, tentatively titled, "Bouncing with Bob." He and the film's director, Sheila Wong, have high aspirations—they want the feature-length film to win an Oscar for best animated film, and they want their new animation idea to win a technical Oscar. They want you to help them create good vendor relationships, so that the vendors can help them create the best possible film.

Deciding on Contract Types

1. Marcus wants to incent the marketing company to create a great marketing campaign for the film. What kind of contract type might you recommend to Marcus and why?

    _____

    _____

    _____

    _____

2. After some discussion, you and Marcus have decided that the overseas contract for artwork should be time and materials. Describe how CCC might implement the pricing for the time and materials contract.

    _____

    _____

    _____

    _____

3. What is the riskiest contract type for CCC? What is the riskiest type of contract for the contractor, and why?

    _____

    _____

    _____

4. What contract type would you recommend to Marcus for the sound production company? Why?

    _____

    _____

    _____

    _____

5. What contract type would you recommend to Marcus for the animation software development firm? Why?

    _____

    _____

    _____

    _____

Exercise 8.2: Creating a Procurement Management Plan

The objectives for Exercise 8.2 are:

- Understand the need for a procurement management plan.
- Understand the elements of a procurement management plan.
- Practice creating parts of a procurement management plan.

Background

As with all knowledge areas, PMI expects you to create a plan to set the strategy for managing the processes for each knowledge area for your project. With procurement management, you will create a plan to describe how you will manage the different processes and standards for your contracts and vendors. Some of the processes you need to document are how you will manage vendor solicitations, including describing the documents and evaluation criteria; how you will obtain contract vendors; and how you will evaluate proposals and make your final vendor selection. You might also describe how you would like your contracts negotiated and how you will manage and administer your project's contracts. If your project is going to have contracts, this is extremely important so that you can be efficient and objective in selecting your contractors. Also, due to this early planning, you can direct the lawyers to include important items in the contract to help make your project successful and to manage the contractors with a more organized approach once they have been chosen. Your plan should detail how you will manage the following procurement management items.

- Justify why you have decided to purchase the services or goods via a contract.

- Describe the types of contracts your project will have and why you have decided on the contract type for the particular goods or services. Describe how you will control the costs/prices of the contracts.

- Describe any organizational policies you have for creating and managing contracts.

- Describe the documentation/specifications required for each contract, including how you will create the contract statement of work (SOW), and to what extent it will be documented and used in the proposals.

- Discuss how processes in procurement and solicitation planning will be managed. You will want to make sure you describe your strategies on the following topics:

  - What procurement documents will you use? Will you need a request for proposal (RFP), invitation for bid (IFB), request for quotation (RFQ), or some other document to receive contract bids?

  - Will you create evaluation criteria for the contract bids, and will you provide the criteria? If you do create evaluation criteria, how will you do it and on what will it be based?

  - How will you solicit bids for your contracts? Will you hold bidder conferences or advertise in industry publications, or use some other form? Are you constrained in some way on how you obtain bids?

  - Once you obtain the bids or proposals, describe the evaluation process, including who will do it and how you will use the evaluation criteria you have prepared. Describe whether you will use any screening or weighting systems, or if you will use any independent estimates to help you evaluate the bids.

  - Describe how you will handle bid protests, if it is possible your organization might receive them.

- Describe the management strategies and actions for administering each contract, including the change control and payment systems that should be used for each contract. You might describe how you will coordinate with your regular project performance reporting, especially for scheduling and performance status. You also might include how you would manage the contracts differently during different phases of the project. Describe how you will manage multiple providers if you have them—will you require joint meetings or separate meetings or a combination of both?

- Document the roles and responsibilities for managing each contract. Will the project manager be the contract manager, or will you have a procurement specialist manage the contract? You might describe the different roles and responsibilities of the procurement department versus the project team duties—what actions can the project team take without working with the lawyers or procurement management department?

- Describe how you would recommend that your project proceed with each contract negotiation, including who would manage the negotiations and who would participate in them. Discuss how disputes might be negotiated.

- Document what will constitute closeout of each contract.

Make sure the procurement management plan is well documented and reviewed by your procurement department if you have one. Although much of the contract is written by lawyers, you can have a great deal of influence on what is expected of the vendor and the product or service to be delivered by setting up this plan early in the project.

In Exercise 8.2, you will help the Creative Cartoon Company create portions of a procurement management plan, based on the need for different contract types and vendors it will require to produce its first full-length feature film.

Recommended Reading: Chapter 6, pp.223–229, and Chapter 9, pp. 330–339, *PMP Project Management Professional Study Guide.*

Scenario

Recently, the Creative Cartoon Company (CCC) has obtained enough capital to create its first feature-length animated film based on its most recent short film, which won several major entertainment awards. CCC hired TPMP several months ago to help it improve project management processes, and now, because CCC has to subcontract some of the work to outside organizations in order to complete the film, the executives are asking you and your company, TPMP, to help them with their procurement management processes. For the new feature film they have decided that they will need outside services for sound production, an overseas cartoon firm to create background artwork, a marketing firm, and an animation software development firm to implement an idea that the producer has for advancing the animation industry to the next level. Marcus Manning is the producer of the film, tentatively titled, "Bouncing with Bob." He and the film's director, Sheila Wong, have high aspirations—they want the feature-length film to win an Oscar for best animated film, and they want their new animation advancement idea to win a technical Oscar. They want you to help them create good vendor relationships, so that the vendors can help them create the best possible film.

Creating a Procurement Management Plan

1. For each service CCC needs to procure (sound production, overseas artwork production, software development, and marketing), describe how you would recommend that CCC manage the scheduling and performance of each contract in unison with the other.

   _____

   _____

   _____

   _____

2. Describe how Marcus should manage CCC's procurement processes for the sound production contract. What procurement document should he use? Should he use evaluation criteria? How should he solicit bids? Once CCC receives the bids, who do you recommend should evaluate the bids and use the evaluation criteria?

    _____

    _____

    _____

    _____

3. Describe whether CCC will use evaluation criteria for each contract, what criteria CCC should focus on, and whether CCC should obtain some independent estimates. Explain your reasoning for each of these items.

    _____

    _____

    _____

    _____

4. Describe what constitutes closeout for each contract.

    _____

    _____

    _____

5. Who should be in the negotiations for each contract, and what might some general negotiation points be?

    _____

    _____

    _____

    _____

6. What are some important items that the project manager needs to consider in administering the contract?

    _____

    _____

    _____

    _____

Exercise 8.3: Creating a Statement of Work (SOW)

The objectives for Exercise 8.3 are:

- Justify the need for a statement of work (SOW).
- Understand the elements of an SOW.
- Practice creating parts of an SOW.

Background

The statement of work (SOW) is perhaps the single most important output from your project procurement management process. A well-written SOW can help you obtain the best product or service from your contractor. You need a SOW for each product or service that you are procuring for your project. The SOW may be derived from the scope statement and, if you are procuring the entire product or service, may actually be the same as the scope statement. Some people may call the SOW a scope statement, which we discussed in Chapter 1, or they may call it the scope of work and, in fact, the SOW is a scope statement focused on just the work required of the vendor. In procurement management, the SOW will be written for contractors to understand the expectations of the work you are requesting. The SOW often follows the same pattern of information the scope statement provides: objectives, description of the product or service, deliverables required, requirements or specifications, assumption and constraints, and time estimates. The only thing you may not provide is the cost estimate, because you usually expect the bidder to provide that. The SOW needs to be written well enough so the vendor knows whether he or she wants to bid on it and whether the vendor can actually provide the work. Vagueness sometimes leads to optimism by vendors—because it isn't clear, they think they can take on the work, and figure out how to handle it along the way. This could be very dangerous for your project.

As the project manager, it would be useful to get involved in the writing of the SOW as soon as possible, so you understand the scope and understand how you need to manage the work. Often, though, you may not be involved up front. Whenever you become involved, make sure you read and understand the SOW thoroughly. This may require reviews with both your team and the working members of the vendor to make sure everyone understands the requirements and expectations.

Once you have chosen a contractor, you may use the initial SOW you created for the bidding, or you may need to create a more detailed SOW for the contract. The closer you can get the SOW you create for the bidding to what you end up with in the contract, the closer your contract pricing and contract contents will be.

You or members of your project team may choose to write the SOW, but sometimes the vendor is better equipped to write it and you may just review it. It is important that the SOW be as clear and detailed as possible. If the vendor or the customer misunderstands any part of it, then disputes are more likely to occur. Initially, if the SOW is not well defined, the vendor may underbid, and if a poorly defined SOW is used in the contract, it may produce unpredictable results. For instance, if the SOW says the widget needs to slim and economical, the vendor could interpret this requirement as being as slim as a ruler and about $5 each, when you were thinking as slim as a measuring tape and about $3 each. At times, the work may simply need creativity and flexibility, so the SOW may focus more on the skills, attitude, and technical expertise of the vendor.

You may use a template, a checklist, or previous contracts to help you prepare a good SOW. The following are some major elements you need to consider in your SOW:

Roles and responsibilities   Make sure that it is clear who is doing what. You need to include who is taking the action and who is participating in reviews. If specific people are needed at certain meetings, or in particular roles, make sure it is clear. If you need the architect of the project in a technical review, make sure the SOW states that.

Security   Discuss any security specifications. Will the product or facilities need any specific security processes or procedures during production, transportation, and on delivery?

Location of work   Make sure you describe where the work needs to be done. Can the vendor work on its own premises, work at the project site, or maybe work in both places depending on the work itself or phase of the project? If there are different locations where the work must take place, put it in the SOW.

Milestones/deliverables   List all expected milestones and deliverables.

Quantities   Make sure you list quantities of everything needed. For instance, specify that you need one report that you can copy, or maybe you want the vendor to provide 15 copies. This may seem minor, but for a 750-page report, the difference can be hundreds of dollars.

Vendor payments   Include how the vendor will be paid or should invoice the work. Make sure it is clear how often payment occurs, what constitutes payment, and what constitutes final payment.

Progress reporting   Be specific about when and how you want the work's progress to be reviewed. For instance, state that you want a report every week showing schedule/budget, and that you want a monthly review meeting with the major vendor team members attending if you feel that is important for project success.

Testing   Describe the testing requirements for the work. You might indicate that you want an independent testing group, or that the vendor can provide the testing but needs to provide testing plans and results for your review.

Quality   Describe the quality required. You may describe that you will accept no more than a .05 percent error rate and leave it up to the vendor to provide that. Or you may require a major quality plan and processes.

Change control   Describe change control requirements, including a general description of the change process.

When you create requests for proposals, invitations to bids, or any procurement documents, always include the SOW. Without it, you might not get the kinds of bids that give you a clear understanding of the work the vendor can provide you.

In Exercise 8.3, you will help CCC create parts of a statement of work so that vendors will know the work they are required to do for CCC's first full-length feature film. You will help CCC understand whether descriptions of their SOW are specific enough for a vendor to bid on or perform their work.

Recommended Reading: Chapter 6, pp.227–228, and Chapter 9, pp.330–333, *PMP Project Management Professional Study Guide.*

Scenario

Recently, the Creative Cartoon Company (CCC) has obtained enough capital to create its first feature-length animated film based on its most recent short film, which won several major entertainment awards. CCC hired TPMP several months ago to help it improve project management processes, and now, because CCC has to subcontract some of the work to outside organizations in order to complete the film, the executives are asking you and your company, TPMP, to help them with their procurement management processes. For the new feature film they have decided that they will need outside services for sound production, an overseas cartoon firm to create background artwork, a marketing firm, and an animation software development firm to implement an idea that the producer has for advancing the animation industry to the next level. Marcus Manning is the producer of the film, tentatively titled, "Bouncing with Bob." He and the film's director, Sheila Wong, have high aspirations—they want the feature-length film to win an Oscar for best animated film, and they want their new animation idea to win a technical Oscar. They want you to help them create good vendor relationships, so that the vendors can help them create the best possible film.

Creating a Statement of Work (SOW)

1. Describe three elements in the SOW that you might recommend that CCC requires from the sound production company. Describe why they would be important in the SOW.

    _____

    _____

    _____

    _____

2. CCC has provided a description of the quality of work it expects from the marketing firm. It says, "marketing materials must be of the highest quality as expected in the entertainment industry." Will this be a good enough description of the quality? What might you do to improve this if you could?

    _____

    _____

    _____

    _____

3. What three elements of the SOW might you recommend as the most important for the animation software development firm? Why?

    _____

    _____

    _____

    _____

4. What are some of the deliverables that might be required in the SOW for the overseas contractors?

    _____

    _____

    _____

    _____

5. Since CCC has never done sound production before, how would you recommend that CCC create the SOW for the sound production vendor?

    _____

    _____

    _____

    _____

6. For the sound production and overseas artwork SOWs, describe any security considerations.

    _____

    _____

    _____

    _____

Exercise 8.4: Evaluating and Selecting the Vendor

The objectives for Exercise 8.4 are:

- Introduce evaluation criteria and why you need it.
- Describe how you use evaluation criteria in selecting a vendor.
- Practice creating and using evaluation criteria.

Background

If you are requesting a proposal or bid from a vendor for a complex product or service, your chances of getting what you want are dramatically increased if you have criteria to evaluate the vendors prior to creating the request for proposal, the invitation to bid, or any other kind of procurement document. You can write the requests focused on what is important to you, and you will be more objective when the proposals or bids are returned to you. You may choose to share the evaluation criteria with the vendors, or you may choose to use it for your internal evaluation processes only. The evaluation criteria may be subjective or objective. You may create the evaluation criteria using weighting factors and scoring to help you decide on what is more important to you. Note that if you are procuring a product or service that is well established on the market you may create this evaluation criteria, but in a simplified manner. For instance, the best price may be the only evaluation criteria you have.

When you plan evaluation criteria, first decide on the tools and techniques that you want to use. You may document this information in your procurement management plan as described in Exercise 8.2.

- What criteria are most important to you? Is quality, technical expertise, price, company experience, previous references, or the vendor's understanding your need most important? List each criterion and describe what you want the vendor to deliver for each.

- Decide if you are going to use an independent estimate for comparisons to the estimates you receive from the vendors. If you do not choose to use it, describe why or how you will be able to know if you have a fair estimate. If you choose to use an independent estimate, describe how you will obtain it and when. Don't forget to put it into your project plan and schedule.

- Document whether you will use a screening system. This means you will use some kind of minimum level of requirements or threshold you expect in the bid or proposal. For instance, you may only accept companies with a demonstrated annual profit because you do not want to take a chance on a start-up or floundering company. You will want to document what you are screening, and eliminate anyone not meeting the requirements immediately. You may or may not want to share this requirement within the request.

- If you decide to weight the criteria, create and document the numerical ratings for each criterion. Again, you may or may not choose to share these weighting factors with the vendors.

Your criteria should be specific to the product or service you are procuring, but the following lists some of the general evaluation criteria you might use:

- Does the vendor demonstrate the best value, lowest price, or some other price comparison advantage? Make sure you distinguish what is more important, and evaluate this for the overall life cycle of your project. Don't forget to include operations in the consideration.

- Does the vendor demonstrate an understanding of your expectations of the product and service, as well as how you expect the vendor to work with you during the project?

- Does the vendor clearly demonstrate the ability to carry out the technical or operational processes needed to perform the work? You will judge this on references, previous performance, skill sets of the employees within the organization assigned to the project, and any awards or technical achievements the vendor can demonstrate.

- Will your project team be able to work with the vendor management team? This criterion is sometimes overlooked. All other qualifications may look terrific, but the management itself might be difficult to work with, or the company processes for invoicing, status reporting, treatment of their employees, and documenting financial transactions may be lax or difficult to deal with. Sometimes contracts are rewarded solely for the relationships between the management personnel of each firm. Although the project manager may have to settle for this kind of decision, it is still important to document evaluation criteria to ensure that the vendor can fulfill the work and attempt to make sure that a bid or proposal is submitted by the vendor.

- Can the vendor fulfill the obligations of performing the work based on the vendor's financial capabilities? If you choose a vendor who is relying on your project to keep it afloat, you have a very large risk on hand if it has to lay off employees during the project.

The other evaluation criteria may be on a more personal level: In other words, is this vendor a good match for your organization's culture and personnel? You may also decide that the vendor needs to pass some face-to-face interviews to make sure your project team or organization feels comfortable with the vendor's team and its management methods despite how good the proposal or bid looks.

Once you have created these evaluation criteria in the planning processes of your project, you will then use them as in the executing process of source selection. Even if you have rigorous evaluation criteria, it is possible that once you receive the proposals, you may find that some vendors are strong candidates for criteria you did not think of or that are hard to measure, such as levels of creativity or reputation. You may decide that new criteria outweigh the criteria you thought were important.

In Exercise 8.4, you will help CCC create some evaluation criteria for a few of its contracts. You will work with Marcus and Sheila to help them determine what is most important for each criterion, and how to input it into their request for proposal as they start to understand what kind of help they need in creating their first full-length feature film.

Recommended Reading: Chapter 6, p. 228, and Chapter 9, pp. 332–335, *PMP Project Management Professional Study Guide.*

Scenario

Recently, the Creative Cartoon Company (CCC) has obtained enough capital to create its first feature-length animated film based on its most recent short film, which won several major entertainment awards. CCC hired TPMP several months ago to help it improve project management processes, and now, because CCC has to subcontract some of the work to outside organizations in order to complete the film, the executives are asking you and your company, TPMP, to help them with their procurement management processes. For the new feature film they have decided that they will need outside services for sound production, an overseas cartoon firm to create background artwork, a marketing firm, and an animation software development firm to implement an idea that the producer has for advancing the animation industry to the next level. Marcus Manning is the producer of the film, tentatively titled, "Bouncing with Bob." He and the film's director, Sheila Wong, have high aspirations—they want the feature-length film to win an Oscar for best animated film, and they want their new animation idea to win a technical Oscar. They want you to help them create good vendor relationships, so that the vendors can help them create the best possible film.

Evaluating and Selecting a Vendor

1.   List the five general evaluation criteria CCC should consider for each contract.

   _____

   _____

   _____

   _____

2.   You will help Marcus create criteria for the animation software development vendor. List four of the top criteria and rank them in importance.

   _____

   _____

   _____

   _____

3. You will help Marcus create criteria for the overseas artwork vendor. List four of the top criteria and rank them in importance.

    _____

    _____

    _____

    _____

4. Why should CCC create evaluation criteria before sending out the requests for proposals?

    _____

    _____

    _____

5. Marcus has a golfing buddy, Davis Neely, one of the co-owners of Thundering Sound Productions. Marcus would like Davis, whom he trusts and has worked with before, to receive the sound production contract. Would you recommend that Marcus still use evaluation criteria?

    _____

    _____

    _____

6. Would you recommend that CCC include its evaluation criteria in each RFP? Why or why not?

    _____

    _____

    _____

    _____

Exercise 8.5: Creating the Contract

The objectives for Exercise 8.5 are:

- Introduce concepts for creating a contract.
- Introduce the parts of a contract.
- Discuss some of the most important parts of a contract.
- Practice understanding how to create parts of a contract.

Background

Once you finally select your vendor, you will need to create the contract so you and your vendor can work together productively. You will start by using templates of your organization's contracts or previous contracts as a basis, collecting the requirements you must include in the contract, and then working with the lawyers and the procurement department (if you have one) to put the contract together. If you need to move more quickly than this process usually takes, you may start the work through a temporary agreement, such as a memorandum of agreement or a time and materials contract.

You may also participate in or have input into negotiations of the contract. It will be in your best interest to get involved early so you can influence the content and quality of the contract. The negotiations can be a prelude to a very good relationship if you go into it with the attitude of creating a good relationship, creating mutually beneficial agreements with enough detail to be unambiguous, and protections for each party. It can be a difficult and arduous task if the negotiation process is not well managed, confrontational, or vague. In such a case, once the contract is signed, it can then end up being a difficult relationship and contract to manage. If there is any way you can help influence the attitude and expertise required for the contract negotiations, try to do so, but often it is out of your hands.

You may not understand some of the language in the contract, and maybe are even frustrated by it, but it is important that you take the time to try to understand the contract, provide as much input to it and then manage it based on your detailed understanding of the work required. The contract explains how you need to manage the contractor, the contractor's work, and your mutual processes so you will need to know those details.

The contract should include the following content details. The information may not reside in sections exactly as stated, but the information should be included somewhere in the contract.

Definitions   Define all the technical terms and other terms particular to the contract to indicate agreement on what is meant for the parties. This is not like a glossary—both parties need to understand the definitions and agree on them.

Scope/statement of work   Description of work or work product you expect from the vendor. You might use the SOW that was in the proposal as a basis, but you will need to review and rewrite the SOW as necessary, based on more current knowledge and any details discovered between the vendor solicitation and contract award.

Roles and responsibilities   Description of who does the work, approves the work, administers the contract, and manages the processes described in it. This also might include who supplies the equipment and facilities.

Technical specifications and deliverables   Provides specific measurements, specifications, and other technical requirements, as well as details all deliverables due for the vendor's work. This might include detailed service level agreements for operations.

Interpretation of requirements   Gives the order of precedence (the order of what is most important) for the project requirements.

Schedule   States the general dates for the milestones or deliverables expected from the vendor.

Quality assurance/control   Describes the inspections or audits expected. This section might include detailed service level agreements as well as scorecard or testing quality expectations.

Warranty/guarantee   Specifies how long the product is expected to last (e.g., guaranteed for five years after acceptance) or an expectation of meeting a particular standard. This section might include express warranties for equipment, workmanship, performance or process, and design. Another warranty to consider is the implied warranty by the seller that what the seller provides is marketable and can be used by the buyer. This is one of those legal agreements that does not have to be written, but which the courts would accept as a good faith agreement.

Contract administration   Describes the processes, time frames, and escalations for contract administration, including the change control procedures.

Price and terms of payment   Includes price information and a schedule of invoicing and payments, including the processes for doing so.

Laws, regulations, and taxes that might apply   Any legal regulations or restrictions specific to your state or project for administering the project. The lawyers would probably create this section. Similarly, an accountant should probably help determine what taxes will be involved.

Provisions   Includes general and special terms and conditions negotiated with the vendor. Lawyers would create this section. It might include incentive/award fee provisions to optimize performance. It might also include who owns what parts of the product or service, especially when it comes to the results of the work, the data involved, or intellectual property.

Provisions for early termination   Describes how the contract would be dissolved and any work produced or payments would be distributed, if for some reason the vendor or buyer cannot fulfill the contract.

Liabilities and insurance   Describes liability if the project or product is disrupted, is delayed, or fails. You should take into consideration damages and indemnity of the vendor or buyer as well as force majeure (acts of God), and the results expected if there are any delays due to natural causes or accidents. Plus, as protection, you should know your insurance needs, such as liability and general business insurance required for worker protection or property damage.

Confidentiality, privacy, and security   Describes confidentiality requirements. You need to determine how you will handle confidential information if the company does not already have a policy.

Employee recruiting   Provisions protecting each party from raiding each other's employees until after a certain time period.

Disputes   Escalations, arbitration, and other ways to settle disputes and the time frames and order in which the escalations should be instigated.

Contract completion   Indicates when the contract is up, which may not be the same as when the product of service is finally delivered. The contract may cover several SOWs, or may be extended for new work. But the contract itself might have an eventual end date. Closure should also center on formal acceptance of all deliverables and formal closure of the contract.

In administering the contract, whether you were part of the negotiations or not, you need to know all the parts of the contract and create project procedures to abide by the terms. A good habit for each contract you manage is to study each major section in detail, and in your own words, write what the contract is stating. This is a lot of work, but will help you in the long run. You can share the important parts of the contract with your team members, so they understand any of its implications as well and how they need to work with the contractor and review the contractor's work. You might suggest that you review the contract with the contractor's team as well. Since you are managing the project, you need to ensure that the work of the vendor contributes to the success of the project and that all team members understand their contractual obligations.

In Exercise 8.5, you will help CCC think about how it needs to approach various contract negotiations, and what might be included in parts of the contracts for vendors as CCC starts it's first full-length animation feature film production.

Recommended Reading: Chapter 9, pp.333–339, *PMP Project Management Professional Study Guide.*

Scenario

Recently, the Creative Cartoon Company (CCC) has obtained enough capital to create its first feature-length animated film based on its most recent short film, which won several major entertainment awards. CCC hired TPMP several months ago to help it improve project management processes, and now, because CCC has to subcontract some of the work to outside organizations in order to complete the film, the executives are asking you and your company, TPMP, to help them with their procurement management processes. For the new feature film they have decided that they will need outside services for sound production, an overseas cartoon firm to create background artwork, a marketing firm, and an animation software development firm to implement an idea that the producer has for advancing the animation industry to the next level. Marcus Manning is the producer of the film, tentatively titled, "Bouncing with Bob." He and the film's director, Sheila Wong, have high aspirations—they want the feature-length film to win an Oscar for best animated film, and they want their new animation idea to win a technical Oscar. They want you to help them create good vendor relationships, so that the vendors can help them create the best possible film.

Creating the Contract

1. What might be some specific warranties or guarantees you would recommend that CCC include in its contract for the artwork and sound production vendors?

    _____

    _____

    _____

    _____

2. What kind of insurance might CCC request from the marketing and software development vendor contracts?

    _____

    _____

    _____

    _____

3. What change control might you recommend be included in the contract?

    _____

    _____

    _____

4. How would you recommend that CCC approach the negotiations for the software development vendor contract?

    _____

    _____

    _____

    _____

5. How would you suggest CCC train its team members to work with the contractors and the contract?

    _____

    _____

    _____

    _____

Answers to Exercise Questions

Answers to Exercise 8.1

Your answers may be somewhat different, but the following answers provide a guide.

1. To motivate the marketing company to create a great marketing campaign for CCC's film, Marcus might decide to use a fixed fee plus incentive contract. Film marketing is a fairly common service, and so the scope is well understood and a fixed fee would be appropriate. However, if Marcus would like the marketing firm to go above and beyond, perhaps an incentive bonus based on a independent market awareness survey or a target for first week box office returns would help provide an incentive for the marketing firm.

2. You and Marcus have decided that you would like to try a time and materials contract for the overseas contractor. To implement this, CCC and the overseas company would create a fixed unit price for each of the art positions needed, such as senior artist and junior artist. However, the work itself to deliver certain sections of the backgrounds would be based on how long it would take to produce them to the level of quality Marcus and Sheila expect. At this time, CCC is uncertain of how long that would take, and it is possible it may need other kinds of artwork from the firm they hire.

3. The riskiest type of contract for CCC is the cost reimbursable contract. The fixed price contract is the riskiest type of contract for the contractor.

4. You might recommend a fixed fee contract for the sound production company. The scope of the work is well known for sound production and though the technical expectations for the animation portion of "Bouncing with Bob" are high, the sound can be of the same quality level as most of the major animated features on the market.

5. Marcus and you, after discussing the uncertainty of the idea for the animation software development, might decide that a cost reimbursable contract is the only kind that a good company will take on for such a new and risky technical advancement. You might recommend that CCC include an incentive to the firm it hires. CCC might award the development firm with a percentage of the film's profit if the new technical advancement wins an Oscar or other technical award. CCC might also consider a contract that sets the foundation for a joint partnership for profiting from the new animation advancement if it is successful.

Answers to Exercise 8.2

Your answers may be somewhat different, but the following answers provide a guide.

1. Marcus needs to manage the sound production, overseas production company, and software development firm together with the overall schedule and team status. Each vendor will have deliverables that need to be on schedule and with a quality that matches the rest of the production. Sheila may need to create a schedule in which parts of the deliverables are provided at certain audit checkpoints, with the entire project team gathering to review quality and progress. Marcus might manage the marketing firm completely separately. He might provide some of the film's scenes for input to the marketing plan. It would be important to treat the vendors as team members, so that their work synchs with the rest of the film.

2. You might recommend that Marcus use a request for proposal (RFP) to lay out the requirements and bids from sound production vendors as part of the procurement processes for the sound production contract. CCC should use evaluation criteria to help define the quality and expectations of the sound production company. Marcus might decide to solicit bids via advertisements in film industry and animation publication magazines. The technical division of CCC should evaluate the bids based on the evaluation criteria.

3. The evaluation criteria CCC will use for two of the four contracts, the criteria for the project, and whether CCC should obtain some independent estimates are included below. Explanations are given for each.

Sound production   Yes, CCC should use evaluation criteria. CCC might focus evaluation criteria on quality, previous experience especially on animated films, and price. CCC should be able to obtain an estimate without an independent estimate based on previous similar jobs.

Marketing firm   Yes, CCC should use evaluation criteria. CCC might focus evaluation criteria on successful campaigns in the past and creative capabilities. CCC might request an independent estimate for the work, or use previous industry productions to decide if the bids are fair.

Overseas art contractor   CCC may choose not to use evaluation criteria for this time and materials contract. They may choose to go with the best bid based on comparing prices from various firms and recommendations from other industry peers. They would not need an independent estimate.

Software development firm   CCC may choose to use evaluation criteria based on the creative capabilities of the software firm, and their willingness to take risks and put some of their own "skin in the game." They may want to see previous experience, but also base criteria on the skills base of the vendor's employees. An accurate estimate based on an independent company's work might be difficult to obtain since the new animation idea has never been tried before.

4.   The following describes what closeout would constitute for each contract. You might recommend to CCC that closeout should consist of a lessons learned document or audit of each contract as well as what is described below.

Sound production   Closeout would be a technical review of the completed film and positive preview audience reaction for the technical sound qualities of the product. Final payment would be provided during the film's release week.

Marketing firm   Closeout would be when the final deliverable is made for the marketing plan. This might consist of the results of a marketing survey, or a calculation of the target box office receipts versus actual box office receipts. Payment would occur when the last deliverable is made and when all terms of the contract have been fulfilled.

Overseas art contractor   Closeout would be when the final artwork is delivered, possibly after the first few audience previews show the work is satisfactory. Payment would be made, however, when the last of the artwork is delivered for integrating with the film and the director/editor have approved the work. If more work is required after the audience preview, an extension to the contract might be required.

Software development firm   Closeout would be when the animation software is at the level of quality to make the animation in the film appear to work seamlessly. Final payment would be made after the preview audience gives the film a positive review.

5.   Marcus, Sheila, and appropriate technical subject matter experts from CCC should be involved in the negotiations for the three technical contracts. The marketing contract may need just Marcus and Sheila involved, with a lawyer who is an expert in marketing contracts. In all cases, the procurement department of CCC and lawyers with particular industry expertise should be involved.

6. Sheila and Marcus need to consider the vendor relationships in administering the contracts and making sure those administration considerations are well detailed in the contract. This might involve creating a contract that ensures regular status reporting and meetings, and a good change control process that everyone is trained on and understands. CCC should consider some kind of continuous improvement meetings to work on correcting issues with the vendors. CCC might also consider bringing the vendors in on major team meetings and perhaps a few celebrations after major deliverable completions, to make sure they feel a part of the film team.

Answers to Exercise 8.3

Your answers may be somewhat different, but the following answers provide a guide.

1. You might recommend that the following three elements in the SOW be addressed for the sound production company:

   Quality   CCC would need to be very specific about the quality, based on measurable and technical production objectives. This will help the vendor understand the equipment it needs to provide and the expertise of the people needed for the work. CCC may need to describe that high quality is not needed for some phases, while for the final edit top quality is needed, as measured by an independent technical auditor.

   Concise requirements/specifications   CCC would need to be very specific about the requirements, such as when sound production is needed for what deliverables. For instance, will sound production need to be delivered for the storyboards, when proofs are created, or when the animation is three-fourths complete? This is necessary for the sound production vendor to lay out the total scope and schedule of its own project.

   Where the work should be done/location of deliverables   It might be important to indicate that the initial work can be done at the sound production company's site, but that during production and post-production, the sound production team may need to be on-site at the animation studio. This will affect the costs, equipment used, and people involved for the vendor.

2. CCC needs to improve the description of quality for the marketing firm to be more objective. One way to do it is to require a deliverable that the marketing company must conduct a survey after a marketing preview and ask the audience specific questions about the production's quality. CCC might also request an independent review of all of the written materials or a focus group to help demonstrate quality levels.

3. The three most important elements of the SOW for the animation software development firm may be:

   Security   Since this is a proprietary project that CCC is hoping will achieve a new animation technology, CCC might require a high level of security and confidentiality. This is important, because the animation vendor not only will need to educate employees to keep work confidential, but may also need to hire special security for delivering trial software.

Quality   CCC would need to be very specific about the quality of the final software product. It might state something like "based on a survey of a typical audience, 98 percent of the survey participants finds the technology to appear 'real looking'." The vendor might need to build a schedule in which the vendor has expert reviews often and audience surveys at appropriate milestones as the animation software is developed.

Roles and responsibilities   CCC may require a lead systems engineer to work with the CCC technical folks in weekly meetings, and the vendor project manager to report at status meetings every two weeks.

 It will be difficult to provide precise requirements. Since this is a new product, the requirements might describe the need for the vendor's flexibility and technical creativity to help solve difficult programming issues.

4.   Some of the deliverables that may be required in the SOW for the overseas contractors could be samples of proposed background styles and colors for CCC to review and approve, draft background artwork based on initial storyboards, final backgrounds, and revised backgrounds after animation is added. Deliverables also might include status reports and art reviews.

5.   Since CCC has never done sound production before, you might recommend that it actually have the leading sound production vendor candidates write the SOW. CCC may send out a request for proposal with a requirement that the sound production company would need to write the SOW and deliver it with the proposal.

6.   For the sound production vendor, CCC may require vendor employees to sign confidentiality statements and perform background checks of employees to make sure they have never divulged secrets on previous assignments. For the overseas artwork vendor, CCC may require the proofs to be sent via secure mail or e-mail services. However, since the art backgrounds may give little away about the movie itself, the security may not need be too strict.

Answers to Exercise 8.4

Your answers may be somewhat different, but the following answers provide a guide.

1.   The five general evaluation criteria CCC should consider for its contracts are competitive pricing and value, vendor understanding of expectations, capability of vendor to carry out technical or operational work, vendor management team fit, and financial capabilities.

2.   The top four evaluation criteria for the animation software development vendor might be technical capability including expertise of personnel, understanding of need (showing flexibility to work with CCC and its new idea), management team fit, and financial capability. The price of the contract is probably one of the least important evaluation criteria for CCC.

3.   The top four evaluation criteria for the overseas artwork vendor might be price, since one of the reasons CCC is sending artwork production overseas is to save money, technical and

operational capability of the vendor to ensure the vendor has the skills to create the artwork, financial capability, and understanding of need. Since the deliverables may be well defined, the management philosophy won't be as important to CCC.

4. The CCC procurement team should create evaluation criteria before sending out the requests for proposals so that they can focus on the specific requirements needed. For instance, since price is the most important aspect of the overseas artwork, CCC can emphasize that the best price with the highest demonstration of technical ability will win over other proposals. That way, the vendors can put together proposals that focus on demonstrating those capabilities. Even if CCC does not include the evaluation criteria in the procurement documents for the vendors, CCC can at least write them with more focus and clarity.

5. Marcus should still use evaluation criteria for the Thundering Sound Productions company. Even though Marcus may have good judgment about his buddy, it will help both CCC and Thundering Sound Productions to make sure that each can fulfill the contract. It will also help the teams create a more robust SOW and eventually, a better contract.

6. You might advise that CCC do the following in sharing the evaluation criteria for each RFP:

    Sound production   Yes, it's important that each criterion is met.

    Overseas artwork   Yes, it's important they understand that the price and technical capability are some of the most important aspects. Showing creativity is not important, so the vendor won't waste time trying to be different from everyone else.

    Marketing firm   Possibly, to make sure the vendor demonstrates a proposal that includes the quality it will provide. CCC might find an advantage to judging the vendor more on the merit of the vendor's own creative ideas, rather than too much direction from CCC.

    Animation software development   Perhaps not. Since CCC wants to build a good relationship with the vendor, it might be important for the proposal to demonstrate some of the creativity and flexibility without CCC hinting that is what is needed. CCC might want to see some independent thinking and for the management philosophy to reveal itself in the proposal itself.

Answers to Exercise 8.5

Your answers may be somewhat different, but the following answers provide a guide.

1. For the artwork vendor, you might recommend that CCC request a warranty/guarantee around the design and workmanship of the artwork. It might include some kind of money-back offer if the work delivered has to be redone more than two times due to quality issues (for instance, the vendor not using agreed-on color selections or not following requirements). For the sound production, CCC might request a warranty/guarantee around the process and workmanship of the sound. If the sound company does not satisfy required sound performance standards that CCC stipulates in the contract, then CCC might request money back if the sound production vendor cannot make it right within a certain time frame.

2. For all vendors, CCC would want to include insurance for indirect losses due to contractor problems. For the marketing vendor, you might recommend that CCC include liability insurance in case any of the marketing material creates lawsuits from offended readers or viewers. For the software development vendor, you might recommend that CCC ensures that the vendor has insurance for key employee loss or liability for poor product design or failure. CCC might also require the normal insurance for fire and other property damage as well, in case damage would occur to the software vendor's work. CCC may want to expressly state in the contract that the vendor must have the business insurance to help recover possible losses that CCC could have due to the contractor's problems.

3. You might recommend that CCC provide a general change control process description, including turnaround times for changes, limiting how long a vendor can have a change in process. You might also include who must approve what according to schedule or budget changes they could produce. CCC might also stipulate and include in an addendum the change form and log that must be used by both parties to manage and track change. This cannot be overstated. By putting it in the contract, it will be much harder for either group to make changes that can make the budget or schedule get out of hand.

4. The CCC procurement team should approach the software development negotiations by making sure they have a well-managed approach. Since the work itself is not well defined, and CCC wants to create a good relationship with the vendor for possible joint selling of the product, the negotiation should be a forum to create the good relationship and mutually beneficial agreements. CCC might ensure that meetings and statuses are required in the contract administration to help systemize the communication that needs to take place between the companies.

5. You might suggest that the CCC project manager review each part of the contract with the CCC team, so that each team member understands what they can and can't do and what is expected in the relationship. For instance, rather than the CCC project manager describing the change control processes to the team members and giving them the form, it would be best to discuss what is actually in the contract, so that the team understands that the processes are not just good business but contractual. The CCC project manager may want to do the same thing with the vendor's team, with the agreement of the vendor, so that everyone has a common understanding of the important obligations.

Chapter

9

Project Integration and Professional Responsibility

THE EXERCISES PRESENTED IN THIS CHAPTER INCLUDE:

✓ Exercise 9.1: Creating the Project Plan

✓ Exercise 9.2: Executing the Project

✓ Exercise 9.3: Change Control

✓ Exercise 9.4: Organizational Structure

✓ Exercise 9.5: Professional Responsibility

Project integration and professional responsibility are some overarching processes and concepts in project management. Creating the project plan is actually done after you have completed all the other planning activities that were discussed in this workbook, such as scope planning, schedule development, or planning for quality. The project plan is the written document that describes these plans, and may refer to the actual planning documents you created in the other planning activities. Executing the project puts your project plan into action. You monitor your results, and take any course corrections to get the project back on track. Sometimes you may even decide you can change course, based on what you learn from performing the planned work. Change control lays out the systems, processes, and documentation you will use to manage the changes that are inevitable on a project. During all phases of your project, the organizational structure influences how much authority and action you can take on your project. Understanding how that structure affects your ability to get things done helps you understand your project management role. Last, professional responsibility describes your ethical obligations and educational growth responsibilities to the project management profession. You may practice every portion of project management impeccably, but if you do not practice it with the best ethical intentions, then you probably will have only short-term success as a project manager. It is important to understand what the Project Management Institute expects from you as a project manager. These processes bring all the other processes together as an umbrella function of project management.

Project Integration Management is covered in the Planning, Executing and Controlling process groups objectives of the PMP exam.

Exercise 9.1: Creating the Project Plan

The objectives for Exercise 9.1 are:

- Describe the project planning process.
- Understand when the project plan is created.
- Describe typical components of a project plan.

Background

There is a point in time on a project when you have completed the planning and are ready to start executing the plan. This point is when one of the project integration management processes—project plan development—is performed. Project plan development takes all the information created in the previous planning processes and integrates it into one comprehensive document that will serve as a guide during project execution and control. This document usually has the formal approval of the project stakeholders. The previous planning processes we described (in earlier chapters) are the processes performed in the other eight knowledge areas. These are processes such as scope planning, schedule development, cost budgeting, quality planning, staff acquisition, communications planning, risk management planning, and procurement planning. There are 21 total planning processes that are incorporated into the project plan.

If the project plan is a comprehensive document that guides you in project execution and control, then what should it contain? In this exercise, we examine the most common components of a typical project plan.

Components of a Project Plan

There are eight common components of a typical project plan: project charter, scope statement, work breakdown structure, project schedule, resource assignments, project costs, risks, and other management plans.

Project charter   The project charter was created during the project initiating process covered in Exercise 1.3. The charter is the formal authorization to start a project. It should be included in the project plan so the original purpose of the project is understood during the life of the project.

Scope statement   The scope statement describes the work that must be done in order to deliver the product of the project. It will cover what features must be included and, in some cases, it will cover what the product must not do. We examined the scope statement in Exercise 1.4. The scope statement is placed in the project plan as a reminder of the features and functionality that must be created.

Work breakdown structure   The WBS, as described in Exercise 2.1, is a tool and technique used to decompose project scope components into smaller and more manageable components or work packages. Its inclusion into the project plan allows the project team to have a reference for the original thinking of what work needed to be accomplished on the project.

Project schedule   The project schedule is created during the schedule development process of the planning phase of a project. It is created with some of the tools and techniques described in Exercises 2.4 and 2.6 on calculating critical path and duration compression. The schedule is documented in the project plan so the project team understands the sequence of the work that must be done. This project schedule should also include all of the major milestones and deliverables for the project.

Resource assignments   Resource assignments need to be included in the project plan so team members understand exactly the work that they are required to do. The resource assignments can be depicted using a resource assignment matrix that was covered in Exercise 5.2.

Project costs   The different elements of project costs should be included in the project plan. Because the project plan usually has a formal approval process, including the costs acts as another guarantee that project funds will be available. The costs that should be included are order of magnitude estimates, budget estimates, and work estimates for each resource. These estimates were covered in Exercise 3.2.

Risks   A section on risks should be included in your project plan. This section will be updated as new risks are identified, quantified, and risk responses are created. The handling of risks was described in Chapter 7.

Other management plans   Through the course of this book, you have had many opportunities to explore management plans, for example, scope management plan in Exercise 1.5 and quality management plan in Exercise 4.1. You may find it necessary to include portions of your management plans in your project plan. Remember this project plan serves as a guide for the project during the execution and control phases. Therefore, you will need to determine which sections should be included to guarantee the objectives of the project.

Be sure to include any other documentation in your project plan that will guide the project to successful completion. This document should act as a litmus test for project personnel when they are in doubt about what to do.

In Exercise 9.1, you will exercise your knowledge about creating a project plan as you help the Sensational Advertisement Productions company create a project plan for their advertising campaign for a new cell phone service.

Recommended Reading: Chapter 7, pp. 266–269, *PMP Project Management Professional Study Guide.*

Scenario

TPMP have brought project management processes to an advertising firm, Sensational Advertisement Productions (SAP), and the project managers at SAP are learning how to use the eight knowledge areas of scope, time, cost, quality, human resource, communications, risk, and procurement management. However, you need to help them start using the processes and tools of what is probably their most important function: integration management. You are working with Pam Rosenbaum, who has been assigned account management functions for a telecommunications client's important new product: a new cell phone that integrates normal service with PDA functions right on the phone, which will be sold at a competitive price with normal cell phone services. The account has several project managers for the various sales campaigns: Michael Harland for the print campaigns, Judy Arakawa for the TV campaigns, and Joseph Matumbo for the telemarketing campaigns. Each project manager is working with marketing managers within the telecommunications company to get direction and approval for the work they will produce.

Because these projects must integrate, and a change in one campaign could affect the other, Pam knows she must create an integrated project plan. Even though the telecommunications company is putting a lot of money into the campaign, SAP still has a tight budget for all its advertising. You will help Pam put together an integrated project plan that guides the work for both SAP and its client.

Creating the Project Plan

1. When is a project plan created?

    _____
    _____
    _____
    _____

2. Describe the project planning process.

    _____
    _____
    _____
    _____

3. Pam is working on the cost portion of the project plan. How should she describe the costs in the project plan?

    _____
    _____
    _____
    _____

4. Name three sections that Pam should include in her project plan.

    _____
    _____
    _____
    _____

Exercise 9.2: Executing the Project

The objectives for Exercise 9.2 are:

- Describe four major inputs into the project executing process.
- Describe the executing processes that are integrated into project plan execution.
- Describe the tools and techniques of project plan execution.

Background

It's show time! You have planned a flawless project and you have baselined the schedule and the budget. Now it's time to start working the plan you have created. At this point in time, you have created your project plan, you understand the organizational policies of your company, and you understand strategies of corrective action and preventive action. With these inputs, you now execute the plan.

Project execution is part of the integration management knowledge area. During this process, you will integrate the other executing processes such as quality assurance, team development, information distribution, and contract administration.

This phase of the project will exercise all of your talents as a project manager. The tools and techniques used in this phase are critical to your success. In this exercise we will spend some time on each of the tools and techniques used to execute the project to successful completion.

Project Plan Execution Tools and Techniques

The five tools and techniques used to successfully execute the project are general management skills, product skills and knowledge, work authorization system, status review meetings, and project management information systems.

General management skills   There are hundreds of books that describe general management skills. These skills cover communication, managing, and team development, among other things. The project manager will utilize all of these skills and more during project plan execution.

Product skills and knowledge   As you execute the project, you will find that the team's knowledge and expertise in developing the product of the project is critical to the success of the project. You will want to monitor this level of expertise and train and retrain your team accordingly.

Work authorization system (WAS)   In order to begin execution of your project, approval is given for a specific team member to begin working on a task. A WAS can be set up very formally or informally. The key is setting it up prior to the work commencing. This system gives the project manager the ability to control the sequence of tasks. It also allows the project manager to stop work that is not planned or is out of scope.

Status review meetings   A status review meeting is any meeting that is conducted to examine the progress of the project. The project manager should set the frequency of the meetings depending on the need for review. Some project managers gather task progress at this meeting and therefore the frequency needs to be set often enough so the project manager has knowledge of potential slippage. A possible litmus test for this frequency is how long a project manager can go without knowing something is not proceeding as planned and still feel comfortable.

Project management information systems (PMIS)   A PMIS is any manual or mechanized tool that helps the project manager collect, analyze, and integrate information about the project.

Outputs of the project execution process are work results and change requests. Using these tools and techniques effectively produces deliverables that enables the project manager to deliver the objectives of the projects as chartered.

In Exercise 9.2, you will test your knowledge about executing the project plan as you help the Sensational Advertisement Productions company.

Recommended Reading: Chapter 8, pp. 289–294, *PMP Project Management Professional Study Guide.*

Scenario

TPMP have brought project management processes to an advertising firm, Sensational Advertisement Productions (SAP), and the project managers at SAP are learning how to use the eight knowledge areas of scope, time, cost, quality, human resource, communications, risk, and procurement management. However, you need to help them start using the processes and tools of what is probably their most important function: integration management. You are working with Pam Rosenbaum, who has been assigned account management functions for a telecommunications client's important new product: a new cell phone that integrates normal service with PDA functions right on the phone, which will be sold at a competitive price with normal cell phone services. The account has several project managers for the various sales campaigns: Michael Harland for the print campaigns, Judy Arakawa for the TV campaigns, and Joseph Matumbo for the telemarketing campaigns. Each project manager is working with marketing managers within the telecommunications company to get direction and approval for the work they will produce.

Because these projects must integrate, Pam has created one integrated project plan. She now knows that she must execute this integrated project plan.

Executing the Project

1. What are four inputs for project plan execution?

    _____

    _____

    _____

    _____

2. What are some of the executing processes that are integrated into project plan execution?

    _____

    _____

    _____

    _____

3. Pam has found that some tasks are being done out of sequence on the project. She also has found work done that is out of scope. What tool and technique of project plan execution needs to be put into place?

    _____

4. Pam uses spreadsheet software to prepare task assignments. This spreadsheet software is also known as what general project management term?

    _____

    _____

5. Pam is having difficulty getting the right information to her project team. What general management skills should Pam use more effectively?

    _____

    _____

6. What are the two outputs of the project plan execution process?

    _____

    _____

Exercise 9.3: Change Control

The objectives for Exercise 9.3 are:

- Introduce concepts for integrated project change control.
- Understand why change control is important.
- Practice creating change control procedures.

Background

One of the most common problems that project managers complain about on their projects is how changes affect their projects, either drastically inflating, extending, or reducing their original scope, schedule, budget, or quality plan. Any change to the original project plan that the client requests or team members decide to implement, can change any number of factors on the project. Although change is inevitable, and even welcome, if appropriate, in order for the project to stay under control, one of your main jobs is to help the team learn how to recognize and manage change and to create good change control processes. You might use or establish systems to help manage the change, and you should create processes and change forms that all of your team members understand and use.

First and one of the most important things you must do is to baseline your project plan. That is, you need to set a stake in the ground that declares the project's scope, budget, schedule, and quality. This needs to be reviewed and approved by your project stakeholders. Second, you need to identify the process for project changes. You need to take into consideration:

- How does someone request a change and who can request a change?

- Where does the request go and how is it documented? What is the system you will use to record and archive your changes?

- How is change analyzed and reviewed?

- What constitutes a change that must be made and how should changes be prioritized?

- Who approves the request? Will you have meetings to manage change within your team and will you also have a configuration control board (also known as a change control board in some organizations) to approve the changes? Does the PM have the authority to approve change that can be handled within the current schedule and budget, or will all changes need to be managed and approved by the change board?

- How is change implemented if approved and what happens if it is not? How will you communicate the changes to project stakeholders?

- How will you monitor the project to ensure no unapproved changes are implemented into the project?

During development of the change process, you also need to document what kind of data you must capture to help you organize and make decisions about the change requests. The following lists some of the data you need to capture for a change request. Some of the data can be recorded immediately, but much of it cannot be determined until analysis.

- Request description (short title and longer description)

- Date request opened and date that the requestor would like to see the change implemented

- Originator and information about how to contact them

- Justification for change

- Change request number (must be assigned via a change control process and should never change)

- Status of the change (for instance, has it just been opened, is it in review, has it been approved, or has it been implemented?)

- Priority (high, medium, low)

- Analysis, which might include the following items:
  - Alternatives or trade-offs
  - How functionality is affected
  - Cost and work estimates to implement

- Risks to project and impacts to quality, scope, budget, and schedule
- Plans to implement change (including what must be changed, such as requirements, project schedule, scope statement, or test plan updates) and date the change can actually be implemented
- Dependent project impacts
- Approval, denial, modifications, and short reason for each
- Sign-offs

To manage this process, you need a log that briefly describes the change request and refers to the change request ID you have established so someone can find the change request easily. The log should include information about the status of the change, and the final disposition of the change. You might use a mechanized change request system, or may keep a log and notebooks to house the changes. You might even use both methods for ease of use. If you establish and document your change processes, your project has a much better chance of success and you will manage change instead of change managing you and your team.

In Exercise 9.3, you will practice change control processes as you help the Sensational Advertisement Productions company create a system for its advertising campaign for the new cell phone service. You will help the account manager learn how to implement change control processes and documentation for all the project managers on her account's projects.

Recommended Reading: Chapter 10, pp. 367–372, *PMP Project Management Professional Study Guide.*

Scenario

TPMP have brought project management processes to an advertising firm, Sensational Advertisement Productions (SAP), and the project managers at SAP are learning how to use the eight knowledge areas of scope, time, cost, quality, human resource, communications, risk, and procurement management. However, you need to help them start using the processes and tools of what is probably their most important function: integration management. You are working with Pam Rosenbaum, who has been assigned account management functions for a telecommunications client's important new product: a new cell phone that integrates normal service with PDA functions right on the phone, which will be sold at a competitive price with normal cell phone services. The account has several project managers for the various sales campaigns: Michael Harland for the print campaigns, Judy Arakawa for the TV campaigns, and Joseph Matumbo for the telemarketing campaigns. Each project manager is working with marketing managers within the telecommunications company to get direction and approval for the work they will produce.

Because these projects must integrate, and a change in one campaign could affect the other, Pam knows she must create a change control process for the overall account, as well as for each individual project. Even though the telecommunications company is putting a lot of money into the campaign, SAP still has a tight budget for all their advertising. You will help Pam put together an integrated change control process that works for both SAP and their client.

Practicing Change Control

1. What is one of the first steps that you will tell Pam to perform to create a change control process?

   _____

   _____

   _____

   _____

2. What kinds of analysis should be performed on the change requests that Pam and her project managers receive?

   _____

   _____

   _____

   _____

3. Joseph has baselined his project plan, and received approval from his client, Bessie Phillips. Days later, Bessie comes to him saying that the president of the company has come up with an idea that must be implemented: they need to add a survey where the telemarketers call customers to ask them to participate in a survey. After the customer answers the survey questions, the telemarketer will try to sell them this cell phone. What should Joseph do?

   _____

   _____

   _____

   _____

4. Why will you recommend that Pam create a change log for the change requests?

   _____

   _____

   _____

   _____

5. Should each project have a separate log and its own change request management?

_____

_____

_____

_____

6. Who should be on the configuration change board?

_____

_____

_____

_____

Exercise 9.4: Organizational Structure

The objectives for Exercise 9.4 are:

- Describe the three major types of organization structures.
- Describe the authority level of project managers in each organization.
- Describe the three levels of matrix organizations.

Background

An area of potential conflict on projects is the way the organization is structured. Different structures create different challenges. This exercise will examine the types of organization structures and their impact on a project manager's ability to execute the project.

There are three major types of organizational structures: projectized, matrix, and functional. Each type of structure will influence the project manager's authority, how resources are committed to the project, and the administrative help available to the project manager. A project manager may have more or less power depending on how the organization is structured.

Projectized organizations   A projectized organization is organized around project management. These organizations have realized that organizing around project management allows it to focus on its primary objective—delivery of projects to realize the corporation's goals. Projectized organizations provide complete authority to its project managers and usually provide administrative support. Personnel assigned to a project are usually committed on a full-time basis. There is very little dotted line reporting in these types of organizations. Figure 9.1 depicts an organization chart for a projectized organization.

FIGURE 9.1   Projectized organization

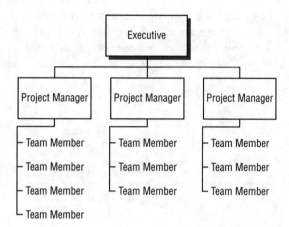

Functional organizations   A functional organization has been established to perform certain functions, such as sales, marketing, or accounting. A functional organization will perform projects but the projects are sometimes confined to a functional area. If projects cross functional boundaries, project managers are challenged to find and keep resources and executive support. Most people believe that a project manager has little or no authority in a functional organization. Figure 9.2 depicts a functional organization chart.

FIGURE 9.2   Functional organization

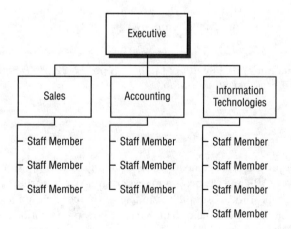

Matrix organizations   Matrix organizations use components of both functional and projectized organizations. There are three levels of progression in a matrix organization that correspond to how projectized or functional the organization is structured. These levels are a weak matrix, balanced matrix, and strong matrix, with strong matrix being very close to a projectized organization. The authority level of the project manager will also vary according to how weak or strong the matrixed organization is. Figure 9.3 depicts a balanced matrixed organization.

FIGURE 9.3   Balanced matrix organization

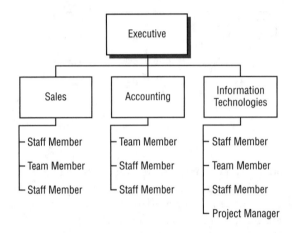

When you are assigned a new project, remember to analyze the organization structure in which you are working. This knowledge will assist you in acquiring resources and understanding the challenges you may face.

In Exercise 9.4, you will test your knowledge about organizational structures as you help the Sensational Advertisement Productions company.

Recommended Reading: Chapter 1, pp. 12–22, *PMP Project Management Professional Study Guide.*

Scenario

TPMP have brought project management processes to an advertising firm, Sensational Advertisement Productions (SAP), and the project managers at SAP are learning how to use the eight knowledge areas of scope, time, cost, quality, human resource, communications, risk, and procurement management. You want them to understand how organization structures can impact their projects. You are working with Pam Rosenbaum, who has been assigned account management functions for a telecommunications client's important new product: a new cell phone that integrates normal service with PDA functions right on the phone, which will be sold at a competitive price with normal cell phone services. The account has several project managers for the various sales campaigns: Michael Harland for the print campaigns, Judy Arakawa for the TV campaigns, and Joseph Matumbo for the telemarketing campaigns. Each project manager is working with marketing managers within the telecommunications company to get direction and approval for the work they will produce.

Organizational Structures

1. What are the three major types of organizational structures?

   _____

   _____

2. What are the three levels of progression in a matrixed organization?

   _____

   _____

3. What do the three levels in a matrixed organization correspond to?

   _____

   _____

4. Pam works for the Vice President of Account Management who in turn works for the CEO. The other vice presidents head organizations such as Sales, Operations, Media, and Direct Mail. What type of an organization is this?

   _____

   _____

5. What is Pam's authority level in this organization?

   _____

   _____

6. If Pam worked directly for the CEO, what type of organization structure would she be working in?

   _____

   _____

Exercise 9.5: Professional Responsibility

The objectives for Exercise 9.5 are:

- Introduce the major concepts of professional responsibility.
- Understand why you need to include professional responsibility in your everyday project choices and management.
- Practice making professional responsibility decisions.

Background

The Project Management Institute (PMI) added a section to the PMP exams about professional responsibility within the past few years. Although project managers might know how to perform all the required technical processes of project management, if they do not work ethically, with regard for customer fairness, and with the latest project management knowledge, then they may still not be doing the best job for their customer. Professional responsibility is based on the *Project Management Professional Code of Professional Conduct.* Read and understand those items listed on the code of conduct. The major elements of the code of conduct are:

- Adherence to the code of conduct, including supporting it and sharing it with others, acting ethically related to taking the PMP exam, and cooperating with PMI in gathering ethics violations information

- Disclosing what could look like conflict of interest or impropriety to customers and ensuring a conflict of interest does not compromise your judgment or duties to the customer

- Advertising your qualifications truthfully

- Complying with all applicable laws wherever you are performing your project management duties

- Respecting intellectual property

- Providing accurate cost and service estimates and expected results of the project

- Sticking to and satisfying the scope of your objectives (unless changed by the customer)

- Protecting confidential information

- Refraining from taking gifts or payments for personal gain (unless conforming to the customs where you are practicing yet still not violating your own customary practices)

There are a few other areas that you need to think about that are not expressly mentioned in the code of conduct:

- Seek growth opportunities in your knowledge of project management practices, including taking classes, reading articles, and attending seminars.

- Stay on top of your industry's practices because your project management skills are coupled with your knowledge of your industry.

- Deal with issues on your project as quickly and with as much fairness as possible, keeping in mind to use problem-solving techniques if you can. Make sure if you have competing stakeholder or customer needs, that you try to resolve the differences fairly and with regard to the objectives of the project.

- Use all your project management knowledge and make sure you use the most significant processes and create the most important outputs from the nine PMI knowledge areas as appropriate for your projects.

- Respect cultural differences by learning about them as needed, following local customs, and making sure that your team is trained on cultural issues as appropriate.

- Communicate as accurately and fairly as possible with your stakeholders. This means accurately reporting status—if it is bad news, report it. Your customers or management cannot make good decisions or help you get back on track if they do not know they need to.

- Protect the community as needed. Although you may be following the requirements of your customer, if you think the project could harm the community in any way, you need to work with your customer to change what could be harmful. If the customer will not change the project, then you may need to report the issue to the community.

To perform ethically in project management, you need to follow general business ethics and on top of those, those items specific to project management. You must practice honesty, integrity, fairness; concern for client, stakeholder, and community interests; continued professional growth and education; and protection of intellectual property and confidential information. You will make sure no conflict of interest clouds your professional judgment and actions as you manage each of your projects. This added piece of project management helps round out your full success in your project management career.

In Exercise 9.5 you will help the project managers of SAP identify and understand the individual elements of professional responsibility. These elements will help them think about their professional responsibility in their daily jobs as they manage the projects for their telecommunications client.

 Recommended Reading: Chapter 12, pp. 429–447, *PMP Project Management Professional Study Guide.*

Scenario

TPMP have brought project management processes to an advertising firm, Sensational Advertisement Productions (SAP), and the project managers at SAP are learning how to use the eight knowledge areas of scope, time, cost, quality, human resource, communications, risk, and procurement management. However, you need to help them start using the processes and tools of what is probably their most important function: integration management. You are working with Pam Rosenbaum, who has been assigned account management functions for a telecommunications client's important new product: a new cell phone that integrates normal service with PDA functions right on the phone, which will be sold at a competitive price with normal cell phone services. The account has several project managers for the various campaigns: Michael Harland for the print campaigns, Judy Arakawa for the TV campaigns, and Joseph Matumbo for the telemarketing campaigns. Each project manager is working with marketing managers within the telecommunications company to get direction and approval for the work they will produce.

Professional Responsibility

1. What are five professional responsibility elements the SAP project managers need to understand?

   _____

   _____

   _____

   _____

2. Last week, Judy found out that the time frame for one of her most important TV commercials might not be available during a major golf tournament, when everyone felt it would be most effective. Judy thinks she can recover, by working some deals with other advertisers. Should she report this issue to Pam and the client, or wait until she knows for sure what will happen?

   _____

   _____

   _____

   _____

3. One of Michael's deliverables is to create a test print advertisement campaign in various markets of Europe. His team will be working with a subcontractor in Europe who will help SAP create the campaign. What does Michael need to do to prepare for that deliverable?

   _____

   _____

   _____

   _____

4. The telecommunications company has shared with Joseph some of the projected sales of the cell phone product. Joseph is thinking that he might make a great amount of money if he were to invest in the company's stocks at this time. What should Joseph do?

   _____

   _____

   _____

   _____

5. What could TPMP do to help support the educational growth opportunities of the project managers of SAP?

   _____

   _____

   _____

   _____

Answers to Exercise Questions

Answers to Exercise 9.1

Your answers may be somewhat different, but the following answers provide a guide.

1. There is a point in time on a project where all of the planning has been completed and you're ready to start executing the plan. This point is when one of the project integration management processes—project plan development—is performed.

2. Project plan development takes the information created in the previous planning processes and integrates it into one comprehensive document that will serve as a guide during project execution and control.

3. Pam needs to cover the costs associated with each campaign, including order of magnitude estimates, budget estimates, and work estimates for each resource. She also should describe the same estimates for the entire project.

4. The typical sections of a project plan are as follows: project charter, scope statement, WBS, project schedule, project assignments, project costs, risks, and portions of other management plans.

Answers to Exercise 9.2

Your answers may be somewhat different, but the following answers provide a guide.

1. The four inputs for project plan execution are the project plan, organizational policies, preventive action, and corrective action.

2. Some of the executing processes that are integrated into project plan execution are quality assurance, team development, information distribution, and contract administration.

3. Pam has found that some tasks are being done out of sequence on the project. She also has found work done that is out of scope. Pam needs to put a work authorization tool and technique into place.

4. Pam uses spreadsheet software to prepare task assignments. This spreadsheet software is also known as a project management information system.

5. Pam is having difficulty getting the right information to her project team. Pam should use the general management skill of communication more effectively.

6. The two outputs of the project plan execution process are work results and change requests.

Answers to Exercise 9.3

Your answers may be somewhat different, but the following answers provide a guide.

1. You will recommend that Pam instruct all of her project managers to baseline their project plans. Pam should also create a change control process and change request forms with

appropriate fields to collect relevant data that all of her project managers must use once they have baselined their projects.

2. To analyze change requests, Pam and her project managers need to include information about alternatives or trade-offs; how functionality is affected; cost and work estimates to implement; risks and impacts to quality, scope, budget, and schedule; plans to implement if the change is approved; and dependent project impacts.

3. When Joseph's client asks him to include a new deliverable for his baselined telemarketing campaign, he needs to take out the change request form, and review the change processes with this client. It does not matter who the change request comes from, the change process needs to be followed and the request needs to be documented and approved.

4. You will recommend that Pam use a change control log, so that the change requests can be managed in an organized fashion, so people can look up and find change requests quickly. It would be difficult to go through each change request, which could be several pages long, to review all the project change requests and their dispositions.

5. Pam should manage the account from an overall perspective, which means the projects should not have their own change requests. Because these projects are highly dependent on one another, the project managers need to know the changes each project is considering so that impacts may be analyzed for the entire program. Although the projects may have several requests that do not impact the other projects, it is important to allow a forum and process to ensure communication. Pam needs to ensure that she is the change control process owner and overall manager. Project managers can manage the change requests within their own project, but make sure they are discussed in this overall forum.

6. The client, Pam, and the project managers should be on the configuration change board. Both SAP and the telecommunications company need to consider the changes to scope, budget, quality, or schedule. You might recommend that an executive from SAP and an executive from the telecommunications client also sit on the board to help ensure that change is prioritized and agreed to.

Answers to Exercise 9.4

Your answers may be somewhat different, but the following answers provide a guide.

1. There are three major types of organizational structures: projectized, matrix, and functional.

2. The levels of progression in matrixed organizations are a weak matrix, balanced matrix, and strong matrix.

3. The three levels of progression in a matrix organization correspond to how projectized or functional the organization has been structured.

4. Pam works in a functional organization.

5. Pam has little or no authority in a functional organization.

6. If Pam worked directly for the CEO, she would be working in a projectized organization.

Answers to Exercise 9.5

Your answers may be somewhat different, but the following answers provide a guide.

1. Elements that TPMP need to review with SAP project managers are as follows: respecting confidential information and intellectual property, continued professional and industry knowledge growth, respecting cultural differences and following the cultural norms, protecting the community, not accepting gifts or payments for personal gain that can cloud professional judgment or actions, complying with the applicable laws, and reporting budget and status truthfully.

2. Judy needs to report the possible loss of her TV spot to Pam and the client. It is possible that either they could decide the spot is not as important as previously thought or they may think of ways that Judy has not thought of to help secure the spots. Also, they may need to consider what they might lose if they do not get the spot, and the impacts to the campaign's objectives. Judy needs to deal with the issues sooner rather than later when the consequences might be much more serious.

3. You will advise Michael to have people on his advertising team study the cultural norms of the test markets they will be in. You will also suggest that his sales team take training in the cultural norms of the European culture they will be working with.

4. During your training on professional responsibility, you have taught Joseph and the other project managers that confidential information must be protected and not used for personal gain. Joseph needs to keep this in mind because he has insider information that can be used for personal gain. It is not appropriate for Joseph to do anything with this information.

5. To help promote the project managers' continued educational growth, TPMP could create a curriculum or suggested growth path for SAP. This might include a project management tier structure with educational achievements required for each tier, participation in local PM activities and seminars, and joining PMI for the professional magazines and information it provides.

Index

Note to the Reader: Throughout this index **boldfaced** page numbers indicate primary discussions of a topic. *Italicized* page numbers indicate illustrations.

T

Project Management Skills for all Levels

Project Management JumpStart™
By Kim Heldman
ISBN: 0-7821-4214-1
US $24.99

Prepare for a project management career—Fast!
Project Management JumpStart gives you the solid
grounding you need to approach a career in
project management with confidence.

◆ The basic skills of a successful project manager

◆ Creating project schedules and determining project budgets

◆ Winning the support of department managers

◆ Monitoring project progress, resources, and budgets

◆ Communication and negotiation skills

Whether you're looking to advance your career as a project
manager or simply strengthen your business skills foundation, the
highly respected PMP certification from the Project Management
Institute is the credential you need to succeed in today's competitive
marketplace.

◆ More comprehensive than any other PMP exam prep package

◆ In-depth coverage of all official PMP exam objectives

◆ Project management case studies included to provide real-world insights

**PMP®: Project Management
Professional Study Guide**
By Kim Heldman
ISBN: 0-7821-4106-4
US $59.99

This workbook presents scenarios and exercises
that allow you to practice your hands-on skills.

**PMP®: Project Management
Professional Workbook**
By Claudia Baca and Patti Jansen
ISBN: 0-7821-4240-0
US $34.99

SYBEX®

www.sybex.com

TELL US WHAT YOU THINK!

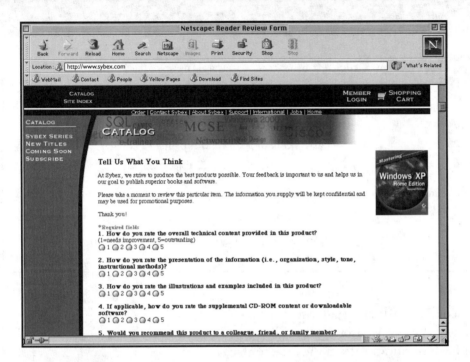

Your feedback is critical to our efforts to provide you with the best books and software on the market. Tell us what you think about the products you've purchased. It's simple:

1. Go to the Sybex website.
2. Find your book by typing the ISBN or title into the Search field.
3. Click on the book title when it appears.
4. Click **Submit a Review.**
5. Fill out the questionnaire and comments.
6. Click **Submit.**

With your feedback, we can continue to publish the highest quality computer books and software products that today's busy IT professionals deserve.

www.sybex.com

SYBEX Inc. • 1151 Marina Village Parkway, Alameda, CA 94501 • 510-523-8233